HATSHEPSUT

QUEEN OF SHEBA

HATSHEPSUT

QUEEN OF SHEBA

EMMET SCOTT

Algora Publishing
New York

Library of Congress Cataloging-in-Publication Data —

Scott, Emmet.
 Hatshepsut, Queen of Sheba / Emmet Scott.
  p. cm.
 Includes bibliographical references and index.
  ISBN 978-0-87586-945-2 (soft cover: alk. paper)—ISBN 978-0-87586-946-9 (hard
cover: alk. paper)—ISBN 978-0-87586-947-6 (ebook) 1. Hatshepsut, Queen of Egypt. 2.
Egypt—History—Eighteenth dynasty, ca. 1570–1320 B.C. 3. Queens—Egypt—Biography.
I. Title.
  DT87.15.S39 2012
  932'.014092—dc23
  [B]
            2012033445

Printed in the United States

TABLE OF CONTENTS

TABLE OF FIGURES

INTRODUCTION

The book that follows is partly biography; but more than the history of a person it is the history of a controversy and of a mystery. It is a history concerned as much with time and context as with personalities. It is the story of the Egyptian queen known to history as Hatshepsut and also of the mysterious queen known to history as the Queen of Sheba, or Queen of the South. These two characters, removed from each other in the textbooks by a little over five centuries, are revealed to be one and the same person.

I was not the first to reach this conclusion: That honor goes to Immanuel Velikovsky, whose 1952 book *Ages in Chaos* acquainted the reading public for the first time with this startling revelation. In line with his proposal that Eighteenth Dynasty Egyptian history needed to be moved down the timescale by five centuries, Velikovsky came to the conclusion that Hatshepsut, the great female "pharaoh", whom conventional history places between 1508 and 1458 BC, must have been a contemporary of Solomon, the most glorious of Israel's early kings, whom history tells us reigned between 971 and 931 BC. Two such extraordinary characters, thought Velikovsky, if they had lived at the same time, must have interacted in some way. Could it be, Velikovsky mused, that Hatshepsut was the mysterious Queen of Sheba, whose meeting with Solomon in Jerusalem had led, throughout the centuries, to such romantic speculation? In the writings of Josephus, the first century Jewish historian, Velikovsky found evidence that the Queen of Sheba had indeed been an Egyptian monarch. According to Josephus, she was "the woman who, at that time, ruled as queen of Egypt and Ethiopia," a woman who was, furthermore, "thoroughly trained in wisdom and remarkable in other ways." Since in Josephus' time "Ethiopia" meant Nubia — and not the modern Ethiopia, which is more properly designated Abyssinia — this strongly implied that she was an Egyptian ruler, and nothing else. If Hatshepsut were the Queen of Sheba, thought Velikovsky, it would be helpful if she had left a record of her much vaunted trip to Jerusalem. Indeed, such a record would almost be required. Does such a record exist, Velikovsky asked, and does it conform to the account of the Queen of Sheba's trip to Jerusalem as recorded in the Old Testament? The record does exist, he said, and it does conform.

At this point he embarked upon a detailed examination of the most famous expedition ever launched by an Egyptian monarch: the journey to Punt, or the Divine Land, recorded on Hatshepsut's wonderful funerary temple at Deir el Bahri. The Divine Land, he concluded, the goal of Hatshepsut's expedition, was Israel.

It is worth emphasizing here that the equation of Hatshepsut with the Queen of Sheba was just one segment of a general reconstruction of history which involved the subtraction of five centuries from the span of Egyptian chronology. His identification of Hatshepsut with the Queen of Sheba was not a starting-point, but a consequence: Velikovsky did not begin by seeing Hatshepsut as the Queen of Sheba and the Punt reliefs as the record of a voyage to Israel. It was the other way round; other considerations entirely — from manifold varieties of evidence — made him conclude, first of all, that Hatshepsut and Solomon were contemporaries, and that, secondly, Hatshepsut must have been the Queen of Sheba. This was a point emphasized again and again by Velikovsky, when he pleaded with his readers to consider the evidence as a whole, and not become bogged down in arguments about a detail here and there. The bigger picture, he stressed, must always be kept in mind. As an example he asked his readers to consider the following: If Hatshepsut was truly the Queen of Sheba, then her successor on the throne, Thutmose III, can be none other than Shishak, the pharaoh whom the Bible blames for plundering Solomon's Temple after the latter's death. His reconstruction and overall thesis, he said, was then, as on many other occasions, put to a crucial test: Was the successor to Hatshepsut on the Egyptian throne a warrior-king, and did he campaign in the direction of Palestine? Did he also boast of plundering a fabulously wealthy temple in that region?

The answer, to all of these questions, was a resounding yes! Thutmose III was indeed a warrior-pharaoh who campaigned in Palestine; and he did indeed plunder a great temple in that region, the contents of which he proudly displayed on the walls of his own temple at Karnak.

Velikovsky was thus able to show that, once Eighteenth Dynasty Egyptian history was moved forward by five centuries, it formed a match, generation for generation, with the history of Israel, which hitherto had failed to agree at all with that of Egypt. The force of the evidence was therefore accumulative. With each new agreement it became increasingly unlikely that the reconstruction was wrong; and so powerfully did Velikovsky make his case that, for a while, very few critics, either specialists or otherwise, cared to cross swords with him.

But criticisms there were — though the most forceful of these only appeared after his death. These proceeded precisely as Velikovsky had in some ways predicted they would: by ignoring the overall picture and focusing upon a questionable detail here and there. And since his equation of Hatshepsut with the Queen of Sheba was one of the most attractive and compelling parts of the reconstruction, it was here that the critics focused their gaze.

One of the problems with hair-splitting is that it obscures the wider picture. If critic and author are involved in a prolonged debate over the meaning of a word here or the interpretation of a sentence there, the central purpose of the discussion can rapidly be forgotten. And this of course is precisely why hair-splitting is such a favorite tool of the pedant: In absence of a coherent counter-argument, this procedure will confuse the picture sufficiently to make it appear the critic has won. If he can also catch the author out on an actual mistake, even a minor one, so much the better. This can now be used as an excuse for throwing out the entire work. And this was precisely the tactic employed by Velikovsky's opponents.

The first, as far as I am aware, to attempt a refutation, was Egyptologist William H. Stiebing, whose objections to the Hatshepsut = Queen of Sheba equation appeared in the journal *Pensée* in 1973. This was followed, after Velikovsky's death, by further criticisms from Peter James (1979) and Michael Jones (1982). The most thorough attacks however came in 1984 from Egyptologist David Lorton and in 1986 from erstwhile supporter John Bimson. The appearance of the latter's paper in particular marked a watershed in the whole Velikovsky debate and proved in the end to be a major factor in the jettisoning of the entire "Ages in Chaos" project by many of its hitherto strongest supporters.

In the course of the present volume we shall have occasion to look at some of the most important objections of the critics. For the present, it is sufficient to note that in general they denied that the biblical Queen of Sheba could be identified as an Egyptian sovereign, and they rejected — predictably enough — Velikovsky's attempt to identify Punt — where Hatshepsut sent her famous expedition — with the land of Israel. The evidence identifying Punt with a region in Africa, they said, was far too convincing to be overturned by Velikovsky's arguments. Both the flora and the fauna depicted on the Punt reliefs, they said, were clearly African, and it was absurd to try to claim otherwise. They claimed too that in several Egyptian inscriptions Punt was named as a southern country — though they also admitted that in several other places Punt is named as an eastern and even (on several occasions) as a northern country.

In his 2006 book, *Empire of Thebes* (which is volume 3 of a general reconstruction of ancient history named "Ages in Alignment"), as well as in various articles published in the journals of the Society for Interdisciplinary Studies, revisionist historian Emmet Sweeney answered some of the more obviously erroneous of these objections, and indeed in *Empire of Thebes* devoted an entire chapter to the topic. Although Sweeney's contribution over the past decade has been valuable, I have come to the conclusion that the Hatshepsut question needs a much more detailed treatment. This is due to the fact that it has become clear that the identity of Hatshepsut is central to the whole topic of Egyptian history and its relationship with the Bible: It is in every respect a pivotal question on whose resolution may well depend our entire understanding of ancient Egyptian and biblical history.

For this reason alone it became apparent to me that it was necessary to answer the critics in at least as much detail as they themselves went. When they attacked Velikovsky's work, they made a mistake common to many pedants: they didn't nit-pick enough: True, they went through the identity of Punt with a fine toothed comb, but they failed to use the microscope. Had they done so, they would have realized that the Divine Land (Punt) is inseparably connected with the god Osiris, who is also inseparably connected with the Byblos region; and they would have found too that the goddess Hathor (Hatshepsut's tutelary deity) is equally strongly connected to Punt and to Byblos, as well as Palestine in general. They would have found further that the "African" animals depicted on the Deir el Bahri reliefs were all at home in Palestine in ancient times; and they would have discovered that frankincense, which nowadays flourishes only in southern Arabia and the Horn of Africa, was anciently cultivated in the Jordan Valley, where it formed an invaluable cash crop coveted even in Roman times by Egyptian sovereigns. And about the Horn of Africa, which they identified as Punt, the critics would have learned that the region harbored no Bronze Age civilization that the Egyptians of Hatshepsut's time could have traded with. Closer examination too would have made them less willing to dismiss Josephus' testimony that the Queen of Sheba was ruler of Egypt, and they would perhaps not have been so eager to jettison the Abyssinian tradition, which also identified her as a queen of Egypt, and which credited her son Menelik with plundering Solomon's Temple.

Some of these points were made by Sweeney in *Empire of Thebes*; though since the publication of that volume ever-increasing amounts of crucially important new evidence have come to light. This new material, I feel, puts the equation of Hatshepsut with the Queen of Sheba on a virtually unassailable basis. Furthermore, in *Empire of Thebes* Sweeney made several errors and omissions which need corrected. He had, for example, argued that Hatshepsut's expedition reached Israel by way of the Mediterranean, and that the party had disembarked at Tyre or Acre before making its way inland. But this route flies in the face of much crucial evidence which strongly supports Velikovsky's original contention that the Egyptian travelers reached Israel via the Red Sea and Gulf of Aqaba and that it was only the return journey which proceeded via the Mediterranean.

Sweeney made other errors that need correcting. For example, many of the "African" animals observed at Deir el Bahri were probably not found throughout the whole of Syria/Palestine, as Sweeney had imagined, so much as in the extremely hot lowlands of the Jordan Valley and the Dead Sea — the Arabah or Ghor region. That, at least, is where they were concentrated. Again, in *Empire of Thebes*, Sweeney passed over the Abyssinian tradition about the Queen of Sheba, whose importance he seems not to have appreciated. Critics such as Lorton and Bimson had claimed that the Abyssinian name for the Queen of Sheba, Makeda, was not sufficiently close to Hatshepsut's throne-name — Makera — to be really significant. This was one of their many mistakes. The similarity is significant, as is the fact that in Abyssinian tradition Makeda's son — Menelik — returns at a later date to rob Solomon's Temple. Furthermore, the name Menelik, or Menerik, is sufficiently close to Thutmose III's throne-name Menkheperre to warrant comment.

In the decision to write this volume I was aware too that the debate had, as it were, to be brought up to date. In *Empire of Thebes*, Sweeney discussed the insights provided by Eva Danelius, who, in several articles, brought forth important new material in support of Velikovsky. He also mentioned several ideas provided by Lisa Liel of Israel and Simon Miles of Australia. Yet he had omitted the work of Hyam Maccoby, whose article on the biblical Song of Songs cast a whole new light on the relationship between Hatshepsut and Solomon. And the work of a host of other scholars, since that time, have added important details about the life and times of Hatshepsut; all of which needed to be brought into the equation.

Having said that, it should go without saying that the evidence presented in the following pages cannot hope to be exhaustive or the last word on the subject. Of necessity, I have had to pass over great quantities of material that would be required in a definitive work. I omit, for example, most of the voluminous material clearly placing the Eighteenth Dynasty in the same epoch as the Early Israelite Monarchy. A small sample of the evidence is indeed examined in Chapter 1; but space did not permit more than a glimpse of the tip of an enormous iceberg. A thorough overview would have required perhaps a small library of books, and it is doubtful if the last word on this topic could ever be said. Suffice to note that the evidence is overwhelming that the Eighteenth Dynasty of Egypt and the Early Monarchy of Israel appeared simultaneously and exerted a mutual influence on each other thereafter — an influence traceable in a thousand ways, in art, literature, religion, and culture in general.

I thus leave out a detailed examination of the Amarna Letters, a huge collection of documents dating primarily from the time of Amenhotep III, three generations after Hatshepsut. Careful analysis of these texts demonstrates beyond question that they belong to the time of King Asa of Judah and Baasha of Israel, three generations after Solomon (a fairly comprehensive consideration of these correspondences is found in Sweeney's *Empire of Thebes*, 2006). I omit also an exploration of the names of Palestinian cities on the Thutmose III's famous list at Karnak — a list mentioning numerous towns and settlements which, according to biblical sources, did not exist before the time of King David and Solomon.

I pass over, too, many intriguing details about the life and times of Hatshepsut and Thutmose III which Velikovsky brought forth. For example, I do not explore the military campaign undertaken in Asia by Thutmose I, Hatshepsut's father. This expedition, during which he "overthrew the Asiatics," was followed by a journey to Retjenu (Palestine), where he "wash[ed] his heart among the foreign countries." (Breasted, *Records*, Vol. 2, Sec. 81) Velikovsky saw in these events the alliance between Solomon and the pharaoh mentioned in 1 Kings 9:16, where the Egyptian monarch took the Philistine city of Gezer by storm and gave it as a dowry to his daughter, who shortly thereafter married Solomon. If Velikovsky was right, here, then one of Solomon's wives, probably his chief wife, was the sister of Hatshepsut.

I do not examine either the question of the sister of the Egyptian Queen Tahpehnes, whom the Book of Kings says was given in marriage to Hadad the Edomite after the latter fled to Egypt in the days of King David (1 Kings 11:19). Velikovsky's chronology placed these events in the time of Ahmose, first pharaoh of the Eighteenth Dynasty, whose chief wife was known as Tanethap, Tenthape, or Tahpenes. Nor do I investigate Genubath, the son of Hadad, who became ruler of Edom in the latter years of Solomon (1 Kings 11:20). As Velikovsky remarked, this man, or his people, seem to appear in the annals of Thutmose III, who refers to the "Genubatye" as having arrived in Egypt with tribute (Breasted, *Records*, Vol. 2, Sec. 474). And I similarly leave out discussion of the princess Ano, a contemporary of Thutmose III, whose canopic jar is housed in the Metropolitan Museum of Art in New York. Velikovsky saw in this woman the princess Ano whom the Septuagint says pharaoh Shishak gave to Jeroboam as a wife after the death of Solomon. We are told that Ano "was great among the daughters of the king, and she bore to Jeroboam Abijah."

These and various other fascinating details are not discussed in the present work for the simple reason that they were never challenged by the critics, and to go over them again would simply be repeating what Velikovsky has already said — and said much more eloquently than I could ever hope to do. What I have tried to do in the following pages is to answer Velikovsky's critics and to bring forward evidence unknown to him — as well as to integrate all this with the work of other scholars such as Sweeney, Danelius, and Maccoby, who have contributed so much to the debate.

What the reader will find in the pages to follow is fairly conclusive proof that Hatshepsut did go on the journey to Punt, a region sacred to her tutelary goddess Hathor. He will learn that she made the journey primarily as a pilgrimage, to strengthen her own claims to the throne of Egypt. The reader will see that the Queen and her party disembarked at Elat in southern Israel and made her way northwards, through the hot depression of the Arabah and on to the Dead Sea. Bypassing the latter, the Queen and her entourage entered the tropical incense-growing region of the Jordan Valley with its "myrrh terraces." Around Jericho she and her followers spotted some of the exotic animals such as the giraffe and the single-horned rhinoceros, which still roamed the Jordan Valley at the time. In Jerusalem itself the Egyptian sovereign met face to face Israel's semi-legendary king Solomon, and was much enamored of him. Evidence is presented to show that they actually became lovers, and that their affection was immortalized in what is perhaps the most celebrated love-song of all time; the biblical Song of Songs, the beautiful love-poem attributed to the pen of Solomon himself.

The reader will find that words, expressions, metaphors and idioms found in the Song of Songs are repeated, often word for word, on the walls of Hatshepsut's temple at Deir el Bahri, and on many other Egyptian love-poems of the early Eighteenth Dynasty. Indeed, the Song of Songs, which was reputedly written by Solomon, may well have been inspired by letters received from Hatshepsut in the years following their brief encounter. The reader will discover too that the temple at Deir el Bahri was almost certainly a direct copy of the Temple in Jerusalem, just as Velikovsky claimed, and that we are thus in possession of a ground-plan of the renowned and mysterious structure.

Finally, it will be shown that Thutmose III was indeed the pharaoh Shishak who plundered Solomon's Temple, and that he left a detailed description of the monument's contents on the walls of his own temple at Karnak. We shall bring forth evidence to show that in Thutmose III's time Jerusalem was the mightiest citadel in Syria/Palestine; hence the claim of mainstream archaeologists, hitherto found in all textbooks, that the latter pharaoh made no mention of Jerusalem in his record of the conquest of Palestine (Retjenu), is untenable. Thutmose III could not have conquered the territory without securing the City of David.

The work that follows, as I say, is not definitive; but I believe that it shifts the burden of proof decisively in favor of Velikovsky and against the naysayers. It is now up to them to refute the material herein outlined, and to prove, by even a single circumstance, that Hatshepsut could not have been the Queen of Sheba.

CHAPTER 1: TWO MONARCHS AND TWO NATIONS

THE WOMAN WHO WOULD BE KING

About thirty-five years after the expulsion from Egypt of the hated Hyksos, the Shepherd Kings of Asia, the Land of the Nile was ruled by one of the most extraordinary persons ever to wear the Double Crown of the pharaohs. This was Hatshepsut, the only woman, as far as we know, who actually proclaimed herself "pharaoh".

Hatshepsut was the elder daughter of Thutmose I by his chief wife Ahmose, and half-sister to Thutmose II, eldest son of Thutmose I by a secondary wife. Upon the death of her father, Hatshepsut married her half-brother Thutmose II and assumed the title Great Royal Wife. By her husband she had one daughter, a girl named Nefrure, though she failed to produce a son. A son was however provided for Thutmose II by a secondary wife named Isis: this was Thutmose III.

When Thutmose II died, after a very short reign — probably three years — Thutmose III was too young to assume the role of pharaoh, and Hatshepsut, his aunt and step-mother, became regent. She seems to have married her daughter Nefrure to the young Thutmose III,[1] but she was not content merely to be the regent and mother-in-law of the pharaoh. Probably before the end of her third or fourth year in this role, she took a further and hitherto unprecedented step, and

---

1 Thutmose III also married a princess named Meretre-Hatshepsut, who was the mother of Amenhotep II. Meretre-Hatshepsut was not a daughter or a close relation of Hatshepsut; though the fact that her name so closely resembled that of the great queen caused much confusion in the past.

had herself proclaimed "pharaoh".[1] This arrangement was detailed in the autobiography of Ineni, a high court official at that time:

> He [Thutmose II] went forth to heaven in triumph, having mingled with the gods; His son stood in his place as king of the Two Lands, having become ruler upon the throne of the one who begat him. His [Thutmose II's] sister the Divine Consort, Hatshepsut, settled the affairs of the Two Lands by reason of her plans. Egypt was made to labour with bowed head for her, the excellent seed of the god [Thutmose I], which came forth from him.[2]

So, while the royal court still designated Thutmose III as co-regent, Hatshepsut ruled as "king." As far we know, this was unique for an Egyptian queen. Several, it is true, ruled alone, as regent, for some time; but none dared to proclaim herself pharaoh. "Pharaoh" by definition was an incarnation of the god Ra, a male deity; so that it was theologically impossible for a woman to hold the position. In order to justify her action, the Queen was compelled to invent a whole mythology in which she was the child of Amon-Ra, specially designed for rule. In her great temple at Deir el Bahri, she portrayed her mother Ahmose (wife of Thutmose I) in conversation with the god Amon, who tells her as he leaves,

> Hatshepsut shall be the name of this my daughter [to be born]. ...
> She shall exercise the excellent kingship in this whole land.[3]

According to Breasted, these reliefs "thus show how she was designed by the divine will from the first to rule Egypt, and hence they proceed to picture her birth, accompanied by all the prodigies, which both the conventions of the court and the credulity of the folk associated with the advent of the sun-god's heir."[4] Such tales however were traditionally told only of princes; applied to a princess, the story became somewhat skewered: "The artist who did the work followed the current tradition so closely that the new-born child appears as a *boy*, showing how the introduction of a woman into the situation was wrenching the inherited forms."[5]

In the rituals of the temple, the fiction of Hatshepsut's masculinity was perpetuated to the extent that she seems actually to have on certain ritual

---

1 William C. Hayes, places her crowning as pharaoh before the end of her second year. See "Egypt: Internal Affairs from Tuthmosis I to the Death of Amenophis III," in *The Cambridge Ancient History*, Vol. 2 part 1 (1971 ed.) p. 317. Since Hayes' time however new evidence has appeared suggesting a somewhat later date.

2 J. H. Breasted, *Ancient Records of Egypt*, Vol. 2 (London, 1951), Sec. 341

3 Ibid., Sec. 198

4 J. H. Breasted, *A History of Egypt* (2nd ed., London, 1951), p. 273

5 Ibid.

occasions dressed as a pharaoh, complete with artificial beard. She is thus portrayed too in many of the monuments which she subsequently erected.

During this time the child (and young man) Thutmose III, theoretically the real pharaoh, was consigned to such "puerile" functions as offering incense in the Temple of Amon, and other ritual roles.

How Hatshepsut managed to carry off what was effectively a *coup d'état*, is not fully understood. In Egypt, inheritance was carried through the female line. She was the only surviving child of Queen Ahmose, who was herself of the blood-line of the earlier pharaohs who had expelled the Hyksos from Egypt.[1] By contrast, Thutmose III was the son of a minor queen, and could not claim pure royal lineage. Even though he was the son of Thutmose II, he was still compelled to marry the daughter of Hatshepsut in order to legitimize his claim. And coupled with her royal blood, the queen had other advantages: Her life and works display not only a driving ambition but also a keen intelligence. Upon becoming regent, she immediately surrounded herself with powerful allies, prominent among whom were the High Priest of Amon, Hapuseneb, the Chancellor Nehesi, the Viceroy (probably of Nubia) Inebny, the Treasurer Thuty, and the Chief Stewards Amenhotep, Wadjrenpowet, Thuthotpe, Senmen, and the latter's brother Senenmut. The last of these was her favorite. Actually, Senenmut's relationship with Hatshepsut has led to endless speculation. He was early made tutor to the queen's daughter Nefrure, in which role he had himself frequently portrayed.[2] He was also an architect, or at least given the responsibilities of an architect; and he it was who received the commission of building Hatshepsut's greatest and most famous monument, her funeral temple at Deir el Bahri. On the walls of the latter structure he was permitted to depict himself praying to Hathor for the queen, "an unparalleled honour," according to Breasted.[3] Such favors bestowed upon a commoner have led to the surmise that he may have been, for a time at least, the queen's lover. And this calls to attention another crucial feature of Hatshepsut: she appears to have been a woman of outstanding beauty. This is certainly the impression conveyed in many of her portraits, and it was an attribute she herself boasted of. She described herself as "exceedingly good to look upon, with the form and spirit of a god ... a beautiful maiden, fresh, serene of nature ... altogether divine." When she mounted

---

1 The early kings and queens of the Eighteenth Dynasty, from whom Hatshepsut was directly descended, were at least partly Nubian. In their veins, and in the veins of Hatshepsut, there flowed the blood of black Africa.

2 Breasted, *A History of Egypt*, op cit., p. 272

3 Ibid., p. 278

the throne, she seems to have been in her late teens or early twenties, in the prime of her life; which makes her ability to command the loyalty and devotion of so many powerful men somewhat easier to understand. The flesh and blood Hatshepsut cannot have borne much resemblance to the androgynous, or shall we say frankly masculine, personage appearing on the front cover of Joyce Tyldesley's 1998 book, *Hatchepsut: The Female Pharaoh.* It is axiomatic that in all periods of history a woman's greatest advantage lay in her ability to attract the loyalty and admiration of powerful men, and we surely cannot credit the stern and angular-featured harridan staring from the cover of Tyldesley's book with that ability. The latter illustration, it would seem, has far more to do with modern feminist ideology than with the actual appearance of the queen.

Fig. 1 Statue of Hatshepsut in Metropolitan Museum of Art, New York. She is depicted dressed in the clothing of a male king, though with feminine form.

The Hatshepsut of the monuments may have invariably been portrayed in masculine attire, but the flesh and blood Hatshepsut would have shown the world a very different visage. We may be reasonably sure that a woman who could describe herself as "exceedingly good to look upon, with the form and spirit of a god ... a beautiful maiden, fresh, serene of nature ... altogether divine," would have spent as little time as possible dressed as a man.[1]

In future ages, the Egyptians looked upon Hatshepsut as a usurper, and her name is never listed among the rulers of the country — her period on the throne being incorporated entirely into the reign of Thutmose III. It was the latter man himself who seems to have begun the process of damning her memory, by defacing her monuments and erasing her name wherever he found it. For all that, she was never viewed in quite the same light as the heretic Akhnaton, who was known simply as the "criminal of Akhet-Aton."

As might be imagined, modern historians tend to take a far more favorable view. Among feminists in particular she is regarded as something of an icon; an early example of a strong woman who showed an extraordinary independence of spirit and strength of character. Others however, especially of earlier generations, were not quite so effusive. So for example in the 1971 edition of the *Cambridge Ancient History*, William C. Hayes describes her as a "shrewd, ambitious, and unscrupulous woman," who delayed very little time before she "showed herself in her true colors" and crowned herself "pharaoh."[2]

Where does the truth lie?

Amidst argument and counter-argument, one thing appears certain: Hatshepsut was not a criminal. We have no knowledge of any assassinations carried out on her orders; a fact which differentiates her dramatically from the only other Egyptian queen with whom she might be compared, Cleopatra. It is conceivable that, as the ruling monarch, she could have had the youthful Thutmose III quietly eliminated and married one of her favorites, thus assuring her position. That she did not do so speaks volumes in her favor.

On the whole, her twenty-year rule is universally regarded as peaceful and prosperous. There is little hint of military activity beyond the usual peace-keeping operations in outlying regions, where the activities of wild tribesmen and bandits needed controlling. She was a great builder, and a large amount of what she constructed still stands. Among these monuments

---

1 These words, we should note, were written after Hatshepsut had been crowned "pharaoh." It is highly likely that her appearances in the dress of a pharaoh were rare, confined to important religious rituals.

2 William C. Hayes, loc. cit.

is what is widely regarded as the masterpiece of Egyptian architecture, the *Djeser-djeseru*, or Splendor of Splendors, which stands on the west bank of the Nile at Thebes, over against a wall of high cliffs. The temple, of which more will be said presently, stood on the site of an earlier shrine of Hathor, Hatshepsut's tutelary goddess.

WHEN DID HATSHEPSUT LIVE?

When speaking of Hatshepsut's life and lifetime, Egyptologists are very confident: The queen, we are told, was born in 1508 and died in 1458. Historians may dissent from these dates, but generally only by a year or two. Similar confidence is expressed in figures and dates provided for other rulers of the Eighteenth Dynasty.

Yet there is much about Hatshepsut and her epoch which seem puzzling, if the dates given in the textbooks are correct. Poetry and prayers from her time seem to find their closest parallels in the literature of the Old Testament, particularly the literature of the Early Israelite Kingdom; yet the latter kingdom is placed over five centuries after the time of the Eighteenth Dynasty. This strange pattern is seen most clearly in the latter years of the Eighteenth Dynasty — about seventy years after the death of Hatshepsut — where one of the hymns composed by the heretic pharaoh Akhnaton repeats almost word for word several verses of Psalm 104.[1] Love-poetry from Hatshepsut's time onwards, as we shall see, bears striking comparison with that famous biblical love-poem, the Song of Songs, said to have been written by Solomon.[2] But Solomon lived five centuries after Hatshepsut. Worse than all this, however, is the fact that the so-called Amarna Letters, a series of royal correspondences dating from the reigns of Amenhotep III and Akhnaton, contain expressions, idioms and metaphors found also in the Old Testament — particularly in the Books of Kings.[3] The letters are invariably

1 According to Breasted, Psalm 104 shows a "notable similarity" to one of the Aton hymns. *History of Egypt* op. cit., p. 371. In the words of John A. Wilson, "The king [Akhnaton] addressed a beautiful hymn to his god, expressing gratitude for the benefits of life. ... It has often been pointed out that this hymn has a remarkable similarity to Psalm 104 in the Bible. Both the hymn and the psalm reflect a common family of ideas, according to which God or the god is praised for his bounties." "Akhenaton," in *The Encyclopaedia Britannica, Micropaedia*, Vol. 1, (15th ed.)
2 See e.g., M. V. Fox's, *The Song of Songs and Ancient Egyptian Love Songs* (Uni. of Wisconsin Press, 1985); also John B. White, *A Study of the Language of Love in the Song of Songs and Ancient Egyptian Poetry*, (SBL Dissertation Series 38, Scholars Press, Missoula, Montana, 1978).
3 There is an enormous literature on this topic. W. F. Albright's "An Archaic Hebrew Proverb in an Amarna Letter from Central Palestine," *Journal of Near Eastern Studies*, 98 (1943), provides several fascinating insights, whilst a more comprehensive over-

written in Akkadian, though occasionally Hebrew (or "Canaanite") words, expressions, and sentences occur. Popular biblical metaphors appear with some frequency. Thus for example, the submission of an enemy is expressed as "to eat dust" in the Amarna Letter written by the people of Irqata, as well as in Isaiah 49:23. Loyalty is expressed by the metaphor "to lay the neck to the yoke and bear it," in the Amarna Letters of Baal-miir and Yakhtiri, as well as in Jeremiah 27:11. There are quite literally hundreds of such parallels.

But it is not only the language of the Amarna Letters that calls to mind the world of the Hebrew monarchs, supposedly five to six centuries later: Towns, cities, and even individuals on the documents often have identical names to those known from the Book of Kings — specifically from the time of Solomon's children and grandchildren. Most strikingly, Jerusalem is mentioned as Urusalim. Until the discovery of the Amarna Letters it was generally assumed that the city did not acquire this name until after its conquest by King David — almost four centuries before the composition of the Amarna Letters. Without exception, biblical texts refer to the settlement as Jebus right up until its annexation by David. Immediately after that, however, it is invariably called Jerusalem.[1] Again, the letters refer repeatedly to a marauder named Labayu, whose capital city is Shechem.[2] Yet Shechem, we know, was not an important center until the time of Jeroboam I, Solomon's rebellious subject. In the First Book of Kings we read: "And Jeroboam built Shechem in mount Ephraim, and dwelt there ..." (1 Kings 12:25). Essentially, he moved his capital to Shechem, but it remained capital of Israel only until the beginning of the reign of Omri, two generations later, who moved his court to Samaria. It seems very strange that in the time of Labayu, supposedly five centuries before Jeroboam I, Shechem would enjoy a similar status, a status only otherwise mentioned in the time of Jeroboam I and his successor Baasha. Labayu of the Letters was a perpetual and dangerous enemy of the king of Jerusalem; which sounds rather like Baasha, the King of Israel, who waged a never-ending war against Solomon's grandson, King Asa. "And there was war between Asa and Baasha king of Israel all their days." (1 Kings 15:32)

view is provided by S. A. Cook, "Style and Ideas," in *The Cambridge Ancient History*, Vol. 2 (2nd ed).

1 A location named Salem, generally believed to be Jerusalem, is mentioned in Genesis as the home of the priest-king Melchizedek. However, since the Book of Genesis was not written until the Persian period, and contains numerous indicators of its late composition (such as the domestic use of camels), the occurrence there of Salem cannot be seen as proof of an ancient origin. In any case, "Salem" is not the same as "Jerusalem." For the recent origin of the Book of Genesis see John Van Seters, *Abraham in History and Tradition* (Yale University Press, 1987).

2 See Y. Aharoni, *The Land of the Bible* (London, 1966), pp. 162-3

Again, a city named Batruna in the Letters was immediately recognized as Botrys (modern Batroun), a settlement which Menander of Ephesus claimed to have been built by king Ithobalos (Ethbaal), the father-in-law of Ahab, and a contemporary of King Asa. (See Josephus, *Against Apion*, i, 116)

If the occurrence of the names of towns and cities centuries before they were expected caused disquiet, the appearance in the Letters of actual individuals known from the time of Solomon's grandchildren and great-grandchildren was perhaps even more worrying. Thus one of the most important and controversial figures of the Letters was a king named Abdi-Ashirta (also written as Abdi-Astarte), king of Amurru. The double-dealing, scheming and aggression of this man made him a real menace to the security of the region. He was eventually put to death, perhaps on the orders of the pharaoh — an event which happened, apparently, just immediately prior to the death of Amenhotep III. His kingdom, Amurru, is generally recognized as Syria, or the Syrian region. Now Abdi-Ashirta has a name identical to that of Abd'Astartus, whom Menander of Ephesus tells us was the grandson of Solomon's great ally King Hiram.[1] Once again, we seem to find an uncanny match between a character of the fifteenth century BC and one of the ninth. The similarities between the two are not confined to names: Both Abdi-Ashirta of the Amarna Letters and Abd'Astartus of Tyre were removed violently from the throne.[2]

The Amarna Letters were written during the reigns of Amenhotep III and Akhnaton, roughly three to four generations after Hatshepsut. That they seem to refer in so many ways to the time of King Asa of Judah and Kings Baasha and Omri of Israel — three to four generations after Solomon — would suggest that Hatshepsut and Solomon were contemporaries; and that the parallels between the love poetry of Hatshepsut's time and the biblical Song of Songs are not coincidental.

Another collection of documents from the same period, the famous Library of King Niqmed of Ugarit, discovered at the modern village of Ras Shamra in northern Syria, points in exactly the same direction. Here we find a written form of Hebrew/Phoenician "surprisingly akin" in terms of vocabulary, grammar, syntax, and idioms, to the Hebrew of the Old Testament.[3] The majority of the Hebrew/Phoenician texts are poems describing the exploits and battles of the gods and the adventures of heroes. Yet, "The mythological pictures of the Ras Shamra poems often employ the same wording as the so-

---

1 Josephus, *Against Apion*, i, 122
2 Ibid.
3 J. W. Jack, *The Ras Shamra Tablets* (T & T Clark, Edinburgh, 1935), p. 10

called mythological images of the Scriptures. Leviathan is a 'crooked serpent' (Isaiah 27:1); it has several heads (Psalms 74:14). Lotan of the poems also is a 'swift and crooked serpent' and has several heads. There is, in one of the poems, an expression put into the mouth of El which sounds like a refer-ence to the great feat of tearing asunder the sea of Jam-Suf [at the Exodus]. And the verb, 'to tear asunder,' used in the Psalms (136:13) is the same (*gzr*). The conclusion drawn from the similarity was this: long before the Exodus and the passage through the Red Sea, the Canaanites of Palestine knew this myth."[1]

The meter of the poems found on these tablets, as well as the division into feet of three syllables or three words, and the balancing of theme (par-allelism) are also found in the Scriptures.[2] According to Claude Schaeffer, the excavator, "These rules are precisely those of Hebrew poetry, and even the language from some of our Ras Shamra texts is entirely Biblical."[3] Even worse, some of the Ugarit documents were composed in an alphabetic script (written in cuneiform); yet this was supposedly at least five centuries before the Phoenicians had developed their alphabet (in the tenth century). More shocking still, this alphabet was not a primitive pioneering effort, but a well-developed system with a long history behind it: "The Ras Shamra alphabet is already so advanced that it implies the existence of a still earlier alphabet yet to be found."[4] Characters and events on the Ugarit documents seem also to recall the time of the Book of Kings. In the famous Poem of Keret we meet a King Daniel, who hurries southwards to meet an enemy known as Terah (or Zerah). On his way he gathers allies from the Hebrew tribe of Asher. This sounds like the war between the Israelites under King Asa (Solomon's grandson) and the Egyptian or Ethiopian king Zerah. But how could docu-ments of the fourteenth century refer to events of the ninth; five hundred years in the future?

Thus the testimony of the written word: Archaeology too, in a thousand ways, seems to place Egypt's Eighteenth Dynasty parallel to the world of the Early Hebrew Kings. It would be possible to fill many volumes with this material, and it has already been examined in some depth by a great many authors;[5] suffice to provide just a couple of examples here.

---

1 Immanuel Velikovsky, *Ages in Chaos* (London and New York, 1952), p. 190

2 J. W. Jack, *The Ras Shamra Tablets*, op cit.

3 C. Schaeffer, *The Cuneiform Texts of Ras Shamra-Ugarit* (Oxford University Press, Lon-don, 1939), p. 58

4 Ibid., p. 36

5 The main work was done by Immanuel Velikovsky in *Ages in Chaos*, and by vari-ous other authors in subsequent years. Much new evidence was added by Emmet

When in the nineteenth century English explorers unearthed the ancient city of Calah (modern Nimrud) in northern Mesopotamia, they discovered there a large number of Egyptian artifacts (mainly scarabs) of the Eighteenth Dynasty.[1] The majority of these were of the pharaoh Amenhotep III, and seemed to have been placed underneath buildings as a form of date-marker. This was normal practice throughout the Near East, and scarabs of pharaohs are regularly found under the foundation-stones of many important buildings. The problem here is that Calah was built by Ashurnasirpal II, father of Shalmaneser III, and contemporary of King Omri of Israel; a man supposedly five centuries removed from Amenhotep III.

Again, we might note the reoccurrence of building-styles in the ninth and eighth centuries which had first appeared in the fifteenth and fourteenth — and had disappeared completely in the interim. Perhaps the most notorious example of this was the famous hilani-house of Syria. The hilani-house was a palace-type structure consisting of a vestibule with one to three supports on the front side, behind which lay a large room with a hearth. Around this room were grouped smaller rooms. It was a style of architecture peculiar to the Hittite states of northern Syria, and described by historian Ekrem Akurgal as "one of the most remarkable architectural inventions of the ancient Near East,"[2] where it appeared in the late ninth, eighth, and seventh centuries BC. One of the first examples was raised by a King Kilamuwa, of Zincirli in northern Syria, a contemporary of Shalmaneser III and his successor Shamshi-Adad IV. However, astonishingly enough, Kilamuwa's hilani-house, which admittedly set the tone of building throughout northern Syria during the eighth and seventh centuries, is strikingly like that of Niqmepa, who reigned in nearby Ugarit. But Niqmepa was a contemporary of the early kings of Egypt's Nineteenth Dynasty — about five hundred years before Kilamuwa.[3]

In ways too numerous to mention, the development of art and military technology tells a similar tale. As just one example we may mention the deployment of cavalry. The first certain appearance of such troops in Egypt is right at the end of the Eighteenth Dynasty, when a single man on horseback is portrayed in the Memphis tomb of Horemheb. A decade later, Seti I had Hittite cavalrymen portrayed on his hypostyle hall at Karnak. In Mesopotamia, however, cavalry first appear four hundred and fifty years afterwards,

---

Sweeney in his *Empire of Thebes: Ages in Chaos Revisited* (Algora, New York, 2006)
1 See A. H. Layard, *Discoveries in the Ruins of Nineveh and Babylon* (London, 1853), p. 282
2 Ekrem Akurgal, *The Birth of Greek Art* (Methuen, London, 1968), pp. 69-71
3 Ibid.

during the reign of Ashurnasirpal II, where they are portrayed on the Nimrud bas-reliefs. Yet the deployment of the Hittite cavalry shown by Seti I displays striking agreement with the deployment of the Assyrian cavalry shown by Ashurnasirpal II. So for example the Assyrian horsemen ride bareback, obtaining a firm grip by pressing the raised knees against the horse's flanks — exactly the method of riding employed by the Hittites portrayed on the monument of Seti I. Again, both the Assyrian cavalry and those of the Hittites against whom Seti I battled employed the bow as their only weapon. Even more importantly, they are used in an identical way tactically: they are invariably used in conjunction with the chariotry. Describing the cavalry of Ashurnasirpal II, Gaston Maspero noted: "The army [of Assyria] ... now possessed a new element, whose appearance on the field of battle was to revolutionize the whole method of warfare, this was the cavalry, properly so called, introduced as an adjunct to the chariotry."[1] More specifically, "This body of cavalry, having little confidence in its own powers, kept in close contact with the main body of the army, and it was not used in independent manoeuvres; it was associated with and formed an escort to the chariotry in expeditions where speed was essential, and where ordinary foot soldiers would have hampered the movements of the charioteers."[2]

But the cavalry of the Hittites, depicted in the monuments of Seti I, are deployed in exactly the same way. How peculiar, that after four and a half centuries the art of horsemanship should have developed so little! And this at a time when, we might imagine, any tactical innovations would have been quickly seized upon. Even worse, why did it take the Assyrians, next neighbors of the Hittites, four hundred and fifty years to adopt the use of mounted cavalry; and why did no one, in the intervening years, realize that putting a saddle on a horse would make it more comfortable for the rider and provide him with a firmer grip; thus making him a far more effective warrior?

It is necessary to emphasize that the evidence presented above represents but a tiny sample of a truly enormous volume of material which seems to point to a strong relationship between the world of the Eighteenth Dynasty, supposedly the fifteenth and fourteenth centuries BC, and the world of the early Hebrew kings, of the tenth and ninth centuries BC. But if there is such compelling reason to associate these two epochs, what might it all mean for Egyptian history?

---

1 Gaston Maspero, *History of Egypt*, Vol. 7 (London, 1906), p. 8
2 Ibid., pp. 9-10

VELIKOVSKY, HATSHEPSUT AND THE QUEEN OF SHEBA

Although scholars have long noted the above anomalies, they accepted them as "puzzles" to be resolved at some future date. None of them, for one moment, questioned the chronology of Egypt. This they believed to be on rock-solid foundations, a belief still generally adhered to in the halls of academia. In the 1940s however one man broke ranks. Typically, he was an outsider, in terms of specialty. That man was Immanuel Velikovsky, a psychiatrist by profession and one-time student of Sigmund Freud. The latter had for a long time been fascinated by the growth of monotheism in ancient Israel and eventually became convinced that a connection must have existed between that faith and the monotheism of Egypt's heretic pharaoh Akhnaton. For Freud, the parallels between Moses' monotheism and that of Akhnaton were too clear to be ignored; and he came to the conclusion that Moses was an Egyptian prince raised at the court of Akhnaton, a conclusion expounded in his famous book, *Moses and Monotheism* (1939). Velikovsky, a young polymath from Russia, who came to study under Freud in Vienna, became in his turn fascinated by the question which so engaged his tutor. Influenced by another of Freud's students, Karl Abraham, Velikovsky then began to look at the possibility that Akhnaton might also have had an impact upon Greek culture, and came to believe that he could have been the source of the legend of Oedipus, the mythic king of Thebes who killed his father and married his mother.

His interest having been piqued, Velikovsky now began to explore Egypt's Eighteenth Dynasty in great detail with a view to establishing what cultural links might exist with the Hebrews and the Bible. At some stage during the 1940s, he came to an astonishing conclusion: the chronology of Egypt, the chronology provided in all the learned textbooks, was wrong; and it was wrong to a dramatic degree. It was, to begin with, far too long, and was out of synchronization with regard to the history of Israel. This was the reason, he said, why so little agreement had been found between the histories of Egypt and Israel — in spite of the fact that the two countries were close neighbors, and that their histories were (according to the Bible) inextricably linked for many centuries. Characters and events which, according to the Scriptures, had a major impact upon Egypt, were apparently unmentioned in the Egyptian sources. And yet, said Velikovsky, the Egyptians did record similar events and characters to those recounted in the Scriptures; only these were placed many centuries earlier by the Egyptologists. By the time of the Eighteenth Dynasty, he said, this dislocation of history was of the order of just over five centuries. As soon as we shorten history by that span of time, the Egyptian record fits into that of Israel like two matching pieces of a jigsaw; and in this spirit he published his first great work on chronology, *Ages in Chaos* (1952).

In *Ages in Chaos* Velikovsky argued that the Eighteenth Dynasty rose to power at the same time as the kingdom of Israel, and that the first pharaohs of that line, Ahmose and Amenhotep I, were contemporaries of Israel's first two kings, Saul and David. He went further, and suggested that one of the most important enemies of Saul and David, the Amalekites, were one and the same as those against whom Ahmose and Amenhotep I waged war, the Hyksos. Thus, for Velikovsky, the Egyptians of the early Eighteenth Dynasty and Israel's first kings, Saul and David, were allies. They had fought together to free both their lands from the yoke of a common enemy. Velikovsky therefore saw clear parallels in the battles waged by Ahmose against the Hyksos with the battles waged by Saul against the Amalekites and the Philistines.

Beginning Egypt's New Kingdom in tandem with Israel's United Kingdom presented Velikovsky with a uniquely fresh and dramatic view of the ancient past; and the histories of the two nations, which had hitherto seemed strangely disjointed and out of touch, began to display remarkable and even spectacular agreement. Both nations, he noted, freed from the oppression and exploitation of the "Shepherd Kings," began now to enjoy great prosperity. For Israel, the foundations were laid by David, but it was only in the time of his son Solomon the realm achieved its splendor. In Velikovsky's words:

"According to the scriptural narrative, Solomon had one thousand and four hundred chariots and twelve thousand horsemen; he reigned over all the land from the river Euphrates to the border of Egypt. The kings of Arabia paid him tribute, and presents were brought from near and far, vessels of silver and gold, garments and spices, armor and horses. He made cedars in Jerusalem 'to be as sycamore trees in the vale of abundance.' He built a palace with a great throne of ivory, and a house of worship. Vessels therein were of gold; of gold were the drinking cups of his palace. Six hundred threescore and six talents of gold came yearly to his treasury as tribute, besides the income from the traffic of the merchants (I Kings 10: 14-15)."[1]

The kingdom of Egypt too, Velikovsky notes, "also achieved grandeur and glory" at this time. Furthermore, the two neighboring realms, "freed form the same oppressor [the Hyksos], entered into trade relations and relations of kinship.

---

1 Velikovsky, *Ages in Chaos*, op cit., p. 103

"King Solomon took an Egyptian princess to be one of his wives, probably his chief wife. The Scriptures do not preserve her name. It is known only that her father, the pharaoh, made an expedition against southern Palestine, the home of the Philistines and the Canaanites, burned Gezer, and gave it as a dowry to his daughter (I Kings 9:16)."[1]

According to the chronology outlined by Velikovsky these events would have occurred in the time of Thutmose I, father of one of the most extraordinary rulers ever to wear the Double Crown of the pharaohs. This was Hatshepsut, the only woman ever to claim the "kingship" of Egypt. Like Solomon, this woman was a great builder who reigned over a nation on the threshold of unparalleled wealth and splendor. "Can it actually be," Velikovsky asked, "that no memory of her [Hatshepsut] was preserved in the annals of Jerusalem?" These two neighboring and powerful kings, he says, "in the process of developing their foreign relations and trade could hardly have been out of touch during the reigns of Solomon and Hatshepsut, neither of whom broke the peace of their countries."[2] Furthermore, "If Solomon was really a renowned king, as the Hebrew sources describe him, then the absence of any contact between this queen and this king is difficult to explain. It would, indeed, be very singular, for these two rulers were no ordinary occupants of throne halls, but very excellent suzerains."[3] Furthermore, since in Velikovsky's chronology ties of kinship had just been established between the two nations, it is seemingly impossible that Hatshepsut could have been ignored in the Hebrew chronicles.

But the records of Israel do not, it seems, ignore Hatshepsut; and for Velikovsky, it was but a short step from placing Hatshepsut at the same time as Solomon to making her identical to Solomon's famous royal visitor, the Queen of Sheba.

There is no question that Velikovsky's equation of Hatshepsut with the Queen of Sheba was one of his most attractive and dramatic insights. Few biblical characters have captured the imagination of successive generations quite like this woman. For centuries the identity of the queen, who appears but briefly in the Book of Kings (and Chronicles), has prompted endless speculating and romanticizing. Whole mythologies have been built around her. For the people of Ethiopia she is — along with her host Solomon — the

---

1 Ibid., pp. 103-4. Velikovsky identified this pharaoh with Thutmose I, who indeed records a military expedition into southern Palestine, after which he "journeyed to Retenu [Palestine] to wash his heart among the foreign countries." Ibid. If Velikovsky is correct here then Solomon's wife would have been a sister of Hatshepsut.
2 Ibid., pp. 104-5
3 Ibid., p. 105

ancestor of the native monarchy. The southern Arabs vie with the Ethiopians in claiming her; and they too regard her as their royal forebear. The passing centuries have not diminished her allure, and to this day she holds a unique fascination for many people. Every year sees the publication of new studies propounding supposedly fresh insights into the identity of the bewitching Queen; yet, for all that, precious little is known about her. Theories proliferate, but hard facts remain hard to come by.

Our only real knowledge of the Queen comes in a very brief description of her visit to Solomon in the Book of Kings (along with an almost identical description in the Book of Chronicles). She is simply identified as the ruler of Sheba who, having heard of the fame of Solomon, came to "try him with hard questions" (I Kings 10:1). She is said to have entered Jerusalem in a great train, carrying enormous quantities of treasure. She was then shown around the city, after which Solomon answered her questions. Everything she saw and heard impressed her, and, upon being presented with a great quantity of gifts, she departed to her own country. And that is all. The entire story occupies no more than thirteen biblical verses.

With such meager information to go on, it is little wonder that the mythologists and romanticizers have had such scope. Even worse, archaeological investigations over the past century failed to discover anything that could confirm either the queen's or even her host's existence. This must be emphasized. A century of excavation in the lands of the Bible has, far from confirming the existence of David's and Solomon's kingdom, brought it into question. By the time of the publication of *Ages in Chaos* many biblical scholars had already consigned these two supposedly great kings to the same fairy-land as the Queen of Sheba herself.[1] It was into this climate that, in 1952, Velikovsky produced his dramatic hypothesis. Not only did the Queen of Sheba really exist, but she was one of the most powerful monarchs of her age, and not only her monuments but actual portraits of her remain! If this were to be correct, if the Queen of Sheba really was identical to Hatshep-

---

1 And this process has become even more entrenched since the 1950s. Not a trace either of David or Solomon, it is now claimed, has ever been discovered, and is unlikely ever to be. This is due to the fact that the early Iron Age remains discovered in Jerusalem have revealed nothing like the mighty and grandiose metropolis of Solomon, as described in the first Book of Kings. See for example *The Bible Unearthed*, (2001) by Israel Finkelstein and Neil Asher Silberman, for the most important recent exposition of this thesis. Velikovsky's solution, of course, was to seek Solomon's Jerusalem in the remains of the late Middle Bronze and early Late Bronze city; and such enough, the settlement of this time (contemporary with Hatshepsut) was a mighty and opulent citadel. See chapters 4 and 5 below for a discussion of this question.

sut, then Velikovsky, by this discovery alone, had made one of the greatest contributions ever to the understanding of ancient Near Eastern history. An achievement worthy of a literary Indiana Jones!

As might be imagined, the reading public was captivated by Velikovsky's hypothesis; and among his academic supporters the identification was long regarded as one of his strongest, as well as most attractive. He was able to show, for example, that the Queen of Sheba was regarded as an Egyptian queen by Josephus Flavius, the first century Jewish chronicler and historian. Abyssinian tradition too, insisted that the Queen came from "Ethiopia" and that it was her son by Solomon, Menelik, who plundered the temple in Jerusalem after the former's death. This inevitably meant that the Queen of Sheba was an Egyptian, since it was a pharaoh, Shishak, who plundered Solomon's temple.

Whilst this evidence indicated that the Queen of Sheba was an Egyptian, other evidence from Egypt seemed to suggest that Hatshepsut had visited the land of Israel. Indeed, the most famous event of the queen's life — it seemed — was a journey or a pilgrimage to a mysterious land named Punt — a region also known as the Divine Land.

THE JOURNEY TO PUNT

Placing Hatshepsut in the epoch of Solomon might indicate that she could have been the Queen of Sheba; but the identification would be far more convincing, thought Velikovsky, if a record of her journey to Jerusalem could be found. Does such a record exist, he asked? It does indeed, he said.

On the western bank of the Nile at Thebes, just beyond the line of cultivated land, stands to this day one of the most remarkable monuments ever built by the Egyptians. This is the *Djeser-djeseru*, the "Splendor of Splendors," the funerary temple of Hatshepsut, a building widely recognized by scholars as one of the finest achievements of Egyptian architecture. The Temple is built against a semicircular wall of cliffs, of white limestone, "which time and sun have coloured rosy yellow," forming an "absolutely vertical barrier," beyond which lies the "wild and desolate valley of the Tombs of the Kings."[1] Against this spectacular background, the Temple, with its elegant colonnades and gracefully ascending ramps, stands out like a jewel. According to Edouard Naville, the monument must be "accounted the most beautiful left to us by Egyptian antiquity,"[2] an opinion shared by art historians in general.

1 Edouard Naville, *The Temple of Deir el-Bahari* , Part III (London, 1907) Introductory Memoir, p. 1
2 Naville in Theodore M. Davis, *The Tomb of Hatshopsitu*, (London, 1906), p. 73

Even today, after thousands of years of weathering and damage, the monument strikes the visitor by its elegance and grandeur.

Fig. 2. The Djeser-djeseru, "Splendor of splendors," Hatshepsut's magnificent funerary monument at Deir el-Bahri. Still widely regarded as the greatest masterpiece of Egyptian architecture

Upon this structure, which lay immediately in front of the tomb she had carved for herself in the Valley of the Kings, Hatshepsut recorded the most significant events of her life. Her birth is shown in the middle colonnade, where she is suckled by the goddess Hathor. Opposite her divine birth is shown — as apparently an equally important event of her life — an expedition to a mysterious region named Punt. Most of the Punt reliefs were destroyed in antiquity, but from the portions that survive we learn that the country — also known as *Ta Netjer*, the "Divine Land" — was a source of incense, a product which seems to have grown in abundance upon terraces prepared by the human inhabitants. The language used about Punt at Deir el Bahri is religious, even ecstatic. It is described as "a glorious region of God's Land," and a "place of delight." The queen tells us that she mounted the expedition to the mysterious land after a "command" by the god Amon-Ra had reached the "Great Throne." We are informed also that after the return of the expedition there was great rejoicing throughout the country, and the queen resolved to "build a Punt" in Egypt. The Splendor of Splendors itself was "the Punt" she spoke of.

Scholars have long wondered about this strange and blessed land, which was known equally as Punt and the Divine Land. The country seemed to have a tropical climate, and there is shown what seems to be a hippopotamus, as well as several other typically African animals, such as a giraffe and a rhinoceros.

Notwithstanding the African dimension, Velikovsky claimed that Punt, the Divine Land, was actually Israel, and that Hatshepsut's expedition to the region was the Queen of Sheba's expedition to the same country. He had many good reasons for doing so. The names used for the country, for example, Punt and the Divine Land, seemed to recall Israel. So for example, the "Divine Land," *Ta Netjer*, was known by Egyptologists to be a "reference to lands lying to the east of Egypt: especially Punt and the lands of incense, but not seldom also to Sinai and the Lebanon region,"[1] whilst Punt (*Pwenet*) seemed to recall Phoenicia, whose eponymous ancestor was known as Pontus.[2]

In the Divine Land the Egyptians were received by an official with the Hebrew name Peruah (Perehu), whom Velikovsky recognized as a provincial governor of southern Israel during Solomon's time.[3] The Puntites themselves were clearly Asiatics, or Semites, slightly lighter skinned than the Egyptians. They presented the visitors from Egypt with gifts of fabulous wealth, including huge quantities of incense and spices, gold and lapis lazuli, as well as wood of various exotic varieties and unusual animals. "Never were brought such things to any king since the world was," wrote Hatshepsut.

Among those presenting gifts were "chiefs of Irem," whom Velikovsky identified as servants of King Hiram, Solomon's famous ally.[4]

Perhaps the most important of the gifts received by the Egyptians were large quantities of incense, as well as a number of incense trees, which were brought to Egypt for replanting. These were called *anti* by the Egyptians, and recognized by modern botanists as frankincense. Velikovsky argued that in ancient times frankincense was cultivated in Israel, and that the "myrrh terraces" described by Hatshepsut were found in the Jordan Valley, where they can be seen to this day by the sides of the steep road leading from Jericho up to Jerusalem.

1 Erman, Adolph and Hermann Grapow, eds. *Wörterbuch der aegyptischen Sprache* (Leipzig, 1926-1963), Vol. V. p. 225

2 According to Sanchoniathon, the semi-legendary Phoenician historian. See Eusebius, *Praeparatio Evangelica* I, x, 27

3 Velikovsky, *Ages in Chaos*, op cit., pp. 114-6

4 Ibid. p. 125

Velikovsky conceded that the Punt reliefs did not show Hatshepsut's meeting with Solomon, but suggested this was because two thirds of the reliefs and inscriptions — including presumably the most politically important parts — were destroyed in antiquity. But he found very good reason to suppose, from the surviving scenes, that Hatshepsut had herself travelled to Punt: not the least of these being the incredible importance placed on the journey in the queen's funerary monument. He went a stage further, and argued that the wonderful temple at Deir el Bahri was itself a copy of Solomon's renowned temple in Jerusalem; and he saw reasons to believe that the rituals and protocols of the other temple were copied by the Egyptians.

The dramatic conclusion was that when we look at the Splendor of Splendors, we are looking at an exact copy of the First Temple of Jerusalem.

BIBLICAL PARALLELS WITH THE PUNT RELIEFS

Velikovsky showed that the description of the journey to Punt, as recounted on the walls of the Splendor of Splendors, had numerous parallels with the description of the visit of the Queen of Sheba provided in the Bible and in other Jewish tradition. The similarities are precise and detailed, and we frequently find the same expressions and turns of speech used in the two sets of literature — two literatures supposedly separated from each other by five hundred years. The most remarkable of these parallels were highlighted by Velikovsky, and indeed formed a central plank in his argument for the identification of Hatshepsut with the Queen of Sheba. A few of these are as follows:

To begin with, the expedition to Punt is explained at Deir el Bahri as the result of a divine command: "... a command was heard from the great throne, an oracle of the god himself, that the ways to Punt should be searched out, that the highways to the myrrh-terraces should be penetrated." Velikovsky commented: "Like the Punt inscription, the Haggada [a collection of Jewish traditions], and Josephus, too, describe this strong, imperative desire that inspired the queen [of Sheba] and that was considered a divine command."[1]

On the Punt reliefs, Hatshepsut praised "the greatness of the marvels, which happened to her," and she wrote: "Never did the like happen to any gods who were before, since the beginning." We also hear that the wonders of Punt were previously known only by rumor: "It was heard of from mouth to mouth by hearsay of the ancestors." In Velikovsky's words, "The queen wished to see with her own eyes the land of which she had heard marvellous

---

1 Ibid., pp. 117-8

reports,"[1] and all of this is strikingly similar to the words put into the Queen of Sheba's mouth in the Scriptures:

> And she said to the king. It was a true report that I heard in mine own land of thy acts and of thy wisdom.

> Howbeit I believed not the words, until I came, and mine eyes had seen it; and behold, the half was not told me; thy wisdom and prosperity exceedeth the fame which I heard. (1 Kings 10: 6-7)

Similarly, Josephus wrote:

> [She] was not able to contain her amazement at what she saw, but showed clearly how much admiration she felt, for she was moved to address the king. ... "All things indeed, O King," she said, "that come to our knowledge through hearsay are received with mistrust ... it was by no means a false report that reached us.[2]

In the biblical account, the Queen of Sheba praises Solomon's kingdom as an abode of happy people: "Happy are thy men, happy are these thy servants. ... Blessed be the Lord thy God." (1 Kings 10: 8-9) This is not unlike Hatshepsut's description of Punt: "It is a glorious region of God's Land. It is indeed my place of delight." Again, in Velikovsky's words, "The manner of expression ascribed to the Queen of Sheba in speaking about King Solomon is not unlike that which Queen Hatshepsut used in respect of herself: 'because the Lord loved Israel for ever, therefore he made thee king ...'" (1 Kings 10:9); 'because he [Amon] so much loves the King of Upper and Lower Egypt, Hatshepsut ...'"[3]

The gifts given and received by the Punt expedition match closely those exchanged between Solomon and the Queen of Sheba. Gold, silver, and precious stones figure prominently in the lists described in the two sets of documents; and, "just as Solomon knew the weight of gold he received, so Queen Hatshepsut knew, after measuring and weighing, the exact weight of the precious metals received in the Divine Land. A scene of the bas-relief shows the queen weighing the objects herself."[4]

Next to gold, silver and precious stones, the most valuable gifts mentioned in both sets of literatures are spices and incense. Thus in 2 Chronicles 9:9 we read, "... neither was there any such spice as the queen of Sheba gave king Solomon;" whilst in 1 Kings 10:10 we hear, "... there came no more such abundance of spices as these which the queen of Sheba gave to king Solo-

---

1 Ibid. p. 121
2 Josephus, *Jewish Antiquities*, VIII, xvii, 171
3 Ibid. p. 122
4 Ibid., p. 123

mon." In the same way, Hatshepsut received vast quantities of myrrh from the land of Punt: "Fresh myrrh (anti) in great quantities, marvels of the countries of Punt. Never did the like happen to any other gods who were before since the beginning." The myrrh was counted in "millions" and found to be "without number." But more than all the other "marvels," as Velikovsky notes, the queen valued some precious trees.

> Thirty-one anti trees, brought as marvels of Punt. Never was seen the like since the world was.

Velikovsky noted that the acquisition of valuable and rare plants was characteristic of Solomon and his time. Thus in 1 Kings 10: 11-12 we read:

> And the navy also of Hiram, that brought gold from Ophir, brought in from Ophir great plenty of almug trees, and precious stones. ... There came no such almug trees, nor were seen unto this day.

It is remarkable that in both literatures the trees are described as wonders the like of which had not been seen "since the world was" (Egyptian) and "unto this day" (biblical).

In both the Punt reliefs and the Scriptures which relate to the time of Solomon we hear that living animals (in addition to metals, minerals and plants) were exchanged as royal gifts. Thus in the tenth chapter of the First Book of Kings we read that apes were brought to Solomon by the navy of Tharshish.

> For the king had at sea a navy of Tharshish with the navy of Hiram: Once in three years came the navy of Tharshish, bringing gold, and silver, ivory, and apes, and peacocks.

Velikovsky notes that apes, as well as gold, silver and ivory were among the gifts received by Hatshepsut from Punt:

> The loading of the cargo-boats with great quantities of marvels of the land of Punt, with ... pure ivory, with green gold of the land of Amu, with ... cynocephali [baboons], monkeys, greyhounds, with skins of panthers of the south ...

As Velikovsky emphasized, the "rare trees, the myrrh for incense, the ivory, the apes, the silver and gold and precious stones were enumerated in both records, the hieroglyphic and scriptural."

The Deir el Bahri reliefs refer to negroes as among the gifts given to the Egyptians by the Puntites (a topic to be discussed more fully at a later stage). This calls to attention a passage of Josephus, which speaks of *kussiim* (negroes) as among the "merchandise" he acquired from the sale of the wealth brought to him by his navy from the "Sea of Tarsus."[1]

> The king [Solomon] had many ships stationed in the Sea of Tarsus, as it was called, which he ordered to carry all sorts of merchandise to the inland nations and from the sale of these there was brought to the king silver and gold and much ivory and *kussiim* [Negroes] and apes.[2]

Velikovsky notes; "It has been supposed that Josephus mistook some other Hebrew word of an older source and read it *kussiim*. The picture of the expedition to Punt proves, however, that Josephus was not wrong: *kussiim*, the dark men of Ophir, were apparently brought by the sailors of Hiram and Solomon."[3]

OBJECTIONS OF THE CRITICS

Virtually all of the claims made by Velikovsky about Hatshepsut and the Queen of Sheba, as well as about the chronology of Egypt in general, were rejected by mainstream historians. Strangely, however, none ventured to identify a single fault in his general chronological arrangement. The issues he raised about the literature were ignored; as were his arguments about the archaeology. Why, he said, were cities and towns, which we know were only built in the time of the Hebrew Kings, already mentioned in the Eighteenth Dynasty Amarna Letters, supposedly some centuries earlier? No answer to this was given. Why did the language of the Amarna Letters and Ugarit documents (when Hebrew was used) so closely match that of Israel during the time of the Kings? Again, no explanation was forthcoming; though placing these two sets of Hebrew/Phoenician literature five centuries apart is the equivalent of dating an English document of Richard III's time (fifteenth century) to that of Winston Churchill the twentieth. Why, he had said, did styles of architecture and art of the Eighteenth Dynasty so closely resemble those of the ninth century; and why was there nothing in between that might fill the gap? No answer. Why did the technology of war during the latter years of the Eighteenth Dynasty — including the development of cavalry warfare — so closely match the technology of war during the ninth century, as portrayed in the artwork of the Assyrian kings? Again, no answer was forthcoming. And why, above all, did the history of Egypt for several generations — from the start of the Eighteenth Dynasty — fit so closely with the history of Israel during the tenth and ninth centuries? Why did the his-

---

1 It is probable that "Tarsus" here, or Tharshish, is Tartessos, the Phoenician colony on the Atlantic coast of Spain.
2 Josephus, *Jewish Antiquities*, VIII, vii, 2
3 Velikovsky, *Ages in Chaos*, op cit., p. 126

tory of Egypt form a precise counterpart with the history of Israel, generation for generation, in parallel sequence, once the five and a half centuries
were removed? Once more, no answer.

What the critics did do, when they eventually did respond, was precisely
what Velikovsky had predicted they might do; and which he had appealed
to them not to do: They sought to find a detail here or there where he might
have made a mistake, and to use these errors to invalidate the whole work.
This was neither a very honest nor academically sound procedure. As Velikovsky emphasized again and again, the force of the evidence he mustered
was accumulative, and individual points could not really be considered
without allusion to the whole. Consider the following: It is an undoubted
fact that, if a five hundred year span is removed from the history of Egypt,
Hatshepsut assumes a place in the tenth century BC and becomes a contemporary of Solomon. It is however an even greater certainty that her successor Thutmose III then becomes a contemporary of Solomon's successors Rehoboam and Jeroboam I, and that, as a consequence, he must be identical to
the pharaoh named Shishak, who plundered Solomon's temple. This cannot
be stressed too strongly. Making Hatshepsut contemporary with Solomon
may still leave some doubt as to whether she is the Queen of Sheba; but the
very same adjustment leaves *no doubt at all* that her stepson Thutmose III is
the biblical Shishak. For whereas the Queen of Sheba is nowhere explicitly
identified as an Egyptian monarch (or so it is widely believed) Shishak is
indeed unequivocally identified as such!

The one identification thus makes the other inevitable. And this is the
whole point of *Ages in Chaos*. Even one proven reoccurrence or "matching" of
a personality or cultural feature after a gap of five centuries would in itself
present a powerful argument for removing those five centuries. But when
such reoccurrences repeat themselves generation after generation, in parallel
sequence, the force of the argument becomes almost irresistible. Each new
parallel does not simply add to the probability that the adjusted chronology
could correct, but multiplies it by many orders of magnitude in a geometric
progression. This too was a point made by Velikovsky all those years ago;
and, like most of what he said, ignored by his critics.

Yet having said that, there is a case for looking at the different identifications proposed in *Ages in Chaos* on an individual basis; for if the picture
presented by Velikovsky is correct, each synchronism should in fact be able
to withstand any cross-examination.

Of course, by focusing on a particular identification, the chances of finding a flaw in the argument are improved. After all, the sum total of what we

know of any character of this far-off time is not great; and doubt could conceivably be cast on a statement made by Velikovsky — or by any historian — about any king or queen of this age. It was perhaps for this reason that the critics focused upon Hatshepsut. Perhaps too they were conscious of the fact that this was one of Velikovsky's most attractive and popular identifications. The Queen of Sheba, in the form of Hatshepsut, was again casting her romantic spell upon the world; and the defenders of academia's bastions were bound to try to break it. Yet even on the question of Hatshepsut, few ventured to cross swords with Velikovsky during his lifetime. A rare exception was Egyptologist William H. Stiebing who, in 1972 published a critical article in the journal *Pensée*.[1] Most of Stiebing's objections were reiterated, in much greater detail, after Velikovsky's death (1979) by David Lorton in 1982[2] and by John Bimson in 1986.[3] It is with the latter two that I shall be mainly concerned in the pages to follow.

The first criticism concerned the identity of the Queen of Sheba. There was no reason, said Lorton and Bimson, to suppose that this woman came from Egypt. If she did come from Egypt, why did the authors of the Bible simply not say so?

The second criticism, or series of criticisms, concerned Hatshepsut's expedition to Punt and the location of Punt. First and foremost, they reiterated the mainstream opinion that Hatshepsut did not travel to Punt. If she did not even go on the expedition, this precluded, *a priori*, the possibility that she could have been the Queen of Sheba. Secondly, and perhaps even more importantly, they argued (again, along the lines of mainstream opinion) that Punt was not in Palestine/Syria, as Velikovsky had claimed, but somewhere in Africa (Eritrea and Somalia being the two favored locations). This was proved, they said, by the very obviously African animals shown on the Deir el-Bahri reliefs — such as a giraffe and rhinoceros — and by the African flora. A major reason for the expedition to Punt was to acquire incense trees — either frankincense or myrrh. But the type of frankincense trees shown on the bas-reliefs are nowadays found only in southern Arabia — though a slightly different variety grows in Ethiopia and Somalia.

---

1 William H. Stiebing, "Rejoinder to Velikovsky," *Pensee* 5 (Autumn, 1973), pp. 10-12

2 See David Lorton, "Hatshepsut, the Queen of Sheba, and Immanuel Velikovsky" (1984) on the world-wide web at www. geocities. com/Athens/Academy/1326/ hatshepsut. html.

3 John Bimson, "Hatshepsut and the Queen of Sheba: A Critique of Velikovsky's Identification and an Alternative View," *Society for Interdisciplinary Studies; Review* 8 (1986)

In line with their rejection of the Punt = Israel equation, Lorton and Bimson also denied that the word "Punt" was related to "Phoenicia" (as Velikovsky had claimed), and they pointed to some Egyptian inscriptions which proved, they said, that Punt was located to the south of Egypt. And the term "Divine Land," they said, whilst *sometimes* being used to denote the region of Israel/Lebanon, did not always denote this territory. Lorton argued that it was a general term for any region regarded as blessed in some way.

The latter point was argued in great detail by Lorton in particular, and so it is one which I shall address in equal detail. As a matter of fact, I hope to demonstrate to the reader that every criticism leveled at Velikovsky was specious and the result of superficial research and a too-willing acceptance of mainstream "expert" opinion.

It is with the first of the above objections, however, the identity and nationality of the Queen of Sheba, that we shall begin.

CHAPTER 2: IDENTITY OF THE QUEEN OF SHEBA

THE TERMS "QUEEN OF SHEBA" AND "QUEEN OF THE SOUTH"

In the Bible Solomon's royal guest is known both as the Queen of Sheba (Book of Kings and Chronicles) and Queen of the South (Gospel of Matthew). Is it possible to identify the Queen's origin from these titles? Commentators throughout the centuries have suggested various solutions, though there has never been any general agreement. There is a region in southern Arabia known as Saba, and the natives of that land have long claimed the Queen as their own. Yet the people of Ethiopia make a similar claim, and the historian Josephus named Saba as the capital of ancient Ethiopia (Nubia, in southern Egypt) and claimed that the Queen of Sheba was ruler of their country.[1] As we shall now see, this author, who is admittedly the oldest written source outside the Bible, was right on the mark: For the Queen of Sheba was almost certainly an Egyptian; and whether or not Hatshepsut, the female "pharaoh" who ruled Egypt during one of its most splendid periods was *the* Queen of Sheba and Queen of the South mentioned in the Bible, she was without question *a* queen of Sheba and *a* "queen of the South."

Let's look first of all at the term Queen of the South. In his article, Lorton asks the question: "Why would [the authors of Matthew's Gospel] ... have said 'queen of the South' when they might so easily have said 'queen of Egypt'?" In the same vein, Bimson comments on what he describes as "the total lack of reference to Egypt in connection with the Queen of Sheba." "If the visiting queen was

---

1 Josephus, *Jewish Antiquities*, VIII, vi, 2.

Hatshepsut," he says, "she should be described as the Queen of Egypt by the Old Testament writers."[1]

If Lorton and Bimson had researched the question more thoroughly, they would have found that the name "king of the South" was a recognized biblical term for the Egyptian monarch. Thus for example in the Book of Daniel the Ptolemaic pharaoh is named "King of the South" on several occasions. It may be that this was not the most common biblical designation for the Egyptian ruler, but its occurrence in Daniel, without any explanatory comments, proves beyond question that it was a well-recognized expression.

> And the king of the south shall be strong ... and shall enter into the fortress of the king of the north ... and shall also carry captives into Egypt ... So the king of the south shall come into his own kingdom and return to his own land (Daniel 11, v.5-9).

It should be noted that the Book of Daniel is generally dated to the first century BC, whilst the Gospel of Matthew seems to have been written in the third quarter of the first century AD. Evidently, during this century or two, "monarch of the south" was a normal term for the Egyptian ruler.[2]

So, whether or not Hatshepsut was *the* Queen of the South mentioned in the Solomon story, she was very definitely *a* queen of the South. She was also, as we shall now see, a queen of Sheba.

The capital of Egypt during the Eighteenth Dynasty was the mighty city of Thebes. Modern Egyptologists still use this name, which we get from the Greeks. Where the Greeks got it has always been a mystery, since the native name of the metropolis, in the hieroglyphs, is read as *w3s.t*, which is interpreted as "city of the scepter," and generally given as Waset, though the "t" was unpronounced. Actually, the glyphs used are that of the scepter — written as Uas-t by Budge — and that of a plant and an arm — written as Shema or Sh-a by Budge: thus Uas-sha or Was-sha). Thebes was also known to the Egyptians as *niw.t rs.t*, which is translated as "southern city," and *iwnw-sm'*, meaning "Heliopolis (No) of the south." Some time ago Lisa Liel of Israel, an authority on both hieroglyphic and cuneiform scripts, pointed out to me that in her opinion the "city of the scepter" title, *w3s.t*, should be read as Se.wa or She.wa, since the spellings of hieroglyphic names vary and in addition are often written not precisely as they should be pronounced. In

---

1 Bimson, loc. cit.

2 The importance and significance of the term "Queen of the South" as indicating an Egyptian monarch was first noted by Martin Sieff in 1975 (*Society for Interdisciplinary Studies, Newsletter*, No. 2. Also in *Society for Interdisciplinary Studies Review*, Vol. 1 (1975) No. 1

fact, spellings often had more to do with aesthetics or religious sentiment than with strict phonetics. Thus the name Tutankhamen is actually written as Amen-tutankh (since the god's name had to come first) and the names of the Senwosret pharaohs of the Twelfth Dynasty appear in the hieroglyphs as Wsr.t.sn. One might also note that various pharaohs whose names are made up of the elements Ka-nefer-re are alternately named Nefer-ka-ra (in actual fact the name appears in the hieroglyphs normally as Ra-nefer-ka). Now, if Thebes' Egyptian name is really Shewa (Sheba) then a whole host of hitherto mysterious facts become comprehensible. First and foremost, we now know where the Greeks got the word Thebes (Theba). A normal linguistic mutation (lisping), one which, as it happens, occurred regularly in the ancient Semitic and Indo-European tongues of the Middle East, turns "s" or "sh" into "th." Thus for example the Persians called Assyria, *Athuria*. Secondly, we know why Josephus called the capital of Ethiopia (i.e. Upper Egypt/Nubia) by the name Saba or Shaba. Finally, we understand the significance of the name of another cult shrine of the god Amon — the oasis of Siwa.

Thus the two titles by which the Queen of Sheba is known in the biblical story clearly identify her as a queen of Egypt. It is simply untrue to say we don't know where she came from. But that is not all. For, as we have seen above, Josephus also described her as "Queen of Egypt and Ethiopia"; and it should be stressed here that in his time "Ethiopia" was the name given to Nubia, i.e. southern Egypt/northern Sudan. And elsewhere Josephus states that in ancient times the capital of Ethiopia was known as "Saba."[1] It is true that he also identifies this Saba with Meroe (in the Sudan), claiming that the city's name was changed to the latter by Cambyses the Persian. This however must be viewed as little more than an example of the conflating and confusing of several separate events, for which ancient historians are notorious. Herodotus does the same on a regular basis. There are in fact excellent grounds for believing that between the reigns of Darius I and Darius II a dynasty of Nubian kings reigning from Thebes vied for control of Middle and Lower Egypt with the Persians. They were finally expelled from Thebes by the second Darius, from which point onwards Napata and then Meroe were their capitals.[2]

But it is not only Josephus who connects "Saba" or "Sheba" with Nubia: in at least three places in the Old Testament the land or city of Saba is located in southern Egypt or Nubia. Thus Gen. 10:7 reads, "The descendants

---

1 Josephus, *Jewish Antiquities*, II, x, 2.
2 For a detailed discussion, see Emmet Sweeney, *Ramessides, Medes and Persians* (Algora, New York, 2007)

of Chus [Cushites-Nubians] are Saba, Hevila, Regma and Sabathacha." Isaiah 43:3 reports, "I have given Egypt for thy atonement, Ethiopia and Saba for thee," and Isaiah 45:14, "Thus saith the Lord: The labor of Egypt, and the merchandise of Ethiopia, and of Sabaim [people of Saba], men of stature shall come over to thee ..."

The clear connection between the terms Queen of Sheba and Queen of the South still however leaves us with the question: Why did the biblical authors prefer these terms to "Egypt"? One possible answer is that the Jewish chroniclers were keenly aware of the Nubian (i.e., "Ethiopian") origin of the Eighteenth Dynasty. To call the Queen of Sheba an Egyptian would thus, perhaps, have been (in their minds at least) a slight inaccuracy. We recall here that a generation or so after the time of Solomon, Israel was attacked by an "Ethiopian" ruler named Zerah. Everyone, even mainstream scholars, agree that this "Ethiopian" king was an Egyptian pharaoh (he is said to have brought an army of Libyans and Ethiopians — i.e., Nubians — against Israel), and the present writer agrees with Velikovsky in identifying this man with Amenhotep II — a man whose Nubian ethnic identity is very clear in the portrayals of him that have survived.

Indeed, as we shall presently see, the blood of black Africa flowed strongly in the veins of all the Eighteenth Dynasty monarchs.

It is perhaps significant too, now that we are on the topic of identifying the Queen of Sheba's homeland, that Josephus gives the Queen of Sheba's name as Nikaule.[1] Given the fact, as Eva Danelius has pointed out, that the Egyptians had no separate "l" and "r," this could be read as Nikaure, which is reminiscent of Hatshepsut's prenomen Makare or Makere. The "Ma" part of Hatshepsut's name is derived from the goddess of truth Ma'at, who was portrayed in a characteristic headdress consisting of two high feathers. As Danelius noted, the only other goddess with a similar headdress was Neith, the great mistress of Sais. "In Josephus' time," she says, "Neit had become the leading female deity in Lower Egypt, having absorbed most of the goddesses of an earlier period. Thus, it might have happened that the picture of a goddess with a peculiar high headdress, details of which were blurred on a cartouche carved about 1000 years earlier, was taken for the symbol of the goddess Neit and the first syllable of Hatshepsut's prenom read accordingly."[2] In

---

1 See e.g., Eva Danelius, "The Identification of the Biblical 'Queen of Sheba' with Hatshepsut, 'Queen of Egypt and Ethiopia,'" *Kronos* I, 4 (1977).

2 Ibid., p. 11. John Bimson (loc. cit., p. 23) claims that Josephus' Nikaule is more probably derived from Herodotus' Nitokris. This is quite possible, but in no way does it invalidate Danelius' point, since Nitokris herself — identified by Herodotus

short, read as Neit-ka-ra. Since the "t" was not pronounced, this would have been vocalized something like Ni-ka-ra — i.e. identical to Nikaule. Danelius notes also that "Wilkinson, one of the first Egyptologists to read the cartouches at Deir el-Bahari, thought, too, that the picture of the goddess was that of Neit, and read the queen's name accordingly: Neit-go-ri."

Before moving on, there is one more point that needs to be stressed. The context within which the Queen of Sheba story appears in itself constitutes evidence which cannot be ignored. The Queen of Sheba who visited Solomon was the ruler of an important and powerful kingdom. This is proved beyond question by the amount of space devoted to her in the biblical account, and precludes the possibility that she was the queen of some desert principality in southern Arabia. Solomon no doubt entertained many princes and princesses from Arabia and other areas, but their visits are not recorded because they lacked significance. From the importance placed on the Queen of the South's visit, it is evident that she must have been the ruler of an extremely powerful nation. This alone would point to Egypt and would possibly, I suggest — even without the evidence mentioned above — be sufficient to identify her as an Egyptian monarch.

SHEBA, CITY OF THE SPHINX

We have stated that Thebes seems to have originally been known as Sheba by the Egyptians, and that Josephus gave the name Saba to the capital of Nubia. Biblical passages furthermore apparently connect "Saba" to the region of Nubia. This leads us to suspect that whilst Wa.she/She.wa may have meant "city of the scepter" in Egyptian, the name may also have been influenced by a Nubian word "Shaba" or "Saba.": Was Sheba a Nubian name; and if so, what did it mean?

The Nubian provenance of the word "Shaba" or "Sheba" is rather obviously illustrated by the fact that two of the great warrior-pharaohs of the Twenty-Fifth Dynasty were called Shabaka and Shabataka; and such being the case it would suggest that Sheba/Theba was in origin a Nubian name. This should come as no surprise given the rather well-accepted Nubian origins of the Eighteenth Dynasty, the line of kings which had its home and base in Thebes.[1] So for example the blue war-crown or *khepresh*, which was introduced into pharaonic iconography by the Eighteenth Dynasty kings, is

---

as a sole queen among numerous male rulers — stands a very good chance of being another alter-ego of Hatshepsut/Makere.

1   See e.g., Flinders Petrie, *The Making of Egypt* (London, 1039), p. 155.

widely believed to represent a negro hair-style, whilst several of the early Eighteenth Dynasty monarchs, most particularly Nefertari, the wife/sister of Ahmose (founder of the dynasty) had distinctly negro features. In Petrie's words: "From the stele of Iufi it is certain that Aahhotep was mother of Aahmes [Ahmose] I, and hence Aahmes and Nefertari were of the same mother. But yet we cannot suppose them to have had both parents alike; Aahmes is always (except once) shown of the same colour as other Egyptians, while Nefertari is almost always coloured black. And any symbolic reason invented to account for such colouring applies equally to her brother, who is nevertheless not black. As Nefertari was specially venerated as the ancestress of the dynasty, we must suppose that it was she from whom the royal succession appears to have been reckoned, and hence her black colour is the more likely to have come from through her father. The only conclusion, if these points should be established, is that the queen Aahhotep had two husbands: the one black (the father of Nefertari), namely, the celebrated Seqenera ... the other Egyptian, the father of Aahmes and his elder brothers Kames and Sekhentnebra, which explains why those three kings are separated from the other children of Aahhotep by her husband Seqenera, and placed in a different line in the tomb of Khabekht."[1]

Petrie was of the opinion that pharaoh Shabaka's name derived from a Nubian word meaning "wild cat" and that the word was actually pronounced something like "Shab" or "Shaba," given that the "ka" element was merely the definite article, an element usually omitted in common speech.[2]

Could it be that Thebes was called after a species of wild-cat?

Greek legend told how the city of Thebes was plagued by a ferocious man-eating monster with a woman's head and the body of a lion or lioness. Velikovsky argued convincingly and in great detail that this legend — that of Oedipus — belonged in Egypt; that the city of Thebes referred to was the Egyptian metropolis and not its tiny Greek namesake.[3] Certainly no one denies that the sphinx is an Egyptian rather than a Greek creature, and even the Greeks told how Hera or Ares had sent the Sphinx from her Ethiopian (Nubian) homeland to haunt the mountains around Boeotian Thebes. It seems

---

1 Petrie, *A History of Egypt*, Vol. 2 (London, 1896), p. 337

2 "The present Nubian for the male wild cat is *Sab*, and *ki* is the article post-fixed. Hence in popular talk it is very likely that the king was known as Sab or Shab, just as the hieroglyphic name Pilak lost its article in the common mouth and became Philae." Petrie, *A History of Egypt* Vol. 3 (1905), p. 284. The "Shaba" part of Shabaka's name is admittedly spelled differently to that of the great metropolis. But this offers no real objection, as variant spellings are to be expected.

3 See Velikovsky, *Oedipus and Akhnaton* (New York, 1960).

clear too that Thebes in Egypt was a major cult-centre of the sphinx deity. The ancient legend of the war between Horus and Set told how the sphinx (the lion-bodied god Harmachis or Har-em-akhet, 'Horus of the Horizon'), as an ally of Horus, proceeded up the Nile Valley from Memphis slaughtering the warriors of Set with his mighty claws. Great numbers of these were killed at Thebes, and there is reliable evidence to suggest that, until the time of Akhnaton, human victims — criminals and prisoners of war — were sacrificed to the sphinx at Thebes.

The name sphinx is Greek, said to derive from the verb *sphingein*, "to bind tight," by reason of the creature's supposed reputation for killing by strangulation. This explanation seems somewhat strained, though it is undeniable that victims of human sacrifice were indeed bound tightly before being dispatched. Yet even if "sphinx" does derive from *sphingein*, it seems probable that the word was also influenced by the name of the city — Theba or Sheba. The latter, meaning "cat" in the Nubian language (or shabak — "the cat") is not far removed from "sphinx," and it seems singularly appropriate that the great metropolis, home of the sphinx-cult and sphinx-myth, should also derive its very name from the same creature.[1]

THE QUEEN OF SHEBA IN ETHIOPIAN TRADITION

It is worth repeating, at this point, that the land we now call Ethiopia was not the same country as that which anciently bore the name. In biblical times, as we said, "Ethiopia" was the name given to Nubia, the region corresponding to the far south of modern Egypt and the northern half of modern Sudan. Modern Ethiopia, on the other hand, centered on the highlands of Abyssinia, is a land which, as we shall see, owes much of its cultural heritage to southern Arabia. Nevertheless, there is no question that Abyssinia was influenced, to some degree, by the civilization of Egypt and Nubia. The later Nubian kingdom, from the fifth century BC onwards, had its capital at Meroe, near the Fourth Cataract. This is just over 570 miles, as the crow flies, from Lake Tana, in the Abyssinian Highlands; and the southern borders of this later Nubian realm were substantially closer to Abyssinia than Meroe. It is known that even before the beginning of the Christian era many Egyptian cultural and religious ideas had reached the country. This movement was only strengthened with the advent of Christianity, and from the second cen-

---

1 It should be remarked that the Egyptian crocodile-god Sebek bears a name similar to that of Shaba-ka. This may be more than coincidental, given the serpentine, dragon-like qualities of the early sphinx-creature.

tury AD, Abyssinia became a Christian land with strong links to the Coptic Church of Egypt.

Bearing the latter point in mind, it is surely significant that the Queen of Sheba occupies a central position in the traditions of the Abyssinians. Indeed, in a very real sense the Queen of the South is regarded as the founding matriarch of the nation; the ancestress of all the nation's royal dynasties. In the words of Budge, the Abyssinians "never doubted that Solomon was the father of the son of the Queen of Sheba. It followed as a matter of course that the male descendants of this son were the lawful kings of Abyssinia, and as Solomon was an ancestor of Christ they were kinsmen of our Lord, and they claimed to reign by divine right."[1]

But whilst the Abyssinians identified and celebrated the Queen of Sheba as ruler of Ethiopia, they were equally unequivocal in identifying her as a queen of Egypt; and the traditions which do so are of a type that could not, as we shall see, have been copied from biblical or other sources.

The great repository of Abyssinian legend and lore is a volume named the *Kebra Nagast*, the *Book of the Glory of Kings*. The existing version is said to be a translation from an Arabic text, which in turn was translated from a Coptic (late Egyptian) one. It contains quotation from the Gospels, and therefore cannot predate the rise of Christianity. According to Budge, it is "a great storehouse of legends and traditions, some historical and some of a purely folklore character, derived from the Old Testament and later Rabbinic writings, and from Egyptian (both pagan and Christian), Arabic and Ethiopian sources. Of the early history of the compilation and its maker, and of its subsequent editors we know nothing, but the principal groundwork of its earliest form was the traditions that were current in Syria, Palestine, Arabia, and Egypt during the first four centuries of the Christian era."[2]

The *Kebra Nagast* asserts that whilst in Jerusalem the Queen of Sheba became Solomon's lover, and returned to her own country pregnant. From this liaison was born Menelik, reputedly the ancestor of all the kings of Ethiopia. We are also told that when she returned to her country, "her officials who had remained there brought gifts to their mistress, and made obeisance to her, and did homage to her, and all the borders of the country rejoiced in her coming. .., And she ordered her kingdom aright, and none disobeyed her command; for she loved wisdom and God strengthened her kingdom." Velikovsky noted that this passage "resembles the story of the festival for

1 E. A. Wallis Budge, *The Kebra Nagast* (English trans. London, 1932), p. x
2 *Kebra Nagast*, pp. xv-xvi

the officials and for the whole rejoicing land, arranged by Queen Hatshepsut after her return from her journey; so do the words 'she ordered her kingdom aright' and that she 'loved wisdom.'"[1] Yet for all that, "there is nothing so extraordinary in these things as to compel the conclusion that Ethiopian tradition about the Queen of the South knows more than the Scripture narrative." Should the Ethiopian tradition however disclose some fact not contained in the Scriptures, but which agreed with what we know of Hatshepsut, then its claim to originality would be greatly strengthened.

Such a fact exists. In the Abyssinian tradition, the Queen of Sheba is called Makeda, whilst the royal name of Hatshepsut, mentioned throughout the Punt reliefs, is Makera. The similarity between these two words is so great that we may conclude with Velikovsky that "only by a rare chance" could it be purely coincidental. That the letter "r" in the original has been changed to a "d" in the Abyssinian is easily explained if we remember that the *Kebra Nagast* is the translation of a translation; passages in Egyptian (Coptic) and Hebrew being translated first into Arabic and then — after being added to and rewritten many times — into Abyssinian. A single scribal error (and there must have been many) would have been sufficient to corrupt the original form of Makera's name. Yet it so happens that this is one scribal error that could have occurred with exceptional ease. Some time ago Don Stewart drew my attention to the fact that the early Hebrew/Phoenician letters "r" and "d" are almost identical. Both are left-facing triangles. The only difference is that the "r" has a tail, though, as Don Stewart points out, sometimes scribes also affixed a "tail" to the "d", making the two letters almost impossible to tell apart. The two appear thus in Phoenician:

It will be admitted, I think, that such a scribal error could have easily occurred.

---

1 Velikovsky, *Ages in Chaos*, op cit., p. 136

Velikovsky surmised that if the name was not handed down by an uninterrupted tradition then it might have been disclosed by an Egyptian of early Christian times who, having seen the Punt texts at Deir el-Bahri, and being able to read them, identified Hatshepsut with the Queen of Sheba. There may in any case have been a tradition current in Egypt that the Punt reliefs represented a voyage to Jerusalem. This surmise is however unlikely in view of the fact that by the third or perhaps fourth century BC the old Phoenician alphabet had passed out of use, at least among the Jews. Clearly there must have been a document or documents, composed in old Hebrew/Phoenician, identifying Hatshepsut with the Queen of Sheba.

It is intriguing to think that had the Coptic or Jewish or Abyssinian scribe whose writings formed the basis of the Abyssinian tradition had read the Phoenician triangular letter in the Queen of Sheba's name as "r" rather than "d", then the Ethiopians would always have called her Makera, and early Egyptologists would have swiftly realized that she could only be the same person as Hatshepsut. This realization, however, would have produced a very different history of Egypt to the one we now find in the textbooks.

The *Kebra Nagast*'s value to our investigation is not exhausted with this disclosure, spectacular though it might be. We find there another tradition of equal or perhaps even greater significance. As we saw, the Ethiopians assert that Solomon and the Queen of Sheba became lovers, from which union was born Menelik, the ancestor of all Ethiopia's monarchs. Crucially, we are further informed, after reaching manhood Menelik returned to Israel to rob the Temple, and, upon stealing the holy Ark of the Covenant by a ruse, fled to Ethiopia, pursued by his father Solomon as far as the borders of Egypt. To this day, the Ethiopians claim that the lost Ark remains in their possession.

Now we know that, after the death of Solomon, the Temple in Jerusalem was indeed plundered, and that all of its treasures, including presumably the Ark of the Covenant, were carried off to Egypt.[1] Biblical tradition is very specific that the culprit was a ruler of Egypt, a pharaoh, to whom the name Shishak is given. That Ethiopian tradition should also assert that the king who stole the Ark was a son of Solomon and the Queen of Sheba makes it very clear that the Queen was regarded by the Ethiopians as an Egyptian monarch.

As we shall see, the real Shishak, the plunderer of Solomon's Temple, was Thutmose III, not the son of Hatshepsut, but the stepson and nephew. He did not rule Abyssinia, but he did rule ancient Ethiopia, which was Nubia

---

1 Though Jewish tradition specifically states that the Ark was not removed by Shishak, but remained in the Temple till the Babylonian Exile.

as far south as the Third Cataract. Clearly then Menelik must, in some way or other, represent the historical Thutmose III; and there is some evidence at least to suggest that the name Menelik can be traced to the pharaoh. Given the notorious interchangeability of the letters "l" and "r", Menelik may originally have been Menerik, and this sounds like a contracted and slightly corrupted version of Thutmose III's throne-name, Menkheperre; the name by which he is most frequently known on inscriptions and correspondences. It is perhaps worth pointing out too that by early Christian times Egyptian pronunciations had changed dramatically from pharaonic usage. Thus Amenhotep was, even by the third century BC, pronounced something like "Amenophe," with the "p" softened and the syllable "hot" unpronounced. It is not impossible therefore that by Christian times, when the Coptic traditions which found their way into the *Kebra Nagast* were being compiled, the name Menkheperre could have been pronounced something like Menkere. There is no great distance between Menelik/Menerik and Menkere.[1]

In Chapter 5 we shall see how Thutmose III/Menkheperre attacked Palestine in his first year of rule and how he plundered the fabulously wealthy temple he found in the region's capital.

---

1 Velikovsky noted that the tradition of Menelik seems to mingle the story of Thutmose III's real plunder of the Temple with his son Amenhotep II's unsuccessful invasion of Palestine. This was a topic dealt with by Velikovsky in Chapter 4 of *Ages in Chaos*, where he reveals that Amenhotep II was identical to Zerah, the king of Ethiopia defeated by King Asa, Solomon's grandson. Interestingly, Amenhotep II was the son of Thutmose III but also claimed to be a son of Hatshepsut (the name is normally given as Merytre-Hatshepsut). This claim is regarded by Egyptologists as most mysterious, and it has been surmised that perhaps there were two Hatshepsuts. However, since the Egyptian language has but a single word for "son," "grandson," and "great-grandson," it is possible, if Merytre-Hatshepsut was not a separate person, and that Amenhotep II may have been a son of Hatshepsut's daughter Neferure, whom we know was married to Thutmose III. Perhaps alternatively Neferure was, at a later stage in her life, known as Merytre-Hatshepsut.

CHAPTER 3: THE MYSTERY OF PUNT

THE QUEEN OF EGYPT *DID* GO TO PUNT

Conventional historians, convinced that Punt was a distant land on the southern shores of the Red Sea, or even further south, assume that Hatshepsut did not take part in the expedition described on her funerary monument. According to them, the journey was deemed worthy of commemoration on the queen's temple precisely because its goal was such a distant and exotic location. They can assert this however only by ignoring a great deal of evidence explicitly stating the exact opposite. So for example an official of the Sixth Dynasty, during the Old Kingdom, casually remarked that he had visited Punt and Byblos eleven times. Quite apart from the fact that this seems to locate Punt beside Byblos, in Lebanon, it also suggests that the mysterious land can have been no great distance from Egypt. The same thing is suggested by the apparent importation of incense from the region as early the First Dynasty,[1] and by the claim of the Egyptians that they themselves had originated in Punt.[2] Relations between Punt and Egypt seem to have been intimate during the Old Kingdom. We know that a son of Khufu (Dynasty 4) had possessed a Puntite slave,[3] and the pharaohs of the Fifth Dynasty organized great trading expeditions to the region. That of Sahure, for example, "brought back 80,000 measures of myrrh, probably 6,000 weight of electrum (gold-silver alloy),

---

1 See Breasted, *A History of Egypt*, op cit., p. 127, where he notes that contact with Punt "may have been made as early as the First Dynasty, for at that time the Pharaohs already used myrrh in considerable quantities ..."
2 See e.g., Flinders Petrie, *The Making of Egypt* (Macmillan, London, 1939), p. 77
3 Ibid.

---

besides 2,600 staves of some costly wood, presumably ebony."[1] Punt's chief importance, however, from the very beginning, was as a source of incense. In the words of Kjeld Nielsen, "the use of incense goes back to the earliest time. One of the earliest written sources referring to *'ntyw* [incense] from Punt is the Palermo stone. The king who imports *'ntyw* is Sahure, the 2nd king of the 5th Dynasty. The [Palermo] stone mentions the Egyptian connection with Punt as a most normal state of affairs. ... Contact with Punt was kept alive first of all by ship. Under Pepi II of the 6th Dynasty a certain Enekhet was slain by Asiatics while building ships for Punt. In the Old Kingdom a ship employed for voyages to Punt was called a gubliya, a term which originally must have designated a ship built for voyages to Gubla or Byblos."[2]

Although the above statement would suggest that Punt be located somewhere in Phoenicia, Nielsen quickly puts his readers "right" by adding; "However, the word [gubliya] soon lost its original meaning and came to signify a ship utilized for ocean-going traffic in contradistinction to the boats used on the Nile."[3] Be that as it may, here we seem to find, right at the start of Egyptian history, one of very many connections between Punt and the region of Palestine/Phoenicia.

Trade between Egypt and Punt continued to be vigorous during the Middle kingdom.[4] The proximity of the territory is also suggested by the victory lists of Thutmose III (of which more will be said presently), which state that the pharaoh had conquered all the regions of Punt in his first year. We know that in his first year Thutmose III conquered all of Palestine as far as the northern borders of Lebanon (Byblos and Baalbek are the most northerly conquests mentioned), and all of Nubia as far (probably) as the Third Cataract (close to Napata). Neither country is far from Egypt; on the contrary, they are the lands closest to Egypt. Yet, if Thutmose III's claims have any validity at all, Punt must be identified with one of them! Again, on the Deir el-Bahri inscriptions and elsewhere, the name Punt is written without the determinative of a foreign land, indicating that the Egyptians considered it in some way connected to their own country.

All of this would suggest that Punt was a region very close to Egypt; a fact which begs the question: Why then would Hatshepsut have immortalized a journey to it in such a grandiose and emphatic way if she did not go there herself? This is a fact that cannot be stressed too strongly. At Deir el-Bahri

---

1 Ibid.
2 See Kjeld Nielsen, *The Incense of Israel* (Leiden, 1986), p. 6
3 Ibid.
4 Petrie, *The Making of Egypt*, op cit., pp. 182-3

the expedition to Punt is part of a pair of adjacent reliefs; one recording the journey to Punt, the other recording the divine birth of the queen. The expedition to Punt seems thus to have been regarded by Hatshepsut as an event of equal importance to her own birth! This alone would virtually demand that she took part in the trip.

Velikovsky quoted several of the surviving Punt inscriptions which he claimed were the words of the queen herself, speaking in the first person, describing her journey to Punt. One of these reads:

> ... a command was heard from the great throne, an oracle of the god himself, that the ways to Punt should be searched out, that the highways to the myrrh-terraces should be penetrated:

> "I will lead the army on water and on land, to bring marvels from God's Land to this god, for the fashioner of her beauty ..." (Breasted, *Records*, Vol.2, Sec. 285)

Velikovsky states that "It was an oracle or mysterious voice that Queen Hatshepsut heard within her, and she thought it was her god."[1] He compares this "divine command" to visit Punt with Josephus' statement that the Queen of Sheba likewise felt a divine command to visit Israel.[2]

Velikovsky goes on to quote another part of the Deir el-Bahri inscriptions which states:

> I have led them [the company of the expedition] on water and on land, to explore the waters of inaccessible channels, and I have reached the myrrh-terraces. (Breasted, *Records*, Vol. 2, Sec. 288)

Taken in isolation, this might be interpreted as a personal statement of the queen, and that is certainly how Velikovsky presented it in *Ages in Chaos*. However, there is a problem; and it is one the critics were only too eager to seize upon. The statement, "I will lead the army on water and on land" and "I have led them on water and on land" are not, as reported on the monument, the words of the queen but of the god Amon. This is made abundantly clear in the inscriptions, and beyond dispute. Lorton used this as proof that Velikovsky was involved in deliberate deception and reiterated the mainstream belief that it proved Hatshepsut did not take part in the expedition.

In fairness to the critics, Velikovsky's statement that the above words were spoken by Hatshepsut does strike one as somewhat disingenuous. Both statements are addressed by Amon to Hatshepsut, on the occasion of the return of the expedition and the presentation to the god of gifts from Punt.

---

1 Velikovsky, *Ages in Chaos*, op cit., p. 117
2 Ibid., pp. 117-8

Furthermore, the surviving inscriptions certainly do give the impression, as Lorton and Bimson said, that the queen did not take part in the expedition.

In order to understand these texts, it is necessary to make a brief summary of what they say, and what the bas-reliefs show.

The first set of inscriptions describe the preparations made for the expedition and the departure from Thebes of the ships. A sacrifice is then made to Hathor, the "Lady of Punt," who was regarded as patroness of the land the travelers hoped to reach. Next, we see Nehesi (or Nehsi), the queen's ambassador, arriving at the shore of Punt, where he is greeted by Perehu (P'-r-hw), a "Chief of Punt," and Perehu's grossly overweight wife, Ity or Ati. The Puntites ask the Egyptians why they had "come hither unto to this land, which the people [of Egypt] knew not? Did ye descend upon the roads of heaven, or did ye sail upon the waters, upon the sea of God's Land? [Or] have you trodden the [pathway of] the Sun-god?"[1] After these preliminaries, Nehesi presents the Puntites with gifts, which are laid out on a table and amount to little more than trinkets. We see "strings of beads, bracelets, daggers, axes, and wooden chests."[2] Next, the Egyptians and the Puntites are shown loading gifts onto the Egyptian ships, which then depart for their own country. These gifts, which are listed in the final inscription, where they are presented to Amon in the presence of the queen, are of fabulous wealth, and include "two kinds of oxen; two species of panther, one of which seems to have been tame, being represented as collared and leashed; giraffes; baboons and monkeys; great quantities of panther skins; ostrich feathers and ostrich eggs; living incense trees; costly woods such as ebony; ivory; antimony, to be used as eye-cosmetic; sacks of incense; gold; silver; electrum; lapis-lazuli; malachite; shells; throw-sticks or boomerangs; and so forth."[3] The queen herself supervised the weighing of the incense and precious metals, and the accompanying inscriptions reads:

> Reckoning the numbers, summing up in millions, hundreds of thousands, tens of thousands, thousands and hundreds: reception of the marvels of Punt.[4]

---

1 Breasted, *Records*, Vol. 2, Sec. 257
2 Arthur Weigall, *A History of the Pharaohs: The Twelfth to the Eighteenth Dynasties* (London, 1927) p. 315
3 Ibid. p. 317
4 Breasted, *Records* Vol. 2, Sec. 278

Some sailors from Punt, including "chiefs of Irem" and "chiefs of Nemaeyu," accompany the Egyptians back to Thebes, and are witnesses at the presentation of gifts to Amon.

The overall impression then, as presented in the surviving inscriptions and illustrations at Deir el Bahri, is that Hatshepsut sent an expedition of her servants to Punt, who presented the natives with a few trinkets, and who were given, in return, fabulously wealthy treasures, which were transported back to Egypt with the help of Puntite sailors.

The above scenario, accepted by Velikovsky's critics and by all mainstream Egyptologists, does however strike one as slightly improbable, to say the least; and it becomes even more improbable the further we look into it.

At the presentation of gifts to Amon in Thebes, the deity addresses Hatshepsut in these words:

> Welcome! my sweet daughter, my favourite ... who makes my beautiful monuments, and purifies the seat of the great ennead of gods for my dwelling, as a memorial of her love! (vol. 2, sec. 286)

This ceremony, we remember, took place at Amon's great temple in Thebes. But why would the god bid Hatshepsut welcome, if she had not been away?

The god continues:

> I have given to thee all lands and all countries, wherein thy heart is glad. I have long intended them for thee. ... I have given to thee all Punt, as far as the lands of the gods of God's Land. (vol. 2, sec. 286)

He goes on to say that,

> No one had trod the Myrrh-terraces, which the people knew not; it was heard of from mouth to mouth by hearsay of the ancestors. (Vol. 2, sec. 287)

Amon then recounts how the

> ... marvels brought thence [from Punt] under thy fathers, the Kings of Lower Egypt, were brought from one to another, and since the time of the ancestors of the Kings of Upper Egypt, who were of old, [they were received only] as a return for many payments; none reaching them except thy carriers. (Vol. 2, sec. 287)

Why, we might ask, did earlier rulers of Egypt have to pay for the treasures of Punt; and why were none of the traders sent by those kings permitted to go near the incense terraces? Why the sudden change of heart on the part of the Puntites, who now not only show the Egyptians the sacred and precious myrrh-terraces, but give them as a free gift enormous quantities of incense and other treasures, as well as living incense bushes to transplant in Egypt? The god then drops us a tantalizing hint: he says that he had,

> ... conciliated them [the people of Punt] by love that they might give thee praise, because thou art a god, because of thy fame in the countries. (Vol. 2, sec. 288)

In short, Amon made the Puntites love Hatshepsut; and that is why they showered such gifts on the Egyptians and showed them the secrets of their wealth!

The surviving inscriptions therefore seem to show that Hatshepsut did not take part in the journey to Punt, but that the Puntites were overawed by the Egyptians and transformed by love of their queen — whom they didn't even meet.

From all of this, it begins to look as if the Deir el-Bahri inscriptions were part of some kind of propaganda exercise, and cannot be seen as recording all events as they actually occurred. The statement for example that the Puntites were surprised at the Egyptians finding their way to Punt, a land which they claimed the Egyptians did not know, is obviously and even outrageously false. It is proved false by the testimony of a multitude of Egyptian sources, which, as we saw, demonstrate familiarity with the country as far back as the Old Kingdom.[1] Furthermore, Amon's statement that he had given Hatshepsut the land of Punt, as her own possession, is quite simply ridiculous, and recognized as such by everyone. And we surely cannot accept the claim of the inscriptions that the Egyptians gave the Puntites mere trinkets and received in return from them the treasures and the secrets of their own country.

In accordance with this, we would be led to suspect that in reality the Egyptians must have presented gifts of great value to the Puntites, and that an Egyptian leader of great importance, most probably the monarch herself, was present in the expedition. And at least two of the statements of Amon hint strongly in this direction: First of all, we saw how Amon welcomed the queen to Thebes. This of course could be interpreted as simply a welcome into the temple precinct; and that is how it is normally viewed. Yet it may also — and more probably — be seen as a statement of welcome *back* to

---

1 The question posed by the Puntites as to whether the Egyptians had reached Punt by the "ways of heaven," which is widely viewed as further evidence of the country's remote location, has a fairly mundane explanation. According to Eva Danelius, this expression, which also occurs in Hebrew, means simply the "high road." See Danelius, "The Identification of the Biblical 'Queen of Sheba' with Hatshepsut, 'Queen of Egypt and Ethiopia.'" *Kronos*, I, 4 (1977)

Thebes. Again, the claim by Amon that he had made the people of Punt love Hatshepsut, strongly suggests that she was present in the country.

On the return of the expedition a great festival was held. The presentation of the treasures of Punt to Amon was only the first act of a joyous celebration which then moved to the royal palace. The historian is frustrated by his inability to actually witness an event of such splendor. From the tantalizing and all too brief description given at Deir el-Bahri we may imagine processions led by the queen herself in all her regalia, surrounded by maidservants and troops, accompanied through the streets of the metropolis by hosts of musicians, singers, and dancers. The whole land rejoiced, we are told, and there is a suggestion that the festival lasted many days. Separate events were held throughout the length and breadth of Egypt. "Why," wrote Velikovsky, "would the queen create such excitement over the visit [to Punt] ... and acclaim it in great festivals, unless she herself were the visitor?"[1] Why indeed! "Would the meeting of some royal messenger," he continues, "with a chief Paruah have been an event the queen would have wanted to immortalize as a thing 'that had never happened'?" The implausibility of such a scenario hardly needs to be stressed.

Yet if Hatshepsut did go to Punt, this still leaves us with the problem of explaining why she was so demure in her claims. If she went to Punt, why did she not just say so?

There is, I believe, a fairly straightforward explanation: In travelling to Punt, the Queen of Egypt was paying homage to a foreign land and a foreign king. No ruler of Egypt ever met a foreign monarch in such circumstances — not at least without some form of reciprocation on the part of the other. Yet Solomon, as far as we know, never visited Egypt. The queen had to come to him. The ruler of Egypt, one of the mightiest and wealthiest lands on earth, visited the king of Israel and paid homage to him![2] Now, as we shall see at a later stage, the journey to Punt had a vital propaganda purpose for Hatshepsut, a purpose which involved her claim to divinity and identity with the goddess Hathor. Nonetheless, her journey to that country, to the court of a foreign king, could not be openly portrayed on her funerary monument without some degree of humiliation. In Velikovsky's words, "The Egyptians would have considered it a dishonor to see a picture of their queen in society

---

1 Velikovsky, *Ages in Chaos*, op cit., p. 117
2 The protocols and etiquette of royal visitations have always been understood and observed. Try to imagine the Great King of Persia, Xerxes, paying a visit to the King of Sparta! None of the Popes, prior to Paul VI, in the 1960s, ever left Italy. If foreign potentates wished to meet them, they had to travel to Rome.

as a guest in the house of a foreign ruler."[1] And so, whilst everyone at the time was aware that the queen had gone to Punt; and the journey (or rather pilgrimage) was celebrated throughout the land upon the queen's return, it could not be reported in this way upon her funerary monument. Such a statement would have been beneath the dignity of a woman who claimed, after all, to be the daughter (and actual incarnation) of Amon.

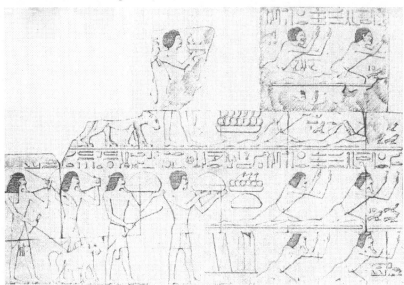

Fig. 3. The presentation of the gifts, from the Punt Reliefs.

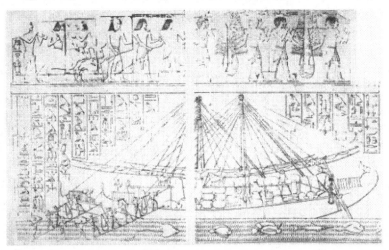

Fig. 4. Loading the Egyptian Ships.

---

1 Velikovsky, *Ages in Chaos*, op cit., p. 120

Fig 5. Incense trees, the main object of the expedition to Punt.

THE LOCATION OF PUNT

It is now that we must confront the most weighty argument brought against Velikovsky. Ever since the discovery and translation of the Deir el-Bahri inscriptions, archaeologists have assumed that Punt was located to the south of Egypt, with most authorities favoring some part of East Africa; usually either Eritrea or Somalia. Yet before proceeding, it must be noted that prior to the discovery of Hatshepsut's temple, it had, on the contrary, been assumed that Punt was to the east of Egypt. Many Egyptian documents speak of Punt as a land to the east, or to the north-east, and it was generally assumed that the mysterious country must have been in Arabia, or perhaps Mesopotamia; though some pointed to the region of Syria/Palestine.

All of this was forgotten after the translation of Hatshepsut's inscriptions, and the evidence that had pointed to Asia was either ignored or explained away. Archaeologists had a very good reason for this geographic relocation: The walls of the "Splendor of Splendors" were fairly packed with illustrations of scenes that could only, or so it seemed, have come from Africa. There was, for example, at least one giraffe. There was also a rhinoceros and, possibly, a hippopotamus. A famous scene, which looks, for all the world, like an African tribal one, shows a Puntite village with rustic-looking houses on stilts, in a tropical-looking scene complete with numerous palm trees, which have been identified as date-palms. Some of the human inhabitants of the area were apparently negroes, and this too pointed to Africa.

The same was true of the region's plant-life. As well as many species of plants that could not be identified, there were several that clearly belonged to Africa. This was most particularly the case with a species of frankincense tree — one of the main objects of the expedition, if the inscriptions are to be believed. Nowadays frankincense only grows in Africa, around Somalia and Eritrea, as well as on the opposite shores of the Red Sea, in southern Arabia.

Taken all together then, the evidence of plants, animals and people seemed unequivocally to place Punt in Africa, most probably in Somalia, or just to the north in Eritrea; and it goes without saying that Velikovsky's critics were very quick to point this out. Indeed, not even Velikovsky denied the African appearance of some of the people and of the animals. His only response to this was the somewhat lame argument that the latter were exotic creatures brought from the far south by Solomon's navy for his royal menagerie.

The "African" nature of the Puntite flora and fauna is a question that will be dealt with at length in due course. However, before proceeding, it has to be stated here and now that in order to sustain a southern, African Punt, Velikovsky's critics, as well as the Egyptological establishment, have had to ignore a great deal of evidence which seemed — equally unequivocally — to place Punt in Palestine, or Palestine/Lebanon. They needed, for example, to ignore or explain-away the fact that Punt was termed the "Divine Land" ("Land of the God"), as was the region around Byblos; and they needed to ignore too the fact that the name Byblos itself seems at times to be connected with the name Punt, and that the goddess Hathor (Hatshepsut's tutelary goddess) was equally the "Lady of Byblos" and the "Lady of Punt". Again, the name Punt (or Pwenet) seemed, as Velikovsky emphasized, to be related to the word Phoenicia, and numerous inscriptions appeared, as we saw, to indicate that Punt lay very close to Egypt, or to the north and east of Egypt, and was regarded by the Egyptians as a land somehow akin to their own.

It is with this evidence, then, that we shall begin.

GOD'S LAND: ITS MEANING AND LOCATION

Hatshepsut's great expedition, which involved a sea voyage, was to a land alternately named Punt (*Pwenet*) and the Divine Land (*Ta Netjer* — or, as David Lorton has rightly translated, the Land of the God). Leaving aside for one minute the origin of the word Punt (which seems, as Velikovsky said, to be identical to the word "Phoenicia", through the country's eponymous ancestor Pontus), it needs to be stated here and now that *Ta Netjer*, the "Land of the God," is unequivocally identified in Egyptian inscriptions with the district comprising the territories between the Sinai Peninsula and the Lebanon. Even Lorton himself admitted the term to be, in the words of Adolph Erman, whom he quotes, a "reference to lands lying to the east of Egypt: especially Punt and the lands of incense, but not seldom also to Sinai and the Lebanon region."[1] I would, for further confirmation, direct the reader to the pages of the *Cambridge Ancient History*, where the country's location is discussed at some length. Thus in the words of Margaret S. Drower, "To the Egyptians, Byblos was the key to 'God's Land', the Lebanon on whose steep slopes grew the timber they coveted."[2] The term God's Land (or Land of the God) is unusual, and one popularly accepted suggestion is that the territory acquired its name by virtue of the resins and gums from Lebanese trees which the Egyptians imported for use in embalming and other rituals. But the region's location in Palestine/Lebanon is not doubted, and is confirmed by a great many Egyptian texts. I will not burden the reader with an exhaustive overview of these, but two or three should serve to illustrate the point. Thus Thutmose III wrote;

> When my majesty crossed over to the marshes of Asia, I had many ships of cedar built on the mountains of God's Land near the Lady of Byblos.[3]

Again, an official of Thutmose III left an inscription of a commission which he undertook to secure cedar from Lebanon. He wrote:

> I brought away (timber of) 60 cubits in [their] length ... I [brought] them [down] from the high-land of God's Land.[4]

An inscription of Thutmose IV tells of:

> Presenting the tribute of Retenu [Palestine] and the produce of the northern countries: silver, gold, turquoise, and all the costly stones of God's Land ...[5]

In order to get round this obvious connection between God's Land and Palestine/Syria, Lorton suggests that God's Land (*Ta Netjer*) was a term used to describe many regions — much as one might describe any favored locality as "God's country." So he asserts that "it cannot be argued from the fact that

---

1 Erman, Adolph and Hermann Grapow, eds. *Wörterbuch der aegyptischen Sprache* (Leipzig, 1926-1963), Vol. V., p. 225
2 Margaret S. Drower, "Syria before 2200 BC," in *CAH*, Vol.1 part 2 (3rd ed.), p. 346
3 John Pritchard, (ed.) *Ancient Near Eastern Texts* (Princeton, 1950), p. 240
4 Ibid., p. 243
5 Ibid., p. 249

ta-netjer is attested in reference to Asiatic regions that Punt was located in Asia." And so, in these words, he transforms *Ta Netjer* into a simple figure of speech. But this, I suggest, is intellectual sleight of hand. We cannot apply the habits and usage of our own profane age onto the Egyptians. The Egyptians would not have misused the word "god" in such a way; and certainly not on official royal and religious inscriptions (even moderns would do no such thing: imagine George W. Bush unveiling a monument in Washington DC describing Texas as 'God's Country'): Besides which, as Lorton himself is keen to emphasize, *Ta Netjer* means the "land of the god." Which god, one might ask? This cannot be a generalized term like today's "God's country." This was a specific territory associated with a specific deity. But which deity?

The word *netjer* or "god" in Egyptian is closely related to the word natron (Greek *natrin*), a sodium-based salt comprising mainly sodium carbonate, used in the embalming process. In fact, the Egyptian word for natron, *ntry*, is almost identical to netjer (*ntjr*). Why this should be so is well understood: the process of mummification was in a sense analogous to deification. Mummification meant the identification of the dead person with Osiris, the first mummy. Osiris himself had a special place in the Egyptian pantheon: he had been Egypt's first ruler and, in a way, the founder of the country. He was also the very epitome of goodness; he it was who struggled against the wicked Set to free the world from evil. Osiris then was benevolence personified, and as recently as 1973 Siegfried Morenz found it "striking that the most human of gods, Osiris, is called *netjer* in a particular context: in quite a number of puns this word is used almost as though it were his name."[1]

So, *netjer* was used specifically to describe Osiris; a divinity occupying a special place in Egyptian belief and devotion. He was also specifically linked to Byblos and to Palestine/Phoenicia. His myth tells us how, after being trapped in a casket by Set and floated down the Nile, his body drifted towards the Phoenician coast, where it was washed ashore and eventually enclosed in a tamarisk tree at Byblos.

Thus Byblos was specifically identified with Osiris. However, it is also recognized that Phoenicia/Palestine was sacred to Osiris because the region furnished many of the gums and resins used in mummification. But which gums and resins? This question is normally passed over with a vague hint that these may have been acquired from the timbers, such as cedar, for which the region was famous. However, as we saw, one material central to mum-

---

1 Siegfried Morenz, *Egyptian Religion* (Cornell University Press, 1973), p. 19

mification was natron, and it so happens that the Jordan Valley, particularly the basin of the Dead Sea, is an important source of natron salt, a source that has been exploited since antiquity.

If we are trying to identify one territory that could accurately be described as the Land of Natron, it would perhaps be the territory on the shores of the Dead Sea.

Another extremely important ingredient in the embalming process was bitumen, and once again the Dead Sea was an important source. Indeed, it may well be that the Dead Sea was the only source known to the Egyptians, and they seem to have imported vast quantities of the material across the Red Sea to Thebes on an annual basis.[1]

Byblos and Palestine/Phoenicia therefore together comprised the "land of the god Osiris," who was also called simply *ntjr*, calling attention to his connection with natron, *ntry*.

And here we find yet another clue: We are told that after Osiris' body had been encased in the sacred tree at Byblos, the ruler of that city, intrigued by the wonderful plant, had it cut down and shaped into a pillar or column, which he installed in his own palace. This was the origin of the so-called Djed Pillar, a symbol sacred to Osiris. Indeed, Osiris was one and the same as the Djed Pillar, which was popularly believed to represent his spine, and ritual representations of the Pillar, like any mummy, were covered in natron salt, wrapped in fine linens and anointed with myrrh.

There seems to me little doubt that Osiris' transformation into a pillar covered in natural salt must be connected with the biblical story of Lot's wife who was transformed into a pillar of salt (probably natron), near the shores of the Dead Sea.

Over the past decade and a half Emmet Sweeney has argued in great detail that the entire story of Abraham (and Lot) refers to a very early culture-bearing migration from Mesopotamia to Egypt, and we shall have occasion to examine this topic in some detail at a later stage.[2] Suffice for the moment to note that it was this migration which appears to have brought literate civilization to the Nile Valley and is thus mythically connected with the earliest phase of Egyptian civilization. Since Osiris reigned in Egypt immediately

---

1 See e.g., Tine M. Niemi, Zvi Ben-Avraham and Joel Gat, (eds.) *The Dead Sea: The Lake and its Setting* (Oxford University Press, 1997), p. 251. Also, J. Rullkötter and Nissenbaum, "Dead Sea asphalt in Egyptian mummies: Molecular evidence," *Naturwissenschaften* (December, 1980).

2 See e.g., Sweeney's *The Genesis of Israel and Egypt* (Algora, New York, 2009).

before the establishment of the human monarchy, it is clear that the legends of Osiris and Lot's wife are connected.

Lot's wife, like Osiris himself (or at least the Djed Pillar), seems originally to have been identical to the Cosmic Pillar or Cosmic Tree; a connection underlined by the very name Lot, which is the same as the Phoenician Lotan (biblical Leviathan), the dragon serpent which wound itself round the Cosmic Tree. (We should note also that the name occurs again in the Greek Latona and even the British Loth or Ludd).[1] According to a large and growing body of researchers of the Velikovskian school, this Tree or Pillar or World Axis may have been an electro-magnetic feature in the form of a plasma funnel or enhanced aurora borealis which was visible in the far north during the Mesolithic, Neolithic and Early Bronze Ages. According to these writers the plasma column appeared in the polar region following a natural cataclysm at the end of the Pleistocene. Velikovsky himself, with his theory of recent cosmic catastrophes, had argued that electro-magnetism plays a much greater role in the mechanics and workings of the Solar System than has hitherto been allowed. In his *Worlds in Collision* (1950) he presented an enormous body of evidence, garnered from traditions throughout the world, to show that a terrible natural catastrophe, caused by the close passage near earth of an enormous comet, had, in the middle of the second millennium BC, effectively electro-magnetically "recharged" our planet. Whilst some researchers have since sought to place Velikovsky's comet and the catastrophe associated with it further in the past, some, including Gunnar Heinsohn and Emmet Sweeney, whose reconstruction of history the present writer favors, would place it more or less where Velikovsky did — in the middle or latter part of the second millennium BC.

Whether or not one accepts Velikovsky's catastrophist ideas, there is no arguing that legends from throughout the world — from virtually every ancient culture — speak of such events, and state furthermore that in the immediate aftermath of the first and greatest catastrophe a crystal-like Pillar (or Ladder, or Tower, or Tree) appeared in the polar region. Ancient peoples tended to see in this feature an attempt by humans (or more frequently by demigods or giants) to reopen communication with heaven, a communication that had been disrupted by the catastrophe.[2] Thus the biblical account places the building of this Tower, the Tower of Babel, in the aftermath of

---

1 See Sweeney's *Arthur and Stonehenge: Britain's Lost History* (Domra Publications, England, 2001)

2 See for example Brendan Stannard, *The Origins of Israel and Mankind: A Unified Cosmogonic Theory* (Carib Publications, 1983).

Noah's Flood, whilst the Greek legend has the Tower constructed by the giants, who sought access to Olympus through it. Norse legends spoke of a great tower of clay constructed by the Frost Giants, who sought thereby to invade the home of the gods.

Traditions from various parts of the world agree that the Cosmic Pillar or Tower was visible for many generations, and its disappearance or "destruction" is recounted in many ancient myths — including that of Abraham.[1]

Though the Cosmic Pillar was originally located at the North Pole (whose name still tells us of the feature), it was later localized by different peoples in different places: Thus in both the Egyptian and the Hebrew traditions the crystal Pillar was located in Canaan.

Before moving on, we should note that the deities associated with this epoch, including Osiris, Abraham, and Min (from whose name that of the legendary first pharaoh seems to be derived), were all phallic. Each of the aforementioned, for example, was associated with the ritual of circumcision. We cannot doubt that this association was in some way or other linked to the then-visible Cosmic Pillar.

We shall have more to say on the connection between Osiris and Abraham in due course.

Thus several quite separate pieces of evidence unite to answer the question: Which god is Ta Netjer, the Land of? The answer is Osiris; and his land is Palestine/Phoenicia. This alone should probably have been sufficient reason to end the debate. Punt *is* the Land of Netjer (Osiris), and the Land of Netjer is Palestine/Lebanon. Yet, as we saw, whilst conceding that Ta Netjer is connected with Palestine/Phoenicia, Velikovsky's critics, and Egyptologists as a whole, insist that the term was also used in connection with another, southern, land which they say is Punt. It is further asserted that whilst Ta Netjer is frequently identified as Palestine/Phoenicia, Punt is never so identified and is clearly a separate region lying to the south of Egypt. These objections shall be addressed in due course. First however let us take a further look at some of the truly overwhelming evidence for placing Punt in Palestine.

THE MYRRH TERRACES OF PALESTINE

Various statements in Egyptian literature clearly link Punt to Phoenicia and Palestine. Velikovsky himself noted an official of the Sixth Dynasty who

---

1 There exists a large and growing body of literature around this topic. Especially informative is Wallace Thornhill's and David Talbott's *The Electric Universe* (Mikamar Publishing, 2007).

casually remarked that he had visited Punt and Byblos eleven times,[1] and in fact no less than three Old Kingdom texts speak of Byblos and Punt in connection with each other.[2] In addition, and this is a point even Lorton has to concede, Punt is *always* described as being to the east of Egypt, whilst a whole series of documents, John Bimson admits, place Punt in the north, and specifically associate the region with known cities in Syria.[3]

But Hatshepsut herself identifies Punt with the Lebanon, and this is a fact strangely overlooked by the critics. Thus in one well-known inscription she writes:

> The myrrh of Punt has been brought to me ... all the luxurious mar-vels of this country were brought to my palace in one collection.... They have brought me the choicest products ... of cedar, of juniper and of meru-wood; ... all the goodly sweet woods of God's Land.[4]

Everywhere else Hatshepsut uses the term God's Land, it is not denied that she is referring to Punt. But here, because she talks of the cedar of God's Land, it is claimed that on this occasion she is referring to somewhere else, namely Lebanon.

With equal clarity Thutmose III describes Punt as located in Palestine/Syria. Three years after his sixth campaign (in which he conquered northern Syria) the pharaoh returned to Palestine to gather the levy. Immediately after describing the tribute obtained from Shinar and Kheta and the land of Na-harin (northern Syria), the register reads: "Marvels brought to his majesty in the land of Punt in this year: dried myrrh...."[5]

The mention here by Thutmose III of Punt as a source of myrrh calls to our attention the fact that a major objective of Hatshepsut's expedition to Punt was the acquisition of incense trees (*anti*) for transplanting in Egypt. This is stressed again and again at Deir el-Bahri. Incense was of course essen-

---

1 J. A. Montgomery, *Arabia and the Bible* (Philadelphia, 1934), p. 176 n. 28

2 P. E. Newberry, "Three Old Kingdom Travelers to Byblos and Punt", *Journal of Egyptian Archaeology* 24 (1938). Newberry denies that these texts prove Byblos and Punt to be adjacent, and claims that they should be read as showing only that these trav-elers had been in the northernmost (Byblos) and the southernmost (Punt) parts of the world known to the Egyptians.

3 The source provided by Bimson is R. Giveon, *Les Bedouins Shoshou des Documents Egyp-tiens* (Leiden, 1971) docs. 6, 20, 20b. Predictably enough, as Bimson tells us, Giveon tries to reinterpret the clear statement of the texts that Punt was in the north by claiming a scribal error. This is a familiar 'solution', used also by Newberry to dis-count the testimony of the 6th Dynasty official who claimed to have visited Punt and Byblos eleven times (though in the latter case Newberry argues that it was the error of a modern translator that was to blame).

4 Breasted, *A History of Egypt*, op cit., p. 280

5 Breasted, *Ancient Records of Egypt*, op cit., Vol. 2, Sec. 486

tial to temple ritual and we cannot doubt that God's Land was so named at least in part because of its association with this sacred material. In the Deir el-Bahri reliefs the incense trees are depicted being loaded onto the Egyptian ships, whilst upon completion of the successful journey the inscription describes how "the best of myrrh is upon all her [Hatshepsut's] limbs, her fragrance is divine dew, her odour is mingled with that of Punt."[1]

Now, in modern times, frankincense grows wild in southern Arabia and north-east Africa, and this was one of the major reasons for looking south in the search for Punt. But, as Velikovsky stated, there is very good reason to suppose that in antiquity the shrub was also cultivated in Syria/Palestine. This is hinted very strongly in a number of biblical passages. Thus in the Song of Songs, reputedly composed by Solomon, we read:

> My hands dripped with myrrh, my fingers with liquid myrrh; Sweeter your love than wine, the scent of your perfume than any spice; Your lips drip honey, and the scent of your robes is like the scent of Lebanon (4:10-11).[2]

Lebanon is apparently here linked with myrrh. But there is more than an apparent link. The records of Egypt inform us repeatedly that Palestine/ Phoenicia was a source of incense. Thus after his fifth inspection of conquered Syria and Palestine, Thutmose III listed frankincense, oil, honey and wine as tribute. After his ninth visit he stated that he had received as "Retenu [Palestinian] tribute of this year" horses, chariots, various silver vessels of the workmanship of the country, and also "dry myrrh, incense 693 jars, sweet oil and green oil 2080 jars, and wine 608 jars."[3] Thutmose III again refers to the great amounts of incense he took from Palestine after his seventh campaign.

In the biblical Song of Songs, the enamored prince (apparently Solomon himself) says to his beloved,

> Until the day break, and the shadows flee away, I will get me to the mountain of myrrh, and to the hill of frankincense. (4:6).

We shall have more to say on the Song of Songs in due course, for it has a very significant connection indeed with the thesis advanced in the present study. For the moment, we ask: Where is the "mountain of myrrh" and the hill of frankincense?

---

1 Ibid., Vol. 2, Sec. 274

2 In an article entitled "The Queen of Sheba and the Song of Songs," which we shall discuss at some length in Chapter 4, Hyam Maccoby highlights the striking similarities between the language of the Song of Songs and Egyptian love poetry of the 18th Dynasty. *Society for Interdisciplinary Studies; Review* 4, No. 4 (1980).

3 Breasted, *Ancient Records of Egypt*, op cit., Vol. 2, Sec. 451

Frankincense (olibanum) falls in clear drops which, when gathered and formed into balls or sticks, turn white. For this reason the precious incense is called "white" in various languages (Greek, Arabic) as well as in Hebrew/ Phoenician (*lebana*, white). Velikovsky identified Lebanah, near Beth-el — about ten miles to the north of Jerusalem — (Judges 21:19) with the "mountain of myrrh" referred to in the Song of Songs. However, there is much evidence to prove that the hill of frankincense was located somewhat further to the east, towards the Jordan Valley.

On her monument, Hatshepsut refers repeatedly to the "myrrh-terraces" of Punt. Now terracing of hillsides for agricultural purposes was extensively carried out throughout Palestine and Syria in antiquity. So heavily was Lebanon terraced that "the [mountain] steps ... was the name given to Lebanon by the Egyptians on account of the terraced character of the mountain slopes."[1] To this day, as one travel writer explains, "Mount Lebanon is extensively terraced and irrigated from copious springs and streams."[2] Yet although the Lebanon was terraced, frankincense could not have grown there. This is a tropical shrub which would quickly succumb to the cold on those slopes. However, there was another heavily terraced region, much warmer, which most assuredly did grow frankincense in ancient times: This was the Ghor or Arabah region, the valley of the Jordan.[3]

Velikovsky himself briefly mentioned that myrrh and frankincense had been cultivated in the Jordan Valley in antiquity. The source he provides is the article "Incense" in *Encyclopedia Biblica*, Vol. 2, col. 2167, where there is mention of classical references to the production there of incenses and spices till late antiquity. In fact, very many classical historians referred to the priceless plants grown in the Jordan region. According to Yadin Roman, editor of Israeli natural history journal *Eretz*, "the Jordan Valley was a major center for the growth of these products [myrrh and frankincense]," whilst "Around Ein Gedi, Jericho, Phasaelis and other Jordan Valley sites extensive agricultural installations have been found for the cultivation of spices ..."[4] These "agricultural installations" were of course hillside terraces, which can

---

1   A. Yahuda, *The Language of the Pentateuch in its Relation to Egyptian* (Oxford University Press, 1933), p. 80

2   Rev. W. Ewing, "Syria" in *Countries of the World* Vol. 6 (Waverley Books, London) p. 3916

3   Much of ancient Israel was heavily terraced for agriculture. See for example, L. E. Stager, "The Archaeology of the Family in Ancient Israel," *Bulletin of the American School of Oriental Research*, Vol. 260, Issue 260 (1985); also Naomi F. Millar, *The Archaeology of Garden and Field* (University of Pennsylvania Press, 1984), p. 64

4   Personal communication, 2nd October, 2009.

be plainly viewed in the area to this day. Interestingly, although in my letter of enquiry to Mr. Roman I had made no mention of Hatshepsut and her
"myrrh terraces," he nevertheless pointed out that the incenses and spices
of the Jordan Valley led to it being "coveted by Queen Cleopatra of Egypt."

It is therefore untrue to state that southern Arabia was the only source of
frankincense known to the ancient world: A far closer and richer source of
the precious resin was found in Israel, a source apparently exploited as early
as Egypt's Early Dynastic epoch. And in this context we should note the passage in Genesis where the Ishmaelites who carry Joseph into Egypt are on
their way from Gilead with "aromatic gum balm and myrrh" (Genesis 37:25).
Gilead is recognized as the country on the east bank of the Jordan.

Before moving on it should be pointed out here that Somalia and Eritrea, which are almost universally identified as Punt, do not grow the type
of frankincense depicted on the walls of Hatshepsut's temple; whilst in the
time of Hatshepsut these regions were primitive lands where the Egyptians
would have found no one to visit or trade with. This is a topic of great importance to which we shall return at a later stage.

The critics of course pointed out that frankincense no longer grows in
Israel; which is factually correct. Yet it *can* be grown there, as numerous
modern horticulturalists have demonstrated. Plant-life, just like animal-life,
can be driven to extinction. Until comparatively recent times the whole of
Palestine was treeless, almost every bush and shrub having been cut down
or grazed to nonexistence over the centuries. When Mark Twain visited the
region in 1867 he remarked on the complete absence of trees and bushes. A
hundred years earlier, Dr Samuel Johnson noted the same thing on his ex-
cursion through Scotland, a country far more naturally wooded than Palestine. And we should note that papyrus, which once flourished in Egypt as far
north as the Nile Delta, is now completely extinct along that river north of
southern Sudan.

There remains to be mentioned the name Punt (*Pwenet*) itself, which, as
Velikovsky stressed, has obvious parallels with the word Phoenicia.[1] I will
not on this issue address the hair-splitting of Velikovsky's critics, but will
leave it to the reader to decide for himself whether he feels it likely that a link

---

1 The Egyptians did use the word "Phoenicia," which they wrote as "Fenku." This
  does not however preclude the possibility that Punt could be a related term. We
  recall that whilst the Greeks spoke of Phoenicia, the Romans, who waged war
  against the Phoenician colonists of Carthage, described their opponents as "Punic."

exists between the two names. It should be remarked that Phoenicia, deriving apparently from the Greek *phoinos*, "red," was apparently a Hellenic rendering (and pseudo-etymological derivation) of a Semitic name something like Pont, since the eponymous ancestor of the Phoenicians was said to be Pontus. Velikovsky in fact suggested that the word Punt derived from the Hebrew *panot*, a term which implies "to face," "to turn to," or "to address"; and Velikovsky noted that throughout the Bible *panot* is used in association with religious practice and worship.[1] Why the Greeks transformed "Pont" into *phoinos* ("red") is not addressed by Velikovsky, but is easily explained by the fact that in the spring-time the Palestinian and Lebanese hills are turned scarlet by a dense crop of anemones which cover the land. And the fact that Phoenicia was identified as the "Red Land" is another clue of crucial importance to our investigation: Hathor, the tutelary goddess of Hatshepsut, was connected with a myth of the world turning red. Thus she was known as the Lady of Byblos, and is so addressed in literally dozens of documents; but we know from several inscriptions that she was linked to Punt as much as to Byblos. Thus for example, one oft-quoted poem to the goddess praises her thus:

> Your eyes have felled the Nubians,
> Oh, great mistress of Punt,
> Delightful source of the north wind,
> Mistress of the pleasant air.

To the above we may also note an inscription in Wadi Gasus, which refers to Senwosret I as "beloved of Hathor, mistress of Punt."[2]

It is just here too that we find another dimension to the Osiris connection. The Greek myth of Adonis was of Phoenician origin. The Greeks themselves actually set the action in Phoenicia, and it is well-known that "Adonis" is but a Hellenic rendering of the Hebrew/Phoenician *adon*, "lord." In the Greek telling of the story, Ares, disguised as a boar, gored Adonis to death, and red anemones sprang from his blood. In the Phoenician/Semitic version, Adonis is the great god Tammuz, lord of the Underworld, who was also killed by a boar, and who was commemorated in a mourning festival named the Adonia.

In the Phoenician version of the story, Tammuz/Adonai was a vegetation god. The Greek version is more specific, and states that Adonis was

---

1 See *Ages in Chaos*, op cit., p. 134. Ralph E. Juergens and Lewis M. Greenberg analyzed the name "Punt" from a linguistic viewpoint and have shown, citing several authorities, that the region clearly refers to Phoenicia. See Juergens and Greenberg, "A Note on the Land of Punt," *KRONOS*, Vol. 1, no. 2 (June, 1975).

2 A. M. Sayed, Discovery at the Site of the 12th Dynasty Port at Wadi Gawasis on the Red Sea Shore," *Revue d'egyptologie*, 29 (1977): 159-160. v.

born from a myrrh tree.[1] From this alone we see that myrrh was specifically connected with the region of Palestine/Phoenicia. It is apparent too that Tammuz/Adonai was identical to the Egyptian Osiris, who was also, we remember, specifically connected to the Byblos area. It was at Byblos, we are told that his body, having been floated down the Nile and washed out to sea, eventually grew into the trunk of a great tamarisk tree.

Here then we are provided with yet another pointer to the location of Punt, as well as a vital clue to the purpose of Hatshepsut's journey to the region. More shall be said on this topic in due course.

There is then an abundance of evidence to suggest that Punt was indeed the land of Israel, or at least Israel/Lebanon, just as Velikovsky claimed. It is true that other names, such as Retjenu (Rezenu), Djahi (or Zahi), or even God's Land were more frequently used than "Punt", a term which seems largely confined to religious literature and poetry. This can be explained by the fact that by Hatshepsut's time Punt may well have had a slightly archaic connotation: an ancient name for the region not then generally used in common speech. Its use in poetry and religious literature would have been analogous to modern poets calling Scotland Caledonia, or naming Britain Albion, or France Gaul.

PUNT: HOMELAND OF THE EGYPTIANS

The land of Punt is not usually accompanied, in Egyptian inscriptions, with the determinative for a foreign country; a fact which illustrates that the Egyptians regarded the region as in some way connected with their own country. Why this should be the case is well understood: the Egyptians claimed to be of Puntite origin. In the words of Flinders Petrie, the Land of Punt was "sacred to the Egyptians as the source of the race."[2] Recognizing themselves to be of Puntite origin, they could scarcely describe the Puntites as foreigners.

According to the thesis presented in these pages, Punt was Israel/Lebanon: Is there anything in ancient tradition to indicate that the Egyptians, or a segment of the Egyptians, had come from that region?

There is much to indicate it.

According to the traditions of the Phoenicians, as recorded by the semi-legendary Sanchoniathon, the Egyptians derived their civilization from them. We are told that Misor, the ancestor of the Egyptians, was the child of the

---

1 Robert Graves, *The Greek Myths*, (Penguin Books, 1955) 18,h
2 Petrie, *The Making of Egypt*, op cit., p. 77

Phoenician gods Amynus and Magus. Misor gave birth to Taaut, the god of letters and inventor of the alphabet, and Taaut became Thoth, the Egyptian god of learning.[1] Sanchoniathon tells us that "Chronos visited the South, and gave all Egypt to the god Taaut, that it might be his kingdom."

Before taking a step further, we note that Misor of the Phoenician tradition is almost certainly identical to Osiris (Asar),[2] the god we have already shown to be peculiarly linked to Byblos, and from whom the entire territory was named Ta Netjer. And the Phoenician claim that Misor was Egypt's first ruler is surely reflected in the Egyptian tradition which named Osiris as the first pharaoh. We note too that Thoth, or Taaut, is said by Sanchoniathon to be particularly linked to the early stages of Egyptian civilization, a statement which appears to be confirmed by the evidence from Egypt herself, where Thoth was especially honored during the Early Dynastic Age.

Now the Jews also claimed that the Egyptians derived their civilization from Israel/Lebanon. In Genesis, Abraham pays a brief visit to the land of the Nile, where his wife Sarai is briefly married to pharaoh. Extra-biblical Jewish tradition however goes much further, and states very specifically that Abraham taught the Egyptians the rudiments of civilization. According to Josephus, for example, before the visit of Abraham, the Egyptians had been virtual barbarians, and it was the Hebrew Patriarch who communicated to them mathematics, astronomy, and a host of other branches of learning. Upon entering Egypt, we hear that the father of the Jews was given leave by pharaoh to:

> ... enter into conversation with the most learned of the Egyptians: from which conversation his virtue and his reputation became more conspicuous than they had been before.
>
> For whereas the Egyptians were formally addicted to different customs, and despised one another's sacred and accustomed rites, and were very angry with one another on that account; Abram conferred with each of them, and confuting the reasonings they made use of ... he demonstrated that such reasonings were vain and void of truth; whereupon he was admired by them these great conferences as a very wise man, and one of great sagacity. He communicated to them arithmetic, and delivered to them the science of astronomy; for, before Abram came into Egypt they were unaccustomed with these parts of learning.[3]

---

1 Eusebius, *Praeparatio Evangelica*, I, ch. ix-x

2 A regular mutation transforms 'm' into 'w' or 'ua' or vice-versa. Thus there is no linguistic objection to Misor = Asar/Osiris.

3 Josephus, *Jewish Antiquities* (trans. Whiston) I, 155-57

Other Jewish tradition, as compiled for example in Ginzberg's *Legends*, states very clearly that Abraham entered Egypt during the reign of the first pharaoh — in other words, at the beginning of the First Dynasty.[1]

Abraham, we note, though settling in Canaan/Israel, was of Mesopotamian origin; and the Phoenicians, as we shall see, also regarded themselves as the descendants of Mesopotamian immigrants.

Neither the Phoenician nor the Hebrew traditions would have much value were they not supported by the findings of archaeology. But supported they are, and in a most spectacular way. This is a topic covered in detail by Sweeney in several publications, and which I propose to deal with here only briefly.[2] To cut a long story short, archaeologists have found that towards the end of Mesopotamia's earliest literate epoch, named Jamdat Nasr, there occurred a great culture-bearing migration which brought Mesopotamian civilization to Syria, Palestine, and Egypt. The first scholar to devote serious consideration to the topic was Flinders Petrie, and the discoveries he made led him to speak of a great migration from Mesopotamia — via Syria/Palestine — to Egypt at the very dawn of history.[3]

Since Petrie's time our knowledge of Early Dynastic civilization has expanded greatly, and the Mesopotamian origin of Egyptian civilization has now become part of accepted wisdom. In the 1971 edition of *The Cambridge Ancient History*, I. E. S. Edwards devoted considerable space to a discussion of the question. "Foremost among the indications of early contacts between Egypt and Mesopotamia," he says, "must be counted the occurrence in both countries of a small group of remarkably similar designs, mostly embodying animals."[4] The artistic parallels are detailed and striking: "Both on the Narmer palette and on the seals, the necks of the monsters are interlaced — a well-attested motif in Mesopotamian art, to which the interlaced serpents found on three protodynastic knife handles may be an additional artistic parallel."[5] Some Egyptian work of the period looks as if it were actually produced in Mesopotamia. A famous ivory knife-handle, for example, found at Gebel el-Araq, "portrays in finely carved relief a bearded man clothed in

1 L. Ginzberg, *Legends of the Jews* Vol. 1, (Philadelphia, 1909), p. 225. "The Egyptian ruler, whose meeting with Abraham had proved so untoward an event, was the first to bear the name pharaoh."
2 In Sweeney's *The Genesis of Israel and Egypt*, op cit., as well as in numerous articles.
3 Petrie, *The Making of Egypt*, op cit., pp. 77-8
4 I. E. S. Edwards, "The Early Dynastic Period in Egypt," in *The Cambridge Ancient History* Vol. 1 part 2 (3rd ed.) p. 41
5 Ibid.

Sumerian costume and holding apart two fierce lions."[1] In Edwards' words, "so close does the composition of this scene resemble the so-called Gilgamesh motif, frequently represented on Mesopotamian seals, that the source of the inspiration can hardly be questioned."[2]

Since these words were written, things have moved on substantially, and more recent studies have revealed in fairly dramatic detail the extent of Egypt's debt to Mesopotamia. In *Egypt's Making* (1990) Michael Rice lists at least a dozen areas of Late Predynastic and Early Dynastic culture that display very specific Mesopotamian influences. David Rohl (*Legend: The Genesis of Civilization*, 1998) looks at even more, going into such detail that he has quite possibly forever silenced whatever lingering doubts may have remained. Foremost among the Mesopotamian parallels examined by Rohl, constituting perhaps the most pervasive material evidence in the Near Eastern sites, is pottery. He showed conclusively that all the new types of pottery introduced into Egypt in the Late Predynastic (Naqada II) age came from Mesopotamia. And along with pottery, a whole host of cultural innovations arrived in the Nile Valley at the time. These included various types of weaponry, but most especially maces with peculiar pear-shaped heads, the semi-precious stone lapis-lazuli, high-prowed boats, building in mud-brick, royal insignia and iconography, cylinder-seals, writing and some vocabulary; and even the names of a few of Egypt's most important gods including that of Osiris' wife Isis (Egyptian Aset), who seems to be derived directly from the Mesopotamian Ishtar.[3] Furthermore, Rohl noted that the actual myth of Isis and Osiris bears remarkably close comparison with that of the Mesopotamian Ishtar and Tammuz. Isis' search for Osiris after his murder is strikingly similar to Ishtar/Inanna's descent into the Underworld in search of Tammuz.

This great migration touched large areas of the Near East. The immigrants settled not only in Egypt, but also, and even more so, in Syria/Palestine and Arabia, and Rohl in particular noted the strong tradition among the Phoenicians that their ancestors had come from Mesopotamia; a tradition that lives to the present day among the Christian Lebanese.[4]

So, we find that archaeology concurs with the traditions of the Phoenicians and the Hebrews in claiming a Syrian — and ultimately Mesopotamian — origin for Egyptian civilization. We find also that the Phoenicians named

---

1 Ibid. p. 42
2 Ibid.
3 Ishtar was known as Astarte among the Phoenicians, and there is little down that Phoenician religious ideas were heavily influenced by those of Mesopotamia.
4 D. Rohl, *Legend: The Genesis of Civilization* (London, 1998), p. 305

Misor (Osiris) as the Asiatic god-king (Sumerian Asar) who migrated to Egypt and communicated to the inhabitants of the Nile Valley the arts of civilization, and that the Egyptians themselves specifically connected Osiris with Phoenicia. We know also that it was in honor of Osiris (Netjer) that the Divine Land (Ta Netjer) received its name, and that this was the appellation applied by the Egyptians also to Punt. And it was from Punt that the Egyptians claimed to have migrated.[1]

EGYPTIAN TEXTS LOCATING PUNT IN PALESTINE

There thus exist manifold varieties of evidence which point insistently to the region of Palestine, or Palestine/Phoenicia as the location of Punt. Yet should all of this evidence, so precise and so detailed, fail to convince, then there also exists a whole series of Egyptian documents and inscriptions, dating mainly from the New Kingdom, which clearly and unequivocally place Punt in Palestine or Palestine/Phoenicia. John Bimson, we noted, was aware of this material, but failed to quote from it in his critique of Velikovsky. David Lorton failed even to mention its existence, and Lorton's behavior is rather typical of mainstream Egyptologists. Bimson himself briefly explained why the texts were ignored, when he quoted R. Giveon as asserting that they had to be the result of a scribal error, or errors.

But the texts have now received a full-blooded reappraisal in the form of an article titled "Locating Punt" by author Dimitri Meeks in David O'Connor's and Stephen Quirke's *Mysterious Lands (Encounters with Ancient Egypt)* (2003). Meeks, who is not, by the way, a supporter of Velikovsky, goes to the original sources, bypassing conventional wisdom as found in the textbooks and guidebooks, and what he finds is most illuminating. He notes, to begin with, that "Texts locating Punt beyond doubt in the south are in the minority, but they are the only ones cited in the current consensus on the location of the 'country.' All the other texts [that locate Punt to the north or northeast], despite their large number, have been ignored."[2]

---

1 It would appear that not all Egyptians, but only those of the ruling elite, the *Iry-pat*, were of Puntite origin. It was from the latter that the Horus Kings of the First Dynasty emerged; and it is evident that the *Iry-pat* were an intrusive Semitic group which came to dominate the native Egyptians, who were of predominantly Hamitic/Berber stock. This is confirmed by the evidence of Egypt's language, which is basically Hamitic, but with a strong Semitic overlay. For a discussion of this topic, see David Rohl, op cit.

2 Dimitri Meeks, "Locating Punt," in David B. O'Connor and Stephen Quirke (eds.) *Mysterious Lands (Encounters with Ancient Egypt)* (University of California Press, 2003), p. 58

The texts placing Punt "beyond doubt" in the south will be examined in due course.

Meeks proceeds to highlight several toponym lists at Soleb, beginning with one of Amenhotep III, which clearly "locate Punt closely to the north of Egypt among places [where] Punt appears to be either between Pehal [in Transjordan] and Shosou, or in the sequence Mitanni, Shosou, Kadesh, Punt, Qutna, Tahse, Yenoam..." "Curiously," says Meeks, "these sequences seem to have sometimes been taken unquestioningly to be the result of error on the part of scribes and sculptors...

"Numerous texts, from at least the Middle Kingdom onwards, describe Punt as the land of the rising sun and locate it in the East, equating it with the eastern horizon."[1]

Centuries after the time of Amenhotep III, Punt is mentioned again, in the monuments of the Ptolemies: "Once the construction of the temple of Edfu was completed, the priests decided to have inscribed on its walls an historic account of the events which marked the ... years that the work had taken. ... In connection with the dynastic feuds between Ptolemy IX Soter and Ptolemy X Alexander I, they note laconically in relation: 'he fled to Punt, his older brother took possession of Egypt and was crowned king again'. ... Other sources record that Ptolemy X [then] fled to Cyprus, but Egyptologists have only mentioned the apparent [north–south] contradiction without further comment. ... However ignorant one might assume Egyptian priests to be, they could scarcely have confused an island north of Egypt [Cyprus] with the depths of Africa."[2] Punt is mentioned again, this time in the Roman period, and once again it is clearly located in Syria/Palestine. Here the region is listed "between Upper Retjenou, corresponding to Palestine, and Pa Bekhen, the mountainous northern part of Mesopotamia ... on the one side and Beiber or Babylon (?) — or a place name in southern Palestine ..." In Meeks' words, "All these texts agree in assigning Punt and its inhabitants to the Near East in more or less direct contact with the land of the Mediterranean coast."[3]

Meeks concluded: "The hypothesis of an African location for the land of Punt is based on extremely fragile grounds. It is contradicted by numerous texts and has only become an established fact in Egyptology because no-one has taken into account the full range of evidence on the subject, regardless of place of such an African hypothesis becomes self evident. The only way to reconcile all the data is to locate Punt in the Arabian Peninsula. The territory

---

1 Ibid., pp. 56-7
2 Ibid., p. 69
3 Ibid., p. 65

of Punt began quite close to that of Egypt, once Sinai had been crossed, in Arabia Petraea or the Negev. It incorporated in a rather imprecise manner the whole coastal zone of the Red Sea down as far as present day Yemen and the actual heart of Punt probably corresponded more or less to YemeniTihama."

Yet even allowing all of the above to be incontrovertible, the critics still have — or claim to have — several trump cards: Perhaps the most important of these are inscriptions which seem unequivocally to place Punt to the south of Egypt, as well as depictions of animals on the Deir el Bahri reliefs that could only have come from Africa.

It is to the former of these two issues that we shall now turn.

THUTMOSE III'S LIST OF CONQUERED LANDS

Both David Lorton and John Bimson, along with the entire Egyptological establishment, assert that the name Punt is found in Egyptian documents associated unequivocally with a southern territory. Did then the Egyptians know of a Punt in the south?

As we saw earlier, before the discovery of the Hatshepsut temple at Deir el-Bahri, it was universally assumed that Punt lay in Asia, with most authorities placing it somewhere in Arabia. However, the reliefs at Deir el-Bahri seemed to point to Africa, and this caused a rethink. All the evidence that had hitherto identified Punt with Asia was now either ignored or downplayed. Even worse, there was now a concerted effort to find inscriptional justification for this geographic relocation. In time, it became part of received wisdom that a number of Egyptian documents do indeed tell of a Punt in the south.

A search of the evidence shows that in fact there are but two: both of which shall now be addressed.

The more important of these is the famous victory lists of Thutmose III in the temple of Amon at Karnak, a series of documents whose importance was emphasized at great length by David Lorton. The lists in question, copied three times, record the names of all the foreign nations and city-states conquered by Thutmose III in his first year. The subjugated regions are not enumerated haphazardly, but follow a definite sequence. In fact, they are named according to their geographical location. Thus, one of the lists, on the northwest facade of the seventh pylon, begins (following Lorton's translation):

> Summary of the foreign countries of Upper Retenu, which his majesty had shut up in the town of doomed Megiddo, and whose children his majesty had brought back as living captives to the town [...]

in Karnak, in his first campaign of victory, as his father Amon, who led him to the goodly roads, had commanded.

It would appear that Upper Retenu/Retjenu is the Egyptian term for the mountainous or upland regions of Palestine/Syria. Megiddo itself is in the land of Israel, as are virtually all of the cities and towns mentioned as belonging to Retenu. After listing these, Thutmose goes on to enumerate states closer to Egypt. He ends, according to Lorton (and this is accepted by Egyptologists in general), with a quite separate and corresponding list of southern states, similarly conquered in the first year. This list begins:

> Summary of these southern foreign countries of the Nubian *'Iwntyw* — people of Khenthenopher whom his majesty had slaughtered, a massacre made of them, the numbers not known, all their inhabitants brought back as living captives to Thebes to fill the workhouse of his father Amon-Re lord of the Two Lands.

Thus there appear to be two separate lists, one comprised of regions to the north of Egypt and the other of regions to the south of Egypt. Somewhat triumphantly, Lorton announces that in all three copies of these lists Punt is clearly and unequivocally placed as the forty-eighth land of the "southern" list. The evidence of these lists, he says, is "in and of itself sufficient to demonstrate that the thesis of chapter III of *Ages in Chaos* [where Velikovsky claims Hatshepsut = Queen of Sheba] cannot be correct."

If the lists said what Lorton claims they say, then perhaps there would be some weight to his argument. But the fact is that they do not say what he claims.

Here is what he says about them: (a) He says that there are two separate lists, copied three times, of the northern and southern states conquered by Thutmose III; and (b) He says that the three lists are identical, and that they all clearly place Punt along with the southern (Nubian) states. Yet the truth is somewhat different. Statement (a) is in fact only partly correct. There are indeed two lists, but they are not entirely separate, in that one list always and only names northern states and the other always and only names southern states. More on this in due course. Statement (b) is quite simply untrue; and with this assertion Lorton is committing an act of *legerdemain* on his readers. Let's look at what he says about the lists. "The three lists," he claims, "are identical, the only differences among them being minor orthographic variations." He continues, "I have quoted the introductory passages at length to show that, despite some variation in wording and some loss of text, the variants are nevertheless explicit as to the fact that one of these is a list of northern countries and the other a list of southern countries."

It is with good reason that Lorton emphasizes the importance of the introductory passages. For it is there that we are told of the lists' contents. But the "minor variation" in wording of the introductions, which Lorton presumably hopes the reader will not question too much, is in fact a *major* variation in wording. Lorton, remember, bases his argument on the assertion that there are two entirely separate lists, one of the northern regions, the other of the southern, and that these lists are copied identically three times. But let's look at what the introduction to the register on the southwest facade of the seventh pylon says: "Summary of these *southern and northern* foreign countries whom his majesty had slaughtered" (my italics). Lorton's comment gives the game away: "For reasons of space in this particular case, the last part of the northern list had to be placed with the southern list." This, I would suggest, hardly constitutes a "minor orthographic variation." The fact that "in this case" the last part of the northern list "had to be placed with the southern list" in fact invalidates his entire argument. Evidently there are not two separate lists, but one continuous list, beginning with Thutmose III's most northerly conquests and ending with his most southerly.

In order to properly understand these registers, the reader should consider the following. The vast majority of the territories and cities conquered by Thutmose III in his first year were in Asia, almost exclusively in Palestine and southern Syria/Lebanon. This being the case, we must suppose that these would take up much more space in his inscriptions than the cities of Nubia. Therefore, quite probably in *all three* copies of the lists, we must expect that "for reasons of space" the "northern" list will overflow into the "southern." That this is so is, as we have seen, explicitly stated on one occasion. On another copy of the "southern" list the introduction, as Lorton himself admits, is lost: Which leaves only *a single list* to which Lorton can point to in support of his thesis.

The reader himself will by now, I am sure, be less certain of accepting Lorton's word on any aspect of this question. His statement that three copies of the Thutmose III lists clearly place Punt to the south of Egypt is exposed as being simply untrue.

I would, at this stage, ask the reader to consider the following: In Velikovsky's theory Punt is identified as Palestine. Now, if as we say, these lists are in fact simply one long list, in a geographical north to south sequence, we must assume that in all of the copies the southernmost cities of Punt/Palestine will be placed right next to the cities of Nubia, which come next geographically to his southernmost Asiatic conquests; and this of course is exactly what we do find. The reference to Punt, "all the regions of Punt," which would appear to come at the end of the list of northern territories, is evidently intended to inform the reader that all the cities and territories listed prior were in the land of Punt.

How then do we explain the one copy of the register where Punt is indeed apparently placed in the south? One of the things Lorton stresses is that in all three copies of the lists Punt is placed as the forty-eighth region of the second or so-called "southern" register. But if Punt occupies an identical position in all three copies, this must mean that all three copies are in fact, just as we surmised, an identical list of "southern and northern" regions. That one of these inscriptions is introduced as simply a list of southern regions can, I would suggest, be explained in the following way. The scribes and craftsmen had indeed originally intended to produce two separate lists, one of Thutmose's northern conquests and another of his southern. But when it came to entering the names onto the prepared registers, it was found that there were far more northern names and these had to continue into the southern list. Having made the mistake once, the scribes corrected the error by describing the other two copies as a list of southern and northern states.

As a historian, I find it astonishing that neither Lorton nor any other Egyptologists are surprised by the inclusion of Punt in the list of lands conquered by Thutmose III in his first year. If, as they unanimously say, Punt was a region of Somalia or Eritrea, are they trying to suggest that Thutmose III conquered these regions? We know in fact that no pharaoh came anywhere near these lands with an army, nor was there substantial contact of any kind between Egypt and the Horn of Africa until the Ptolemaic period, at the earliest. On the other hand, we have a rather precise knowledge of the lands Thutmose III did conquer in his first year. These were: Lebanon and southern Syria, as far as Byblos and Baalbek, and the whole of Palestine, as far as Edom and the border regions of Midian.[1] He also conquered parts of Nubia, possibly as far south as the second or third cataract.[2] From this information alone it becomes absolutely essential to place Punt either in Palestine or in Nubia; yet since the journey to Punt was regularly undertaken by ship from Thebes, this leaves Palestine as the only possible location that would fit the bill.

---

1 Breasted, *A History of Egypt*, op cit., pp. 293-4
2 Ibid. pp. 317-8

PUNT AS A "SOUTHERN" BOUNDARY?

There is, it is said, one other written source — mentioned by Bimson and frequently alluded to in the literature — which is held to prove Punt a southern country. This is the famous inscription on the shaft of a fallen obelisk at Karnak where a passage celebrates Amon's goodness in establishing Hatshepsut's kingdom. The god, she says, has made her "southern boundary as far as Punt."

On the face of it, this seems to be fairly powerful evidence against Velikovsky's thesis. If that is truly what the inscription says, then everything else we have argued, powerful though the evidence might be, is brought into question. Before taking a more detailed look at the inscription and its interpretation, let's have a look at the fuller text:

> He [Amon] hath made my kingdom, the Black Land, and the Red Lands are united under my feet. My southern boundary is as far as Punt ...; my eastern boundary is as far as the marshes of Asia, and the Asiatics are in my grasp; my western boundary is as far as the mountain of Manu ... my fame is among the Sand-dwellers altogether. The myrrh of Punt has been brought to me ... all the luxurious marvels of this country were brought to my palace in one collection ... They have brought me the choicest products of cedar, of juniper and of meru-wood; ... all the goodly sweet woods of God's Land.[1]

A couple of things should be noted here: First and foremost, whilst the queen supposedly here refers to her "southern" boundary (i.e. Punt), she apparently makes no mention of her northern boundary, but instead moves on immediately to her eastern boundary, which she declares to be as far as the marshlands of Asia. Her western (Libyan) border is next described, but she remains silent, apparently, about her northern boundary. This should immediately cause us to pause. Of all her boundaries, those to the north of Egypt — from which direction she was most frequently attacked — were her most important. In that direction lay the mighty empires of Hatti, Mitanni and Assyria. It could of course be argued that the "eastern" boundary by itself deals with all the lands of the Asiatics; and certainly the queen claims to have the Asiatics in her "grasp." It may be argued also that the reference to the northern boundary could originally have been located in one of the lacunae. Nevertheless, it does seem strange that Punt is placed immediately next to the reference to the east, and that later on (as we saw earlier) Punt is named in conjunction with God's Land, which here however is said to be the source of cedar-wood, the typical product of Lebanon. Even more to the point, the eastern border is here described as extending as far as the marshes

---

1 Breasted, *Ancient Records of Egypt* Vol. 2, Sec. 321

of Asia. Now Punt itself is frequently described as to the east of Egypt (a fact admitted by all), whilst in numerous inscriptions (one of which, by Thutmose III, was quoted above) the "marshes of Asia" are clearly adjacent to God's Land and Byblos.

Strange then that Hatshepsut too should mention the "marshes of Asia," of God's Land (Lebanon) next to Punt (also God's Land, but in this case supposedly to the south of Egypt).

Secondly, if Punt truly marked the southern extent of Egypt's rule, this means (according to conventional ideas) that Hatshepsut was claiming to rule everything to the south as far as Eritrea (or Somalia). Even taking into account the normal bombast and exaggeration of Egyptian royal inscriptions, this seems a fantastically improbable claim.

Still, the inscription, we are told, does apparently describe Punt as Egypt's 'southern' border. If that is true it constitutes an inescapable fact which no interpretation can get round. What then is the solution?

Assuming that Breasted translated the inscription literally (which he frequently did not)[1] the text still poses no real problem. It is apparent that Punt may here be used simply as a measure of distance. All the queen seems to be saying is that her southern border, in Nubia, is as far distant from Thebes as her northern border, in Punt. And indeed Arthur Weigall, on the authority of Lepsius, translated the sentence as "My southern frontier is as far off as the lands of Pount."[2] Scholars who were able to "explain" the Sixth Dynasty official's eleven visits to Punt and Byblos as a reference to eleven visits to the northern and southern extremities of the Egyptian world should have no

---

1 In one notorious example, highlighted by Eva Danelius, Breasted translated "bearded ones of Punt" as "southerners of Punt", a fact which should warn us to deal cautiously with the claims he makes. Danelius loc. cit. p. 14. Danelius comments further, "... it is commonplace to remark that translation is interpretation. But while interpretation has to be cut down to a minimum when translating, e.g., from one modern European language into another, related one, interpretation becomes unavoidable when translating from Egyptian hieroglyphs into modern European diction. In the case of the Punt-reliefs, hieroglyphs fill the space left empty by the pictures, the 'letters' beings written in adaptation to the space available. They are partly arranged in horizontal lines — to be read from left to right, or from left to right — partly in vertical columns. There are no punctuation nor other diacritical marks. Thus, it is left to the reader to decide where a sentence ends and a new one begins; whether or not there is direct speech, and by whom, etc. Furthermore, while Naville translated line by line, Breasted broke the text up into sections not to be found in the original, and even added headings which are sometimes more confusing than helpful. "
2 Arthur Weigall (*A History of the Pharaohs: the Twelfth to the Eighteenth Dynasties* (T. Butterworth Limites, London, 1927), p. 310), quoting Lepsius, *Denkmäler aus Aegypten und Aethiopien*, Vol. 3, pp. 22-4.

quarrel with this interpretation. Since the land of Israel was a great distance to the north of Thebes, this would mean that she was claiming to rule Nubia almost as far south as Meroe — which we know in fact to be the case.

In his article Bimson did quote another ancient text which he claimed seemed to locate Punt to the south of Egypt. This was the well-known legend of "The Shipwrecked Sailor," a tale preserved on a single papyrus, that of Leningrad 1115, and dating from the Twelfth Dynasty. The evidence contained in this story is ambiguous, to say the least, and is therefore rarely alluded to in the debate. Why Bimson should have used it as a proof of Punt's southern provenance is perhaps indicative of a certain clutching at straws.

In the legend a returned mariner recounts how he and a shipful of others set out for the "mines of pharaoh," which must surely be in the region of Sinai. In virtually every other reference to these mines it is very clear that the turquoise and copper mines of the Sinai Peninsula are what is referred to. And this impression of a voyage to the north, towards the Mediterranean, is further strengthened by the fact that the island onto which the sailor is cast by a storm is described as the "Island of the Blessed." This is invariably, in all Mediterranean cultures, placed in the far west. The great serpent which dwells on this island describes himself as the "Lord of Punt." In other words, he is a deity — the serpent or dragon deity; identical no doubt to Lotan of the Phoenicians and Leviathan of the Jews.

If the evidence then points so decisively to the north, how is it that Bimson felt justified in seeing the story as pointing to the south? The answer comes at the beginning: Here the sailor tells how he and his companions, on their journey home, finally reached Wawat (Nubia). From this Bimson (and several others) concluded that the traveler must have sailed north to reach Egypt. Yet it is very clear, from the context of the story, that the lost sailor's home was in Nubia. Furthermore, it is specifically stated that he reached Wawat by ship — in other words, by way of the Nile. He must have sailed from the north.

Thus one can now assert that not a single Egyptian source unquestionably places Punt in the south. Contrast this with the scores of documents which beyond all doubt place *Ta Netjer* (according to Hatshepsut one and the same as Punt) in the vicinity of Byblos and the Lebanese region or Palestine. Add to this perhaps a dozen or so other documents which specifically refer to Punt itself (sacred to the goddess Hathor) as being in the area of Palestine/

Lebanon (also sacred to Hathor) and I feel there should no longer be any reasonable doubt as to the country's true location.

The supporters of the southern Punt theory must also answer the conundrum posed above. Since Punt appears in a list of territories conquered by Thutmose III, this would compel Egyptologists to place it somewhere in Nubia. But of course it cannot have been located there, because the Hatshepsut reliefs clearly show, and refer to, a sea voyage. Thus Punt has to be, as the only other alternative, placed somewhere near the southern end of the Red Sea, say in Eritrea or Somalia (the latter two regions being in fact the favored location for Punt). But such a location is equally impossible, since Thutmose III states that Punt was a conquered territory. The list, after all, is introduced with the words, "Summary of these foreign countries of the Nubian people of Khenthenopher whom his majesty had slaughtered, a massacre made of them." No one in his right mind of course would suggest that Thutmose III or any other pharaoh conquered Eritrea or Somalia; but this is the unavoidable and inevitable consequence of placing Punt to the south of Egypt.[1]

It is a pity scholars do not always think out the consequences of their statements before making them.

THE FLORA AND FAUNA OF PUNT

We now come to the greatest problem encountered by Velikovsky and by anyone suggesting that Punt be located in Israel: The Deir el-Bahri reliefs show a number of African people and apparently African animals, such as at least one rhinoceros and a giraffe. For Bimson, and for many of his readers, this was decisive evidence in proving an African location for the territory: decisive enough to make them ignore or forget all the other evidence that clearly located Punt/the Divine Land in Palestine/ Phoenicia. But if Punt really was Israel, why then such an African influence: why the large amount of space devoted to seemingly African animals and people with clearly negroid features? This is a question that cannot be ignored. Velikovsky himself suggested that the African elements were imports, and stressed that the Puntites themselves were not negroes but Semites or Hamites. This in fact is true. The Puntites look very much like the Egyptians and, curiously enough, sport long pointed beards of a type worn in Egypt only by the pha-

---

1 Nor was there in Eritrea or Somalia, in the time of Hatshepsut or Thutmose III, any civilization or culture of the type portrayed at Deir el Bahri that the Egyptians could have traded with. This topic, of fundamental importance to the whole debate, is examined in greater detail below.

raoh.[1] (This should come as no surprise given the fact, noted above, that the earliest Egyptian monarchy, the Horus kings of the First Dynasty, claimed to have originated in Punt; and calls to mind too the strong links we know to have existed between Palestine/Phoenicia and the god Osiris).[2]

But where then do the negroes and African animals come in?

The answer is in two parts. First and foremost, whilst the negroes may indicate an African element, the animals very definitely *do not* belong to Africa. All of the creatures depicted on the Punt reliefs thrived in the Syria/Palestine region during the time of Hatshepsut.

One of the animals depicted on the walls of the *Deser-djeseru* was unquestionably a giraffe. Giraffes of course are nowadays found only in Africa, and this has misled many people into seeing them as proof of a southern location for Punt. However, as Bimson admits, giraffes were found on the borders of Syria and Arabia in classical times — a fact noted by Diodorus, who calls them "camel-leopards."[3] In Roman times giraffes were occasionally displayed in Italy and, as often as not, they seem to have been gifts or plunder from Syria or northern Arabia. Thus in AD 248 the emperor Philip the Arab, a Syrian, celebrated the millennium of Rome's founding with a display in the Circus of numerous exotic creatures, including ten giraffes.[4] This is said to have been the largest number of such animals ever to appear in Rome, though the emperor Aurelian is reported to have marked his triumph over Zenobia, queen of Palmyra (in Syria) in 274 AD with a presentation of several giraffes.[5] Furthermore, the Bible itself (Deuteronomy 14:5) seems to speak of giraffes in the region of Sinai and the Negev, whilst Alessandra Nibbi notes the occurrence of a rock-cut drawing of a giraffe in Sinai.[6]

The giraffe then can at best show that Punt *may* have been in Africa. The rhinoceros however more probably points to Asia. Once again, as with the giraffe, people have simply thought "Rhinoceros — Africa." But the rhinoceros portrayed at Deir el-Bahri appears to be of the Asian one-horned species, *Rhinoceros unicornis*, and cannot represent either of the two contemporary African species, both of which have two horns. The one-horned rhinoceros has

---

1 Abdel-Aziz Saleh, "Some Problems Relating to the Pwenet Reliefs at Deir el-Bahari," *Journal of Egyptian Archaeology* 58 (1972) pp. 140-158

2 As noted earlier, Flinders Petrie remarked that the Land of Punt was, "sacred to the Egyptians as the source of the race." *The Making of Egypt, op cit.*, p. 77

3 Diodorus ii, 50-1

4 *Historia Augusta*, xxxiii, 1

5 Ibid., xxxiii, 4

6 Alessandra Nibbi, "The Shipwrecked Sailor Again", *Göttinger Miszellen* 24 (1977), p. 54

never been attested in Africa. Again, this is a fact that Bimson himself concedes.[1] A single-horned rhinoceros is portrayed on the Black Obelisk of Shalmaneser III, along with an elephant and an oryx, all of which are described as "tribute" of Musri.[2] The Obelisk's purpose was to record the tribute of the peoples of western Asia (Jehu of Israel is shown bowing before the Assyrian king), though it seems that the source of the one-horned rhino (Musri) was Egypt. Nevertheless, all of the lands of Palestine/Syria were at that time regarded as under the suzerainty of Egypt. It should be remarked too, in this regard, that during this epoch large herds of elephants — of the Asiatic variety — roamed throughout northern Syria.[3]

As noted above, in antiquity the entire Near East was home to most of the creatures associated nowadays only with Africa. It is well-known, for example, that lions occurred in great abundance throughout the region, and were extensively hunted for sport by Assyrian kings as well as Egyptian pharaohs. What is not so well known is that in ancient times basically all of the animals now associated with the African savannah roamed the Syria/Palestine region. These populations were remnants of an earlier time when the entire Sahara and Arabian deserts were well-watered grasslands.[4] Thus the *Illustrated Bible Dictionary* supplies the following rather surprising information about the non-human inhabitants of the area in biblical times:[5]

(a) **Elephants**. "The Asiatic elephant was once found as far west as the upper reaches of the Euphrates [northern Syria]." Vol. 1 p.58

(b) **Lions**. "At one time lions were found from Asia Minor through the Middle East and Persia to India ... The last Palestinian lion was probably killed near Megiddo in the 13th century." Ibid.

---

1 J. Bimson (loc cit) suggests that the one-horned rhino may have once occurred in northern Africa, since early Egyptian hieroglyphs included a pictogram of such a creature. This is not impossible, since the rhinoceros, giraffe and elephant were all common in Egypt until near the end of the Early Dynastic period. But the same creatures also roamed Syria/Palestine, where they survived till much later owing to the more favourable climatic conditions.
2 A. T. Olmstead, *History of Assyria* (New York and London, 1923), p. 142
3 Breasted, *A History of Egypt*, op cit., pp. 270-1
4 See e.g., K. W. Butzer, "Physical Conditions in Eastern Europe, Western Asia and Egypt Before the Period of Agriculture and Urban Settlement", in *The Cambridge Ancient History*, Vol. 1, part 1 (3rd ed), p. 68 "Between the First and Fourth Dynasties, the second major faunal break, characterized by the disappearance of the rhinoceros, elephant, giraffe, and gerenuk gazelle in Egypt, culminated in the modern aridity. "
5 *The Illustrated Bible Dictionary* 3 Vols. (Hodder and Stoughton, 1980).

(c) **Leopards and Cheetahs**. "It is possible that Heb. *namer* refers to both the true leopard and the cheetah, or hunting leopard, and also to one or two other spotted wild cats of Palestine." Ibid.

(d) **Gazelles**. "Two wild species [of gazelle] are found in Palestine: the dorcas and Palestine gazelles, both standing under 70 cm." Ibid.

(e) **Hippopotami**. The hippopotamus "lived in the lower Nile until the 12th century AD and, much earlier, in the Orontes river in Syria (and perhaps elsewhere in SW Asia) until after the time of Joseph, so it is well known in Bible lands." Ibid. p.61

(f) **Ostriches**. "The ostrich finds mention in several [Bible] passages ... Jb 39: 13-18 is clearly a description of the ostrich, a bird which once lived in the Middle East." Ibid. p. 62 (note: an Assyrian portrayal of this bird is shown on the same page).

(g) **Crocodiles**. "In biblical times the Nile crocodile was found from source to mouth of the Nile. While its distribution north of Egypt in that period is unknown, returning Crusaders reported crocodiles in the Zerka river, which runs into the Mediterranean near Caesarea and is still known locally as the Crocodile river." Ibid. p.65

Even within the past hundred years Palestine/Lebanon was still home to the Syrian bear and the leopard, whilst the gazelle, ibex and hyena still occur, along with the wild pig, jackal and wild cat.[1]

So, all of Syria/Palestine, as well as Arabia, supported typically "African" wildlife in ancient times. Yet there was one region of Palestine that was peculiarly African in its flora and fauna: The Jordan Valley and Dead Sea basin, also known as the Ghor or the Arabah region, has a unique climate, as well as flora and fauna. The Jordan, rising on Mount Hermon, descends quickly as it flows south, first to Lake Hula, then to the Galilee, and finally south to the Dead Sea. This latter is the deepest point on the surface of the earth, with the shoreline standing at an astonishing 1,292 feet below sea level. The Sea of Galilee itself is 682 feet below sea level. Owing to its low elevation, the valley, which constitutes the northernmost portion of the tectonic fault-line known as the Great Rift Valley (a fault-line which runs down the Red Sea as far as Central Africa), has a tropical climate, and, even to this day, its flora, as well as smaller fauna, peculiarly "African."[2] We are told also that the region's vegetation is "akin to that of the Sudan and the low-lying parts of

1 H. C. Luke, "Palestine" in *Countries of the World* Vol. 5 (Waverley Books, London), p. 3072
2 Ibid.

Abyssinia." One of the plants native to the low-lying parts of Abyssinia is of course frankincense. Here grew the 'Balm of Gilead' tree and the 'Apples of Sodom.'"[1] According to *The International Standard Bible Encyclopedia*, "The most common trees and plants of the Jordan valley are the castor-oil plant and the oleander, flourishing especially about Jericho, several varieties of the acacia tree, the caper plant, the Dead Sea apple (Solanum Sodomaeum) the oser tree of the Arabs, tamarisks, Agnus casti (a flowering bamboo), Balanites Aegyptiaca (supposed to be the balm of Gilead), Populus Euphratica (a plant found all over Central Asia but not West of the Jordan), and many tropical plants, among which may be mentioned Zygophyllum coccineum, Boerhavia Indigofera, several Astragali, Cassias, Gymnocarpum, and Nitraria."[2] Frankincense too, in ancient times, grew there, on the terraced hillsides just above the valley-floor. The latter region, however, was a combination of papyrus marsh, a veritable "sea of slime,"[3] and a "jungle" inhabited by animals such as lions, a region "which only the bravest dared enter."[4]

As might be expected, the area's unique animal-life was a favorite subject of ancient artists. We have already noted how Diodorus of Sicily refers to the giraffe living on the "borders" of Syria and Arabia (evidently the Ghor region); and depictions of such creatures are not uncommon among the ruins of ancient synagogues and other important buildings in the area. Yadin Roman is of the opinion that there were indeed "giraffes and lions and other large wild animals in the Jordan (Ghor) Valley" into Roman times and even later.[5] Fascinatingly, the animal-life is a mixture of African and Indian. We are told that "Of the mammalian characteristic of this general region, 34 are Ethiopian and 16 Indian, though there is now no possible connection with Ethiopia or India."[6] We recall at this point the large herds of Asiatic elephants that anciently inhabited northern Syria, and the single-horned (Asiatic) rhinoceros portrayed at Deir el-Bahri and on the Black Obelisk of Shalmaneser III.

So, far from proving Punt in Africa, the evidence of the flora and fauna points once again to western Asia; and more specifically and crucially, to the Jordan Valley and Dead Sea basin. The importance of this cannot be emphasized too strongly; for it was here too that we found the cultivation in ancient times of frankincense and spices — on terraces which are still plainly

1   Ibid. p. 3071
2   George Frederick Wright, "The Jordan valley," *International Standard Bible Encyclopedia*, (1915) www.bible-history.com
3   Ibid., p. 3070
4   Joyce M. H. Reid and H. H. Rowley (eds) *Atlas of the Bible*, (London, 1956), p. 16
5   Personal communication, October 2, 2009.
6   George Frederick Wright, loc. cit.

visible to this day — and where, as a consequence, we placed the "myrrh terraces" mentioned by Hatshepsut at Deir el-Bahri. Now we find that it was in
this very place that giraffes and other large "African" animals roamed around
in biblical times.

Fig. 6. Various supposedly "African" animals displayed on a sixth century church
in Mount Nebo, Jordan, close to the Jordan Valley.

It must — at least in part — have been the unique biology of the Jordan Valley which gave the region its "Holy Land" designation. Above all, the
occurrence there of frankincense, the indispensible accoutrement of temple
ritual, would have conferred upon the territory a special significance. The
only other source of frankincense known to the ancient civilizations of the
Near East was southern Arabia, but the remoteness of this territory would
have rendered its exploitation — in early times at least — somewhat im-
practicable. Thus it was the Jordan region, from Early Dynastic times at least,
that was the Holy Land or Divine Land of the peoples of Egypt, Syria and
Mesopotamia. We recall that it was from a myrrh tree of the Jordan Valley
that Adonis/Tammuz was born; and it seems likely that Osiris' birth, or re-
birth, from a tree in the area, must have originally been placed in the Jordan.
In later times, it is true, he was pictured as emerging from a tamarisk tree at
Byblos; yet the association with Byblos is probably explained by the fact that
the Egyptians obtained most of their Jordan Valley incense from the hands of
Phoenician traders operating from Byblos and Tyre.

The Jordan Valley, then, with its unique animal and plant-life, was the "Divine Land" of the Egyptians. Yet, as we saw, it was the appearance of those same unique animals and plants on the Deir el-Bahri reliefs that was most decisive in convincing scholars they should relocate Punt from Asia (where they had hitherto placed it) to Africa.

It is evident that, irrespective of what route Hatshepsut took to Israel, and the purpose of her journey there — both of which shall be discussed presently — her travels took her, at some stage, through the basin of the Dead Sea and the Jordan Valley. The exotic creatures displayed at Deir el-Bahri were still found in these hot and well-watered regions, having been previously hunted to extinction in other areas of Syria and Palestine. They were spotted by the royal expedition its journey to the myrrh terraces and to Jerusalem, and portrayed on the walls of the Deir el-Bahri temple because of their scarcity.

SEA-LIFE ON THE PUNT RELIEFS

According to conventional historians, and Velikovsky's critics, the journey to Punt involved a long voyage in the Red Sea, beginning at the port of Quseir. This meant that the royal party needed to cross a stretch of hostile desert before even beginning the voyage to the mysterious region. It is further stated that the journey home was by ship, and we are told very clearly that "the ships arrived [back] at Thebes." Since a journey to Eritrea or Somalia by ship from Thebes is impossible, historians have had to postulate an incredibly complex itinerary on the part of the royal expedition. The problem was outlined thus by Arthur Weigall over eighty years ago: "... the detailed representations sculptured on the walls of the temple [at Deir el Bahri] show apparently the same ships both on the Nile and on the sea, and there is nothing to suggest any transshipment ..."[1] How does one get from the Nile to the Red Sea? Weigall was forced to postulate a canal linking the two: "... the journey was made down the Nile and thence by way of the canal through the Wady Tumilât which ran into the Bitter Lakes and so to the Red Sea."[2] But we now know that no such canal existed in the time of Hatshepsut. Work on a waterway connecting the Nile and the Mediterranean with the Red Sea was begun, hundreds of years after Hatshepsut, by Pharaoh Necho II. This was completed in the Persian age.[3] But there is no mention anywhere of such

---

1 Weigall, *A History of the Pharaohs: The Twelfth to the Eighteenth Dynasties* (London, 1927), p. 313
2 Ibid.
3 Herodotus, ii, 158

a channel in the time of the Eighteenth Dynasty. This being the case, modern historians tell us that the ships which left Thebes sailed only a very short distance north — to Koptos — where the entire party disembarked, and began a long overland trek to the Red Sea coast at Quseir. Arriving there, the group then boarded different ships and began the voyage to the southern shores of the Red Sea. The journey home repeated the same process in reverse.

If the outward journey via Koptos and Quseir strikes one as improbable, then the homeward journey along the same route appears absurd: For whereas on the outward journey the ships leaving Thebes would at least have had the advantage of sailing downstream to Koptos, on the way back they would have had to sail upstream — a much slower and more laborious enterprise. In fact, by going from Quseir to Koptos, loading the ships and then sailing upstream to Thebes, the expedition would have potentially added another day or two to their journey. And it must be remembered that on the way home the expedition party was burdened with the gifts received in Punt — which included numbers of very large animals such as giraffes and cattle. Loading these onto ships would have been an immensely difficult and time-consuming task at the best of times. Instead of doing this, why did the expedition not simply move along the Wadi Hammamat from Quseir and then, about a day's journey from the Nile Valley, simply veer slightly to the south-west by one of the many paths that criss-cross the region, and arrive safely back at Thebes a day or two earlier? Such a route, which would be absolutely required by commonsense, is however rejected for the simple reason that the Deir el-Bahri reliefs tell us very clearly that the ships "arrived at Thebes."

The evidence then suggests that whilst on the outgoing journey the ships may have sailed northwards along the Nile as far as Koptos, from which point the expedition ventured overland towards the port of Quseir, there to board new ships bound for Punt, on the return journey the Egyptian adventurers most probably entered the Nile from the Mediterranean and sailed south to Thebes.

That the outward and inwards journeys were by way of two different bodies of water is indicated by the sea life illustrated on the walls of the Deir el-Bahri temple. The majority of the fish and other sea creatures portrayed at Deir el-Bahri are regarded as typical of the Red Sea. In the words of Eva Danelius: "According to the unanimous opinion of all the ichthyologists the seawater fishes represented belong to the Indian-Ocean-Red-Sea fauna, and so do the crustaceans."[1] However, even the ichthyologists are puzzled by the presence of several creatures which do not fit the mould. I myself am not qualified to comment upon this topic, though I would point out that, notwithstanding the skill of the Egyptian artists, it is not always easy to determine exactly which species is being portrayed. I am indebted to Jill Abery for bringing this to my attention. She notes that "The insects frequently referred to as 'bees' (e.g., on columns at Karnak) are definitely *not* bees — the length of their antennae indicate some species of parasitic wasp. Either the translation/transliteration is inaccurate or the depiction is."[2]

In addition to these uncertain species there are several which clearly point not the Red Sea but to the Mediterranean. Thus at least one lobster, a species not generally found south of the Mediterranean, occurs on the Deir el-Bahri reliefs. This is admitted by John Bimson, though he states that one class of lobster has recently been confirmed in the Red Sea, and that another has been found in the Indian Ocean.[3] Nevertheless, the creature can hardly be said to be typical of these southern waters. Bimson makes much of the occurrence of a freshwater turtle (*Trionyx triunguis*) on the reliefs, and sees this as proof of a southern location. But freshwater turtles thrive not only in the Nile, which admittedly flows into the Mediterranean, but "groups have been found living off the coast of Turkey."[4]

The evidence of sea-life is therefore at best inconclusive. Some evidence, as for example the lobster, points to the Mediterranean. Other evidence, such as the turtle, held to point to the Red Sea, can now be shown also to point to the Mediterranean. These two details in themselves, combined with the ambiguous nature of many of the portrayals (Jill Abery informs me that the "freshwater" turtle only needs to be depicted with slightly larger front flippers and it could be marine), tend to make us suspicious of the confident assertions of the ichthyologists regarding the provenance of the various types of fish (most of which, incidentally, are admittedly found in both the Red Sea and Mediterranean).

In short, the overall picture suggests that two different bodies of water, both the Red Sea and the Mediterranean, are being illustrated at Deir el-Bahri. This is precisely what we should expect from Velikovsky's reconstruction of events.

---

1 Danelius, E. and H. Steinitz, "The Fishes and other Aquatic Animals on the Punt Reliefs at Deir el Bahri" *Journal of Egyptian Archaeology* 53 (1967), p. 17
2 Jill Abery, personal communication (July, 2003)
3 J. Bimson, loc. cit., p. 25, footnote 51
4 *Longman Illustrated Animal Encyclopaedia*, ed. Dr Philip Whitfield (1988), p. 412

ETHNIC IDENTITY OF THE PUNTITES

This brings us to the second supposedly irrefutably African element present in Punt, namely the negroes. Surely, it will be said, these at least must point to Africa. How are they to be explained if we locate Punt in Asia?

To begin with, let me reiterate an important point, one usually overlooked by Velikovsky's critics. The Puntites themselves were very definitely *not* negroes. This is a fact stressed by numerous Egyptologists. Quite the contrary, rather than being southern-looking, they are described as a "long-haired Hamitic people, similar in physical type to the Egyptians themselves."[1] Other writers see them as a mixture of Hamites and Semites, whilst the governor is described as a "tall, well-shaped man" with "flaxen" hair; his nose "aquiline, his beard long and pointed." We are told that "The Puntites are painted red, but not so dark as the Egyptians."[2] It will, I think, be admitted that this hardly sounds like a description of the natives of Eritrea or even southern Arabia. Particularly striking is the "flaxen" (light blond) hair of the governor. It is of course possible that what Naville saw as blond was simply gray; but even if this be the case, the physical features and skin-color of the Puntites does not point to Eritrea.

The ethnic identity of the Puntites was a topic examined by Dimitri Meeks. He notes: "The general appearance of the Puntites in the temple of Hatshepsut and other sources is similar to those people of the Near East and their skin is the same color as that of the Egyptians. ... When Puntites and Africans are depicted on one and the same monument, care is taken to bring out the physical differences between them, as in the tomb of Amenomose at Thebes. ... Here the Puntites have none of the characteristics of the Africans, on the contrary, they exhibit some features which are peculiar to them alone, and others which are found elsewhere. ... Proponents ... recognized that the Puntites were not black Africans."[3] Again, "The Puntites and Nubians are clearly regarded as different ethnic groups, living in different places. ... The black-skinned population whose leaders ('the great men of Punt' ... referred to in the texts) are always slender individuals with pale skin and short beards. The presence of black Africans in a secondary position is relation to the population of 'notables' with the paler skins may evoke the trade in slaves."[4]

---

1 W. C. Hayes, "Egypt: Internal Affairs from Tuthmosis I to the Death of Amenophis III," in *The Cambridge Ancient History* Vol. 2, part 2 (3rd ed), p. 330
2 E. Naville, *The Temple of Deir el-Bahari*, Part III, op cit, pp. 12-3
3 Meeks, loc. cit., p. 58
4 Ibid., p. 61

Meeks also noted that in toponym lists, where the figure of a native of each city or country is shown, the figure for Punt is always that on an Asiatic.[1]

Although a century ago Naville had accepted that the Puntites were Caucasians, he nonetheless placed Punt in Africa. He speaks of "the real Puntite population of Hamitic race ... [as distinct] from the negroes who also inhabited the land of Punt."[2] He also suggested that the Puntite governor's wife, Ati, had some features which looked typically African: "Her stoutness and deformity might be suggested at first sight to be the result of disease, if we did not know how from the narratives of travellers of our own time that this kind of figure is the ideal type of female beauty among the ... tribes of Central Africa. We can this trace to a very high antiquity this ... taste, which was adopted by the Puntites, although they were probably not native Africans."[3] The grossly obese appearance of this woman was in fact a fruitful source of conjecture for several decades. Thus in 1891 Amelia Ann Blanford Edwards wrote: "Maspero suggests that the Princess Ati may be suffering from *elephantiasis*; but Mariette is of the opinion that the Egyptian artist has here represented not merely the wife of the chief, but the most admired type of the women of the Somali race. The complexions of [her] whole family are painted a brick red, and their hair black, thus showing that they are not of the negro race."[4]

Since the above words were written a very different view has prevailed. In the words of Eva Danelius, "A detail on the murals which seemed to hinder its identification with an Asiatic country consists of the picture of the 'abnormally fleshy wife' of the Puntites' governor. The obesity of the wife was considered proof that the scene was in Africa, where wives are artificially fed and fattened. This supposition, however, has ... become obsolete. In a very thorough study, made possible thanks to the 'superior gift of observation of the Egyptians,' it could be shown that the unhappy woman suffered from a progressive dystrophy of the muscles, a malady the cause of which was not known and against which no remedy had been found to this day. The sickness is hereditary and the first signs seem to have been observed by the artist also on her daughter, who follows behind her."[5]

The Puntites then are clearly of Caucasian appearance, with some characteristics even of Indo-Europeans. It should be noted here, in this context,

1 Ibid., pp. 56-7
2 Naville, op cit., p. 36
3 Ibid., pp. 36-7
4 Amelia Ann Blanford Edwards, *Pharaohs, Fellahs and Explorers* (New York, 1891), p. 285
5 Danelius, loc. cit., part 3, pp. 12-3

that at least one of Thutmose III's portrayals of Syrian/Asiatic captives show several of them with blue eyes and fair hair.[1] How is this to be explained? I would suggest two possibilities. Perhaps the Phoenicians, whose voyages to western Europe (Spain and Britain) are well-known, had by this time acquired through intermarriage a European genetic element. Alternately, and more probably, the Indo-European features may have derived from the military ruling caste of the region, the Indo-Iranian *mariyanna*, who were prominent in Syria/Palestine during this epoch.[2]

These then were the typical Puntites. Nevertheless, people of clearly negro physiognomy are indeed portrayed on the reliefs. They are described as "people of the south." Velikovsky suggested that they seem to have been slaves, presented to the Egyptians along with the other gifts. This interpretation has been criticized, but it is perfectly legitimate. In order to illustrate Velikovsky's point, I present here in full the passage of the Deir el-Bahri inscriptions, as it is given in *Ages in Chaos*:

> The loading of the cargo-boats with great quantities of marvels of the land of Punt, with all the good woods of the Divine Land, heaps of gum of anti, and trees of green anti, with ebony, with pure ivory, with green gold of the land of Amu, with cinnamon wood, Khesit wood, with balsam, resin, antimony, with cynocephali, monkeys, greyhounds, with skins of panthers of the south, with inhabitants of the [south] country and their children.
>
> Never were brought such things to any king since the world was.

In the above passage the word "south" was added to the description of the "inhabitants of the country and their children" by Velikovsky, and is not found in Breasted. As might be expected, he was severely criticized for so doing; and on hindsight he should perhaps have made it clear that this was an addendum of his own. Yet his reason for inserting the word was perfectly legitimate. These people, along with their children, were clearly gifts, part of the tribute given by the Puntites to the Egyptians. The Puntites would presumably not have given their own people to the Egyptians as slaves; and the fact that these "inhabitants" are listed as gifts immediately after the "skins

---

1 See, for example, G. Rawlinson, *History of Ancient Egypt* Vol. 2 (London, 1881), p. 244. Rawlinson notes that many had recognized "in this remarkable picture an actual representation of the oppressed Hebrews." However, he goes on to say that though the countenances "have a Semitic cast," they "are certainly not markedly Jewish ... They have light hair and in several instances blue eyes."

2 In Sweeney's *Empire of Thebes: Ages in Chaos Revisited*, there is presented compelling evidence to suggest that the Mitannians were allies of both the Egyptians and the Hebrews in their battles against the Hyksos, who were one and the same as the Old Assyrians.

of panthers of the south," indicate clearly that they are of the same region as the panthers.[1]

Attempts therefore to portray the negroes as natives of Punt flounder on this very clear statement of the inscription.

Interestingly, Velikovsky found in the statement of the Deir el-Bahri inscriptions that negroes were given as gifts by the ruler of Punt to his guests an echo of a similar statement in Josephus, where we read:

> The king [Solomon] had many ships stationed in the Sea of Tarsus, as it was called, which he ordered to carry all sorts of merchandise to the inland nations and from the sale of these there was brought to the king silver and gold and much ivory and *kussiim* [Negroes] and apes.[2]

Velikovsky wrote; "It has been supposed that Josephus mistook some other Hebrew word of an older source and read it kussiim. The picture of the expedition to Punt proves, however, that Josephus was not wrong: kussiim, the dark men of Ophir, were apparently brought by the sailors of Hiram and Solomon."[3]

The Punt reliefs refer to the "chiefs of Irem" as one of the groups presenting gifts to Hatshepsut and to Amon, on the return to Egypt. It seems that the "chiefs of Irem" were men of a seafaring race who accompanied the Egyptians back to Thebes. According to Velikovsky, these seem to have been subjects of King Hiram of Tyre, Solomon's famous ally. Now the entire story of Solomon was intimately connected with Tyre and its king. The Tyrians were Phoenicians; part of that great race of seafarers whose voyages across seas and apparently even oceans were famous in antiquity. We know that Solomon permitted Hiram to equip a fleet at Elat, in the south of Israel; and the First Book of Kings informs us that from this port, Hiram's sailors brought back to Israel, from Ophir, 420 talents of gold.[4] The same book emphasizes again and again that Solomon owed his great wealth to the "gold of Ophir." The latter region has been generally connected with Africa (it seems indeed to be a contracted form of the Egyptian Khenthenopher), and over the years various attempts have been made to find "King Solomon's Mines" in the southern half of the continent, which to this day is a gold-rich region.[5]

---

1 Furthermore, when Hatshepsut mentions the southern land of Kush it is almost invariably described as "the vile Kush." This is very different from her normal description of Punt, which is a "glorious region of God's Land" and a "place of delight."
2 Josephus, *Jewish Antiquities*, VIII, vii, 2
3 Velikovsky, *Ages in Chaos*, op cit., p. 126
4 1 Kings 9: 26-28
5 The statement that the journey to and from Ophir took three years would certainly suggest a district in southern Africa.

These attempts are probably not mistaken. It is unlikely that the Africans on the Deir el-Bahri reliefs were Nubians, but hailed from much further south. As we shall shortly see, archaeology has now demonstrated that negroes — apparently from the Horn of Africa — were indeed living in southern Israel during the time of the Eighteenth Dynasty, where they seem to have formed an important part of the workforce involved in mining.

The Africans, it would then appear, occupy such a significant position in the reliefs because they were one of the wonders of the Divine Land: people from the "ends of the earth" brought back to Punt/Israel by the Phoenician seamen in Solomon's employ.

So, not only do the Africans on the Deir el Bahri reliefs fail to present any real problems for the Hatshepsut = Queen of Sheba identification, they may actually add further dramatic light on the biblical description of Solomon and his fabulously opulent kingdom.

ERITREA AND SOMALIA IN HATSHEPSUT'S TIME: A PRIMITIVE LAND

The Egyptological establishment is nowadays fairly unanimous in placing Punt at the southern end of the Red Sea, either in Eritrea or Somalia, or a combination of these two places. The reasons for this have been examined above. Yet such a location, we have seen, immediately raises the enormous problem of accounting for the fact that Thutmose III claimed to have conquered Punt — all of Punt — in his first year. No one in his right mind would suggest that any pharaoh ever ruled these territories: Aside from the logistical problems of a military expedition to such remote regions, there is no archaeological justification for such a supposition. Not a trace of anything that could be construed as implying Egyptian rule, or even substantial contact with Egypt, has ever appeared.

Yet the first year of Thutmose III's reign did see major military activity; the conquest of Israel/Canaan. He could, and did, claim to have conquered all of that territory.

But locating Punt in Eritrea/Somalia raises an even greater problem. Actually, it is an insurmountable one. The earliest Egyptian contacts with Punt occurred during the Old Kingdom, in the time of the Fourth Dynasty, as a matter of fact; though there is a suggestion of even earlier connections. The Old Kingdom references make it clear that Punt was a territory well-known to the Egyptians, and there is strong suggestion that it was a country which had attained a level of civilization comparable to that of the Egyptians themselves. Certainly by the time of the New Kingdom Punt was a trading partner of Egypt, and the record of Hatshepsut's expedition suggests a cultured region inhabited by people of mixed Hamitic/Semitic stock, who cultivated exotic plants like incense and mined for gold and other precious materials. One of the gifts given to the Egyptian visitors was lapis lazuli, a product of Afghanistan. This alone suggests an extremely active and international trading economy. As such, the archaeologist would expect to find, in Punt, the remains of a thriving Bronze Age culture. Indeed, if the reports of Punt emanating from Old Kingdom inscriptions are anything to go by, he would expect to find plentiful remains even of an Early or at least Middle Bronze Age civilization. Now, we ask ourselves the crucial question: Can Eritrea/Somalia produce the required remains?

The answer, sadly for Velikovsky's critics, is a resounding no!

Neither Eritrea nor Somalia has received the type of intense archaeological attention accorded to Egypt or Syria/Palestine. Nevertheless, a substantial amount of work has been done in both territories; and from this a fairly detailed picture of the region's cultural and ethnic history has emerged. We now know, for example, that the area was colonized by groups of Arabs from across the Red Sea at various times during the first millennium BC. From the intermixing of these newcomers and natives there developed the great and venerable civilization we now call "Ethiopia." But this Ethiopia had nothing whatsoever to do with the Ethiopia of the Bible, which was Nubia. The Arab incomers were literate metal-workers who introduced high civilization into what had previously been a Neolithic territory. The crucial question for us is: When did they arrive? Ironically enough, John Bimson devotes considerable space to this topic in his critique of Velikovsky. He sought to show that these Arab immigrants were the "Puntites" with whom Hatshepsut and the other Egyptians traded. For all that, he has to admit that the main Arab settlement took place only in the 8th century BC! (though according to Velikovsky's chronology Hatshepsut's expedition would have occurred in the 10th century). In order to get round this difficulty he quotes a number of sources which claim Arab settlement from the early Iron Age.[1] The problem is (and Bimson himself is well aware of this) that Solomon's early Iron Age, of the 10th century, is an Iron Age that exists only on paper. It has no archaeological confirmation. That is precisely why Velikovsky was compelled to

1 The sources provided by Bimson are the following: J. Doresse *Ethiopia* (London, 1959); A.H.M. Jones and E. Munroe *A History of Ethiopia* (Oxford, 1935); R. Greenfield *Ethiopia: A New Political History* (London, 1965); A.K. Irvine 'The Arabs and Ethiopians' in D.J. Wiseman (ed.) *Peoples of Old Testament Times* (Oxford, 1973); G.W. van Beek 'Recovering the Ancient Civilization of Arabia', *Biblical Archaeologist* XV: 1 (1952); W.F. Albright 'The Chaldaean Inscriptions in Proto-Arabic Script' *Bulletin of the American Schools of Oriental Research* 128 (1952).

identify Late Bronze Age Palestine with the Palestine of David and Solomon. In short, the Arab settlements in Eritrea would have needed to commence in the archaeological Bronze Age for Hatshepsut and Thutmose III to have found any high culture there. But no such settlements have ever been found. And of course the problem becomes even more acute when we remember that there was frequent intercourse between Egypt and Punt during the Old Kingdom. Eritrea/Somalia should therefore, if it was Punt, have had an Early Bronze civilization.

The nonexistence of any Bronze Age culture in this area, should, in itself, be sufficient to bury once and for all the notion of an African location. The only southern region that could qualify would be Yemen, but this only exacerbates the problem of Thutmose III's conquest of the territory.

Egyptian artifacts do eventually appear in Eritrea/Somalia, but not before the Age of the Ptolemies, in the third century BC. In the words of Timothy Insoll, "items of Egyptian provenance found in either Ethiopia or Eritrea and dating before the Ptolemaic period are unknown. ... In fact, the bulk of objects of Egyptian provenance date from the Aksumite period, i.e., after the first century CE. ..."[1] We recall again at this point the words of Dimitri Meeks: "The hypothesis of an African location for the land of Punt is based on extremely fragile grounds. It is contradicted by numerous texts and has only become an established fact in Egyptology because no-one has taken into account the full range of evidence on the subject, regardless of place of such an African hypothesis."

The failure of the Egyptians to make any substantial contact with the Horn of Africa before the Ptolemaic Age was almost certainly due to the unique difficulties and dangers of navigating the Red Sea. These were discussed at length by Charles Ginenthal in Volume 3 of *Pillars of the Past*. He quotes U. Vermeulen and D. de Smet whose work focuses on the situation during the Middle Ages, but which would also have pertained in antiquity. According to them, "[There are] dangers ships encountered in sailing from the south to the northern Red Sea. Classical Muslim geographers and travelers mention the erratic winds which blow in the Red Sea and the hazards involved in navigating this sea. Our sources all comment about the difficulties encountered with shallow waters and the numerous rocks, corals and islands. [The n]orth-south direction was safer and the pilot would in all

---

1 Timothy Insoll, *The Archaeology of Islam in Sub-Saharan Africa* (Cambridge University Press, 2003), p. 40

probability sail down the centre to avoid the treacherous banks and reefs near the coasts for which the Red Sea is notorious. The route, there, became difficult with islands, rocks and irregular currents, not to mention the danger of sailing in the dark of the night."[1] Ginenthal quotes H. W. Tilman on the navigational hazards faced even by modern yachts:

"Even without pirates the Red Sea provides enough problems for the small-boat sailor ... strong currents, baffling winds, steep seas, scattered reefs and [in modern times] partially lit shores. Another navigational hazard [in daylight] is caused by refraction [of light from the surrounding desert lands]. ... On one occasion a light with a range of 14 miles was seen when we were 37 miles distant. ... Thus owing to the displacement of the horizon, sights, particularly sun sights, are liable to considerable error."[2]

Lin and Larry Pardey provide further information:

"North- or southbound, the Red Sea can be a real test of your seamanship and navigation skills. Sandstorms can reduce visibility to less than 100 yards, though during the most favorable transit months sandstorms are not too common. Currents throughout the Red Sea are variable, especially so near the reefs ...

"Because the Red Sea is flanked by hot deserts, a refraction phenomenon ... causes daytime sights to be in error up to 20 miles east or west [from shore].

"To be becalmed ... in the confined areas of the Gulf of Suez ... can be a real problem."[3]

In Ginenthal's words: "[T]he problem was to keep away from the shore with its rocks and submerged reefs. At night this was not possible, so ships anchored near shore or at the shore overnight, but during daylight the distance to the shore was distorted by refraction, so ships could run aground or be carried aground by the changing currents and erratic winds when the sailors misinterpreted these distances. What further exacerbated these problems was the reduced ability to turn these ancient ships quickly when dangers approached. ... Therefore even if one could see the danger ahead, a strong current and accompanying wind into the direction of the hazard would not necessarily allow the ship, even manned by rowers, to avoid striking it. Even in the times of the Ptolemies, when ships were more advanced

1   Charles Ginenthal, *Pillars of the Past*, Vol. 3 (Ivy Press Books, New York, 2011), quoting U. Vermeulen and D. de Smet, *Egypt and Syria in the Fatimid, Ayyubid and Mamluk Eras* (Leuven, Belgium, 2005), p. 359
2   Ginenthal, op cit., quoting H. W. Tilman, *Eight Sailing/Mountain-Exploration Book* (Leicester UK, Seattle WA, 1987), p. 619
3   Ginenthal, op cit., quoting Lin and Larry Pardey, *The Self-Sufficient Sailor* (Pardey Books, 1999), pp. 290-1

than the ancient Egyptian vessels, the very same problems existed, as J. P. Mehaffey states: 'The navigation of the Red Sea is very carefully described, with all its dangers, which the Ptolemies sought to diminish by leaving wrecked ships where they had stranded by way of warning.'[1]

Having said all of that, it is nonetheless clear that some ships had reached the southern shores of the Red Sea during the time of Hatshepsut. These ships came not from Egypt however, but from southern Israel, and they were manned by the greatest sailors of antiquity, the Phoenicians. Contact with the Horn of Africa is made rather explicit by the Deir el-Bahri reliefs, noted above, where the Puntites present the Egyptians with various gifts "of the southern country," as well as people of the southern country. The aforementioned gifts include products typical of tropical Africa, such as ebony, ivory and leopard-skins; whilst the people are clearly negroes. If, as we believe, the Puntites were Israelites, then the "southern land" in question must have been the Horn of Africa, or at the very least the southern shores of the Red Sea. It cannot have been Nubia, for the Egyptians themselves controlled the latter territory and there would in any case have been little point in presenting them with gifts from a region so familiar to them.

The "southern land" then was almost certainly the region of Eritrea and Somalia, or perhaps even further south, and the connection between Israel and that part of the world in the epoch of the Eighteenth Dynasty has been confirmed, as we noted above, by the discovery of burials of at least one or perhaps two negroes from that region in the southern Negev. These were found during a dig conducted by B. Rothenberg in 1964. He reported that a shallow pit dug into the red sand contained "a stone structure, 2.30 by 2.0 m. and about 1 m. high. ... Clearing out the inside a skeleton was found at its bottom. ... The tomb contained no other objects. ... Examination of the bones by Dr. Haas of Tel Aviv University showed that, in fact, 'there were skeletal remains of two individuals. The first one, almost complete, is an adult male, 25–30 years old, with peculiar proto-negroid features. The second one, found without calvarium, was an adult of 18-22 years. No racial diagnosis of these [second] remains was possible [owing to the absence of the skull].' According to Dr. Haas, the Timna skull, with its peculiar anthropological typological features, could not in any way belong to a population originating from the Syria-Palestine area, but an African origin is strongly indicated. It is

---

1 Ginenthal, op cit., p. 406

similar to the proto-boscopoid type found in ancient Ethiopia and at Nagada in Egypt."[1]

No attempt was made by the excavators to explain this African presence, though the Scriptures hinted very strongly that Phoenician sailors in the employ of Solomon had brought negroes from the southern regions via the port of Elat. From the same region, apparently identical to the fabulous land of Ophir, they brought great quantities of gold. And in this context we recall note that one of the products of the "southern land" presented by the Puntites to the Egyptians was "precious stones" and another was gold.

So, there must have been *some* contact between the civilizations of the Near East and the Horn of Africa in the time of Hatshepsut, yet it cannot have been intense and seems to have been confined to the purchase of slaves and such products as ebony and gold. The latter material may eventually have been mined by the Jewish and Phoenician sailors themselves, which mining gave rise to the legend of "King Solomon's Mines." Gold is still found in the Horn of Africa to this day.

RECAPITULATION

Thus the evidence of Punt, regarded by Velikovsky's critics as crucial in refuting the Hatshepsut = Queen of Sheba equation, in no way says what they affirmed. Indeed, as we look further into the question of Punt's identity, it becomes more and more astonishing that anyone could locate it anywhere other than Palestine/Lebanon. As we saw, before the discovery of the Hatshepsut reliefs in the middle of the 19th century, it was universally assumed that Punt should be located in Asia. The Deir el-Bahri reliefs, however, with their "African" elements, caused a rethink. Everything that had previously identified Punt with Asia was then either reinterpreted or simply ignored. But the supporters of the African Punt theory, as well as those who deny the Egyptian origin of the Queen of Sheba, are now involved in a truly epic amount of ignoring.

Regarding the identity of the Queen of Sheba:

1. They need to ignore the fact that "ruler of the South" was a recognized biblical term for the Egyptian monarch.

2. They must ignore the fact that 'Shewa' or 'Sheba' was almost certainly the original pronunciation of Wa.she, the normal Egyptian name for Thebes.

3. They must ignore the evidence which suggests the Queen of Sheba was ruler of a powerful kingdom, not a desert principality.

---

1 B. Rothernberg, *Timna, Valley of the Biblical Copper Mines* (Thames and Hudson, London, 1972), p. 103

4. They must ignore the fact that Josephus specifically identified her as the "Queen of Egypt and Ethiopia (Nubia)."

5. They must ignore the fact that Abyssinian tradition makes the Queen a native of "Ethiopia," names her Makeda (close to Hatshepsut's throne-name Makera), and claims that it was her son by Solomon (i.e., Shishak, king of Egypt), who plundered Solomon's temple.

Regarding the identity of Punt:

1. They must ignore the evidence which suggests it was a mighty kingdom, otherwise the queen of Egypt would not have decorated an extremely important part of her funerary monument with a visit to it.

2. They must ignore the evidence which suggests Punt was very close to Egypt, otherwise Thutmose III could not have conquered it in his first year (this alone absolutely excludes Eritrea and Somalia).

4. They must ignore the fact that Byblos is always associated with *Ta Netjer*, the "Land of the God," and that Punt too is always associated with *Ta Netjer*.

5. They must ignore the fact that Palestine/Phoenicia was specifically linked to the god Osiris, and that "netjer" was a word used specifically for Osiris — indicating that the land of *Ta Netjer* was a region sacred to Osiris.

6. They must further ignore the fact that Osiris' connection with Phoenicia/Palestine was partly a result of the fact that the latter region was a source of materials used in embalming, particularly natron; and that the richest source of natron, as well as bitumen, was the Dead Sea basin.

7. They must ignore or reinterpret the numerous Egyptian inscriptions clearly linking Punt with Byblos and with other territories in the Lebanon/Palestine region.

8. They must ignore or "reinterpret" the fact that the goddess Hathor was specifically linked to Byblos and named the "Lady of Byblos," and that she was also specifically linked to Punt and named the "Lady of Punt."

9. They must ignore or "reinterpret" the obvious similarity between the names Punt (*Pwene*) and Phoenicia.

10. They must ignore the fact that Punt was described as a land of "myrrh terraces," and that the Jordan Valley was anciently famous for its frankincense and myrrh, which grew upon the terraced hillsides near Jericho.

11. They must ignore the fact that one of the gifts given to the Egyptians by the Puntites was lapis lazuli, a product of central Asia, whilst another was "green metal of the land of Amu," which suggests copper from Asia.

12. They must ignore the fact that the Egyptians claimed to be of Puntite origin, whilst the Phoenicians held that the Egyptians had come from their land; and this Asiatic origin of Dynastic Egyptian civilization is confirmed archaeologically.

13. They must ignore the fact that communication between Punt and Egypt was apparently halted in the Hyksos age (as hinted by Hatshepsut). Yet the Hyksos (in Avaris/Sinai) could scarcely have prevented communication between the southern Egyptians in Thebes and the people of Eritrea or Somalia.

14. They must ignore the fact that at least one of the animals displayed on the Deir el Bahri reliefs, the rhinoceros, has only ever been attested in Asia, whilst the other, supposedly "African" animals, have all been attested in Asia, and that in the time of Hatshepsut large numbers of elephants, lions and other supposedly typical African animals roamed throughout Syria/Palestine, most especially in the Jordan valley.

15. Perhaps most crucially of all, they must ignore the fact that during the time of the 18th Dynasty (never mind in the period of the Old Kingdom) there was no high civilization in Eritrea or Somalia (or southern Arabia, for that matter) that the Egyptians could have traded with or conquered.

CHAPTER 4: THE JOURNEY TO PUNT AND ITS MEANING

THE ROUTE TO PUNT

Velikovsky argued that Hatshepsut had reached Israel by sailing northward from Egypt's Red Sea port of Quseir, disembarking at Elat (near the ancient fortress of Eziongeber) at the head of the Gulf of Aqaba, then travelling overland by foot, or covered palanquin, past the western shore of the Dead Sea and into the Jordan Valley. There is no question that Israel can be reached by this route, and we know that Egyptians did in fact often travel to Punt via the port of Quseir. But it was primarily evidence from the Bible which led Velikovsky to favor the Red Sea route. He noted, for example, that the account of the Queen of Sheba in the Book of Kings is placed immediately after the description of the construction of the port of Elat. He noted too that the Egyptian party was welcomed to Punt by an official named Perehu, a man whose name was identical to that of Paruah, an official, apparently, of the court of Solomon. According to 1 Kings, 4:17, Paruah's son Jehoshaphat was appointed by Solomon to administer the territory of Issachar, which implied that Paruah himself, at a slightly earlier stage, was an important functionary in Solomon's time. Although Jehoshaphat — and by extension his father Paruah — are linked in the Book of Kings to the territory of Issachar in north of Israel, Velikovsky claimed this was an error on the part of later editors, and that he should rightfully have been associated with Alat (or B'alat), which is mentioned in the preceding verse. Alat, said Velikovsky, must be the same place as Elat.

In Velikovsky's own words: "Among the twelve governors of King Solomon — at a later period of his reign (when some of the officials were sons-in-law) — one was a son of Paruah (I Kings 4:17). Jehoshaphat, the son of Paruah, was governor of Ezion-Geber and Eloth; his father, apparently, administered the same region."[1]

The problem, of course, is that the biblical passage referenced does not place Jehoshaphat in the south of Israel, but in the north. Velikovsky explains the discrepancy in a footnote: "It appears that the last word of I Kings 4:16 belongs to the next verse, and the last word of 4:17 to the following verse. The reading should be: '... and in Aloth Jehoshaphat the son of Paruah.' In this case the son remained governor where his father had served in the same capacity, Aloth and Eloth being the same." He also notes that, "In a context having no relation to the question presented here, Albright (*Journal of the Palestinian Oriental Society*, V [1925], 35) made the same suggestion that the place Aloth be transferred to the next verse, into the domain of Jehoshaphat, son of Paruah."[2]

I have to admit that I was originally doubtful of this claim: The need to postulate a corruption of the biblical text in order to prove a point seemed to be stretching things. On the other hand, Velikovsky's identification of Perehu, the "chief of Punt," with Paruah, seemed very strong. Could it be, I thought, that Paruah, as the text seems to imply, was governor of a northern territory, bordering the Mediterranean? It seemed to me that a voyage straight down the Nile into the Mediterranean would leave one on the shores of Israel in about the same time as a laborious journey cross-country to the Red Sea coast, followed by a voyage along the dangerous route north through the Gulf of Aqaba. I was also of the impression that the houses on stilts, which Hatshepsut's expedition encountered shortly after landing in Punt, were perchance the residences of inhabitants of Lake Hulah or the northern Jordan Valley, which was in antiquity a region of papyrus marshes much given to flooding.

That was before. I am now convinced, however, that Velikovsky got it right; that the expedition did proceed through the Red Sea route and disembark at the port of Elat. The crucial evidence was brought forward by Eva Danelius, who proved, I think beyond reasonable doubt, that Elat and the valley leading towards the Dead Sea, the Arabah, were regions crossed by the Egyptian expedition.

1 Velikovsky, *Ages in Chaos*, op cit., p. 115
2 Ibid.

Some of the most compelling evidence brought forward by Danelius in this regard concerns Perehu's obese wife Iti or Ity, who is shown along with her husband greeting the Egyptian travelers. In Danelius' words: "The Governor of Punt and his wife are introduced by name: he is called P'-r-hw; her name was Eti (or Ati). According to Naville, these names have 'no ethnographical significance.' Naville was wrong: As Velikovsky has shown, these names are Biblical names from the period of David and Solomon. A certain Paruah was the father of one of Solomon's twelve governors; a man named Atai was a member of the Ierahmielim, a Bedouin tribe affiliated with Judah, who lived in the northern Negev. Another man of the same name was one of the 'men of might' who joined David when he hid in the wilderness above the Dead Sea, and in Ziklag, because of Saul. According to Hebrew usage, the daughter might have been presented with her father's name: Bat (=daughter of) Atai."[1]

Thus both Perehu and his wife can be linked directly to southern Israel, at just the right time in history.

The fact, noted earlier, that the "ways of heaven," (the route to Punt mentioned by Perehu) probably refers to a route leading from Egypt to southern Israel via the mountainous regions of central Sinai, also points to Elat as the disembarkation point. The road crossing the Sinai Plateau descends precipitously as it approaches the coast near Eziongeber, falling 800 meters in a distance of three miles. If the "ways of heaven" mentioned by Perehu really means "the high road," then this route is particularly appropriate.

Other evidence points in the same direction: The negroes, for example, who are pictured prominently at Deir el-Bahri, could only have come to Israel (assuming that Punt is Israel) by way of the port of Elat. Danelius noted that the remains of at least one negro, and possibly two, originating in the Horn of Africa, have actually been found in the Negev region, and suggests they were brought there by Hiram's navy during the time of Solomon.[2] The negro burials appear to date from the time of the Egyptian New Kingdom, and there seems little doubt that they were slaves put to work in the mines of the Arabah, a region rich in various minerals, particularly copper.

According to Danelius, the scene of the expedition's disembarkation, as portrayed at Deir el-Bahri, strikingly resembles Elat. The date-palms growing at the water's edge are there to this day, even if the houses on stilts have disappeared. "...the reliefs," she says, "show an amazing similarity to charac-

---

1 Danelius, loc. cit. Part III, pp. 13-14
2 Ibid., p. 13, her source being Rothenberg, op cit.

teristics of the northern end of the Gulf of Aqaba, unknown at the time when Velikovsky wrote his reconstruction but to a very small circle of explorers.

"The drawings show meticulous care for details to a degree justifying the supposition 'that the expedition to Punt was accompanied by one or more draftsmen who made careful studies of what they saw there ...' On the picture reproduced on plate LXIX, palm trees and other trees, high enough to shade houses on poles, and cattle, go right down to the edge of the water which swarms with fish and other aquatic animals. Such plant and animal life is 'not to be found by the shore, nor do date palms grow in the sand and pebbles of the beach,' concluded Naville, Maspero and other Egyptologists, who, therefore, looked for a suitable harbor 'at some distance inland, safe from the high tides of the Red Sea.' This opinion, however, is difficult to uphold in light of the fact that the aquatic animals reproduced are typical specimens of the Indian-Ocean-Red-Sea-Fauna.

"The Egyptologists were not the only ones to remark on this unusual combination of nature. Procopius, who lived in the sixth century AD, mentioned the date palms growing along the coast of Aila (=Aqaba) ... And the well-known Arab writer Al-Mukadassi (10th century) describes the place just as it was shown on the mural of Hatshepsut: 'There are many date-trees, and an abundance of fish.'"[1]

Fig. 7. Modern Eilat, with date-palms still growing along the shore.

1 Ibid., p. 12

The territory just to the north of Elat is rich in minerals, particularly copper; and it is here that we encounter a striking echo of the Punt expedition as recounted at Deir el-Bahri. One of the gifts presented to the Egyptians, as we saw, was "green gold" of the land of Amu. Leaving aside the fact that it came from the land of the Amu, or Asiatics, we must wonder at the term "green gold." There is no such thing, of course, as green gold; so there must be some kind of translation mix-up. According to Danelius, "... the Egyptian sign translated 'gold,' if used as a determinative, is actually to be translated 'precious metal.' In combination with a sign for 'white,' it means 'silver.' That is why it was suggested [by Professor Polotzky] to see in 'green gold' an expression for 'copper,' which is stark green in its natural state, coming to the surface in broad green bands across the hills bordering the Arabah."[1]

The copper mines of Timna, just eighteen miles north of Elat, were worked intensively from the Chalcolithic Age onwards, and were always considered an important source of the metal by the Egyptians.

And if all this fails to convince, Danelius also noted that a shrine to the goddess Hathor, dating from the time of the Egyptian New Kingdom, was located at Timna. Hatshepsut's expedition, of course, brought gifts to Punt, "for the life, prosperity, and health of her majesty to Hathor, mistress of Punt." Since, as noted earlier, Hathor was universally known as the Lady of Punt, could it be, thought Danelius, that Hatshepsut founded a shrine to the goddess in Punt, or at least brought offerings to an already-established shrine in the country?

The precise date of the Timna shrine is uncertain: it is claimed that the structure, as it now exists, does not precede the reign of Seti I, at the beginning of the Nineteenth Dynasty. However, this structure bears a very close resemblance to another shrine of Hathor belonging to Amenhotep II at Deir el-Bahri. This latter, in a cave, "was only slightly altered; it is 'about 10 feet long ... it has been lined all round with slabs of sandstone ... the roof is a vault consisting of two stones abutting against each other and cut in the form of an arch. There never was any pavement: the [Hathor] cow stood on the rough rock.' The cow in this cave has the name of Amenhotep II."[2] According to Danelius, "It is this cave-shrine which shows the greatest affinity with the Hathor-Temple at Timna. The naos at Timna is 2.70 meters, compared

---

1 Danelius, loc. cit., Part III, p. 13. In a footnote Danelius notes that the normal word for "copper" is *bia*, but this term may have been used only for finished products. She quotes Gardiner (*Egypt of the Pharaohs*, p. 43) as noting that from "Dynasty XVIII onward Syria is spoken of as sending tribute of copper."
2 Danelius, loc. cit., Part III, p. 17

to 'about' 10 feet (approximately 3 meters) at Deir el-Bahari. Its walls were built of white sandstone which, as the excavator remarks, had to be carried here from quite a distance, and it was leaning 'against the face of a huge picturesque eroded formation at the southwestern end of the Timna massif' in a similar way as the shrine in the Nile valley leaned against the cliff which bordered it in the west. As to the roof, there was no need of one, 'because the overhanging rock served as an excellent protection.'"[1]

It should be noted that the earliest Egyptian temple at the spot, in Stratum IV, had been thoroughly destroyed down to bedrock at some time in antiquity. We are told that, "... apart from walls 1 and 3 and some parts of the naos, no architectural details of the original first temple structure survived what must have been a thoroughly wanton destruction; and there was no archaeological evidence to identify the destroyer of this first temple. ... A new temple was built on top of the ruins of the original temple structure, utilizing some of its architectural elements. ... Unfortunately [there was] little help in dating the destruction of the first temple as the effects of the destruction went right down to bedrock ..."[2] The writer of these words added: "It seems that the first temple was built by Sethos I, (1318-1304 BC.), destroyed or abandoned during the reign of Sethos II (1216-1210 BC.), and the second temple was reconstructed by Ramses III (1198-1166 BC.). However, it should be remembered that there is no definite archaeological evidence for this, although it does appear to be a logical solution which fits the historical picture of the period and the meagre stratigraphical evidence."[3]

But in view of the fact that the temple bears closest comparison with one of Amenhotep II, Hatshepsut's grand-nephew, might we not, thought Danelius, be justified in dating its foundation to a slightly earlier date?

It should be noted too that the Timna structure is very similar to a Hathor sanctuary at the turquoise mines in Sinai, where Hathor, the "Lady of Turquoise," was the protectress of the workers.[4]

In summary, Danelius has presented several compelling reasons for identifying southern Israel, particularly the Arabah Valley and the Negev, as the route to Punt. These are as follows:

---

1 Ibid.
2 Rothenberg, op cit., p. 130
3 Ibid., p. 131
4 Ibid., pp. 149-151

The flora and general layout of Elat, with its date-palms growing down to the seashore, corresponds very well with the description of Punt at Deir el Bahri.

The Puntite governor Perehu and his wife Ati both have names associated with the southern Negev region during the time of David and Solomon.

The "green gold" of the land of Amu is almost certainly copper, and the Arabah region was a major copper-producing area in antiquity.

The shrine of Hathor at Timna shows that the territory was sacred to Hathor, and Hathor was, of course, the Lady of Punt.

To these we might add the fact that the Dead Sea, with its deposits of natron and bitumen, seems to have particularly associated with Osiris, in whose honor the Divine Land was thus named. And it is apparent too that some of the most productive incense and spice-growing territories in Israel were located not far from the Dead Sea, particularly around Ein Gedi, Phasaelis and Jericho.

There seems little doubt then that it was by way of the Gulf of Aqaba that Hatshepsut's expedition reached Israel.

A JOURNEY THROUGH A STRANGE LAND

As the Egyptian fleet sailed northwards through the blue-green waters of the Gulf of Aqaba it must have seemed to the Queen that she was approaching an enchanted region. To the left the rugged peaks of Sinai hugged the shore, whilst to the right the somewhat smaller mountains of Midian could be seen in the distance. These were regions traversed by the Israelites many generations before when they fled serfdom in Hatshepsut's homeland. No doubt the Egyptian queen would have known the story well, and it may have colored her view of the country and people she was about to visit. Great prodigies occurred in those far-off times, the most spectacular of which — the parting of the Red Sea's waters — was said by one tradition to have occurred at the Straits of Tiran, at the very entrance to the Gulf of Aqaba. On either side of the Gulf stretched the lands of the Midianites, an Arab people with whom Moses, leader of the slaves, had been allied through marriage.

As the Egyptian fleet approached Elat the impression of enchantment would have been reinforced. All around the shore grew a profusion of luxurious date palms, whilst behind and amongst these stood the homes of the inhabitants themselves — on stilts. Houses on stilts were by no means uncommon in antiquity, and whole villages of them existed in Europe during Hatshepsut's time. They were thus constructed either for defense or to protect against flooding. The latter would have been the reason for these examples in Elat. The whole of the Negev and ancient Edom is periodically washed by heavy rainfalls, which can briefly turn the wadis into raging torrents. It was these rainfalls which fed the underground springs which in turn provided nourishment to the date palms on the shore. Several wadis converged in ancient Elat, and so the inhabitants designed their homes to protect against these periodic downpours.

Overlooking the settlement would have stood a much more substantial building, the fortress residence of the governor Paruah himself, situated at Ezion Geber, just a short distance from the port of Elat. It would have been to this structure that the queen's attention would have been drawn first.

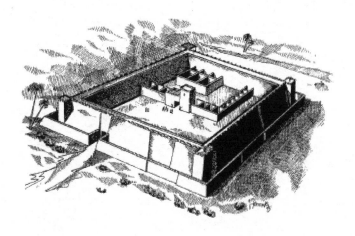

Fig. 8. Reconstruction of ancient fortress at Elat/Ezion-Geber.

Surveying the scene, Hatshepsut must have wondered what adventures lay in ahead in the strange land to the north — the mythical home of the Egyptian people themselves and the land sacred to Osiris and Hathor.

The heralds, led by the Nubian general Nehsi, would have disembarked earlier than the main party; and the meeting between Nehsi and Paruah is portrayed at Deir el-Bahri, together with a faithful rendering of the small gifts the two exchanged. After these preliminaries, the queen herself would have come ashore and been guided to Paruah's residence, where she no doubt spent the night. After perhaps a day or two recuperating, the Egyptian party would then no doubt have set out towards the north, probably accompanied by some of King Solomon's royal bodyguard. The Egyptian queen would likely have travelled most of the way by palanquin, though she may also have periodically ridden on a chariot, all the better to view the wonders of the region through which she now passed. About eighteen miles north of Elat the royal party would have arrived at Timna, where copper had been mined since remote antiquity. Here the royal party would have paid homage to the goddess Hathor, patroness of the land. All caves were sacred to Hathor, and a small cave beneath a rock precipice still named the "Pillars of Solomon" was especially associated with her. Here the Egyptians may have performed sacrifices.

Fig. 9. The Hathor Shrine at Timna.

Fig. 10. The so-called "Pillars of Solomon" at Timna.

Around Timna the Egyptian party would have been shown the "green gold," or, more accurately, "green metal" of the land of Amu, which was mentioned at Deir el-Bahri as one of the wonders of Punt.

Moving northwards in the direction of the Dead Sea the Arabah valley sinks below sea level and becomes increasingly hot. Essentially, it now forms part of the Jordan Valley, though without the Jordan flowing through it. Nonetheless, there were and are numerous oases which sustain a rich tropical flora and fauna. These oases also had human inhabitants, who created terraces and cisterns everywhere to collect precious rainwater for plant cultivation. We know that Ein Gedi, on the western shores of the Dead Sea, was a major centre of incense and spice cultivation. And in this hot region the Egyptians would have encountered creatures more commonly associated with Africa. There were gazelles, giraffes, zebras and even, apparently, a sub-species of Asiatic rhinoceros. These would have astonished the Egyptians, who faithfully depicted them at Deir el-Bahri. The same creatures are shown in dozens of mosaics in churches and synagogues from the Roman and Byzantine epochs.

Fig 11. Botanical garden with tropical vegetation at a kibbutz in Ein Gedi.

Bypassing the Dead Sea on the western side, the Egyptians would now, at Jericho, have arrived at the very centre of the incense-producing region. To this day the whole landscape is heavily terraced, and ascending the steeply inclining road which leads to Jerusalem, the queen's party would have moved through a veritable forest of frankincense trees. It is likely that the king of Punt, Solomon himself, went out to meet the queen's party before it arrived in Jerusalem. At what stage of the journey the historic encounter occurred is impossible to say; but we may be sure that the two monarchs made a deep impression upon each other. This is the stuff of legend and of romance. Very strong traditions, both in Israel and other lands, indicate that they became lovers, as we shall see.

Fig. 12. Ancient agricultural terracing, much of it still in use, near Jerusalem.

PURPOSE OF THE EXPEDITION

In Chapter 3 we suggested that the expedition to Punt had some form of propaganda purpose, and even a cursory look at the Deir el-Bahri temple shows that Hatshepsut regarded the journey as a defining moment of her life. That is certainly how she wished it to be seen, if we consider its prominence and reporting on the walls of her funerary monument.

Why should this be the case? For mainstream academics the answer is simple: Punt was such a distant and exotic region that a successful voyage hither would constitute a propaganda coup in itself. For those of us who hold by Velikovsky's position however and see Punt as Israel/Lebanon, a region not far from Egypt and well-known to the natives of the Nile Valley, its importance in Hatshepsut's eyes is a little more difficult to explain. Was it because, as Velikovsky seemed to believe, that she was overwhelmed by the opulence and splendor of Solomon and his court? Certainly, if Hatshepsut was the Queen of Sheba, then the traditions about her would suggest that she was indeed awestruck by the Hebrew king and his wonderful realm. And the description of Punt which we find on the walls at Deir el-Bahri would lead to a similar conclusion. Yet there is a problem. No matter how much a reigning monarch may have been enamored of another ruler and his kingdom, this would surely be insufficient reason to immortalize a visit to him on one's funerary monument; and above all to portray that visit as the defining event of one's life.

There must have been another reason.

At Deir el-Bahri Hatshepsut had written that "a command was heard from the great throne, an oracle of the god himself, that the ways to Punt should be searched out, that the highways to the myrrh-terraces should be penetrated." We are informed also that the god Amon wished the queen "to establish for him a Punt in his house," and that this "Punt" should contain living incense trees. Whether or not Hatshepsut believed her god to have spoken to her, there was nevertheless a very good political reason for her to travel to Punt. In order understand this, we have to remember the queen's unique — and uniquely difficult — position. Officially, to begin with, she was acting as re-gent for her stepson and nephew Thutmose III. Midway through the second or perhaps third year, however, this pretence was dropped, and she began to rule as pharaoh. As has been emphasized a thousand times, for a woman to assume this role was wholly unprecedented; and there was therefore a pressing need to legitimize her position. This she did in two ways: On the one hand, she had herself portrayed as a man, complete with artificial beard; and she seems to have appeared thus attired at some official religious and political functions. On the other hand, she began to identify herself more and more closely with a deity, a female deity: the goddess Hathor. Just as every pharaoh was a living incarnation of Amon-Ra, so Hatshepsut now promoted herself as an incarnation of Hathor. An ordinary woman might be deemed illegitimate as ruler: a goddess could not be so easily dismissed.[1]

The queen could not, of course, openly proclaim herself identical to Ha-thor: such heresy may have proved a step too far. But she could insinuate, in a thousand ways, her identity with the goddess. And this she never lost an opportunity to do. At Deir el-Bahri there was a special shrine devoted to Hathor. Naville, who excavated it, believed "the shrine of Hathor to have been originally a cave where, according to tradition, the queen was suckled by the goddess and where, at the end of her life, she 'joined' her divine nurse." Hatshepsut identified herself with the goddess, "thus deifying herself and

---

1 Hathor, as the patroness of childbirth and other feminine concerns, was particu-larly worshipped by women throughout Egyptian history. She was very closely identified with Isis, the wife of Osiris, the Lord of Punt and Byblos. The connection between Hathor and Isis was so close that both bore the title "Lady of Byblos."

claiming the same worship."[1] The murals in the hypostyle hall at Deir el-Bahri show a festive procession on the Nile in honor of Hathor's "sacred birth." The text reads: "Hathor, she reneweth her birth. Thebes is in joy/Me-ke-re, while endures ... the sky, thou endures." According to Naville, "we see clearly the confusion which exists between the goddess and the queen, a confusion which is intentional."[2]

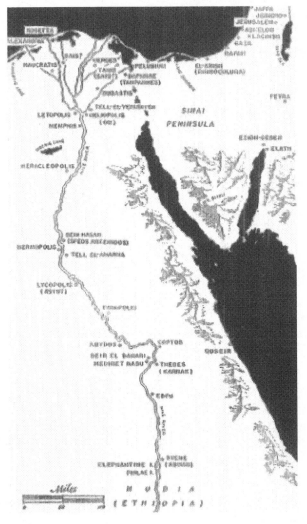

Fig. 13 Egypt and Israel in antiquity.

Thebes, capital of Egypt, is of course far to the south of Jerusalem; hence the Jewish term for the Egyptian monarch as "King (or Queen) of the South".

As we saw, the Punt reliefs are part of a pair located in the middle colonnade of the temple. The other half of the

1 E. Naville, *The Temple of Deir el-Bahari*, Part IV, (London, 1907), Preface.
2 Ibid., p. 2

pair, the "matching" part, shows Hatshepsut's divine birth from Amon and her being suckled by Hathor. Thus the two sections celebrate central events of the queen's life specifically connected with her tutelary god and goddess.

We have already seen that Punt was specifically connected with Hathor. She was the Lady of Punt; and we have seen why: The anemone-reddened Palestinian and Lebanese hills in the spring represented for Egyptians the blood-red earth which was a sign — according to the Hathor myth — that the destruction of humanity had ceased. In visiting Punt/Lebanon, Hatshepsut was reinforcing her identification with Hathor. Hence the ecstatic language of the Deir el-Barhi inscriptions when they speak of Punt.

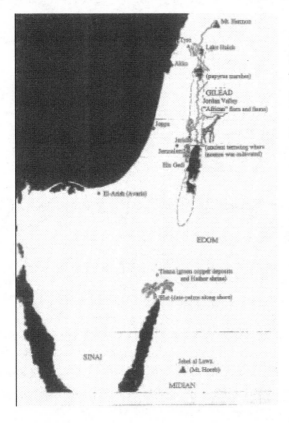

Fig. 14. Hatshepsut's probable route to Jerusalem would have taken her through regions of unusual topography supporting exotic flora and fauna.

The journey to Punt, and its reporting at Deir el-Bahri, was pure propaganda. It was a pilgrimage; but it was also, for the queen, a journey home; a journey to the land of the goddess whom she claimed to be the incarnation of.

That, at least, was its official and original purpose. Later, however, a far more personal motive would enter the equation.

WAS THE KING OF ISRAEL SHOWN ON THE PUNT RELIEFS?

Given the widespread misconceptions about Hatshepsut and the land of Punt I wish here to repeat a point I made earlier on several occasions: It constitutes a profound mistake for a historian to ignore the wider context within which events take place. What Velikovsky's critics — as well as the entire Egyptological establishment — require us to believe, when viewed in context, is astonishingly improbable. We are asked by them to accept that Hatshepsut, the ruler of Egypt, devoted her funerary monument to an expedition (in which she did not even take part) to deliver trinkets to the natives of a semi-primitive region somewhere along the African coast of the Red Sea; a region which was nevertheless so close and so unremarkable that Thutmose III could claim to have conquered and annexed it in his first regnal year. Most readers, I think, will agree that such a scenario is vanishingly implausible. The whole logic of the expedition and its reporting suggests that Punt, though close to Egypt, was indeed a remarkable and powerful kingdom, and that furthermore the Egyptian queen herself led the expedition to its shores. Logic further insists that the Egyptian travelers must have been granted an audience with the Puntite ruler.

That is the logic of the situation. But the critics, in all fairness to them, can point out that no portrayal of the Puntite king is preserved; nor is there, according to Bimson, any space on the walls of the Deir el-Bahri temple where a meeting between Hatshepsut and the Puntite monarch could have been illustrated. What then is the solution? Why is the meeting not shown?

To begin with, we recall that about two-thirds of the illustrations were destroyed in antiquity. Why these segments were effaced we can only guess, but we would be on strong grounds if we argued that these constituted the most politically sensitive parts of the monument. I have been to Deir el-Bahri and confess that I found even the surviving illustrations difficult to discern. How anyone can be sure what the reliefs once contained is beyond me. Velikovsky pointed to the existence of two oversized figures, one of which evidently belonged to Hatshepsut herself: "In the low row [of the Punt reliefs] there appear to have been huge figures, one of which was the queen, as part of her cartouche between the two defaced fields is still recognizable. But if it was a text that was erased and not a likeness, what was peculiar in this text that it had to be erased by the order of her jealous successor, Thutmose III?"[1] Breasted, convinced that Hatshepsut did not accompany the expedition to Punt, identified the figure as that of "a great stone statue of the queen to be

1 Velikovsky, *Ages in Chaos*, op cit., p. 120

erected in Punt."[1] But this was an idea forced upon him only by his conviction that she did not go on the expedition. The other figure is not discernable, though Velikovsky believed that it may well have been Solomon.

Whether this surmise was correct we shall never know. However, it should be noted that even if the King of Israel was not shown on the monument, there is a simple and straightforward answer, one we have already hinted at: A visitation of one monarch by another is an act loaded with symbolic significance. As ruler of a mighty empire, the Queen of Egypt could scarcely allow herself to be portrayed paying homage to a foreign ruler on his own soil. Quite simply, it was beneath her dignity. This was all the more true when we consider that Solomon never reciprocated. There is no evidence that he visited Egypt. And as we saw in Chapter 3, this is almost certainly the reason why the queen makes no direct reference to her being present in Punt during the expedition, preferring instead to portray the Puntites as overawed by her splendor from afar, and delivering into the hands of her servants the wealth and secrets of their country.

In addition, we need to consider that the great temple at Deir el-Bahri was a funerary monument and as such was concerned primarily with religious themes. Egyptian monarchs did not emphasize political events on funerary architecture. Hatshepsut's journey to Punt, the Divine Land, was above all a pilgrimage. She herself was perhaps the most devoted of all Egyptian rulers to the goddess Hathor, and Punt was the land sacred to Hathor, the "Lady of Punt." The temple's purpose was to celebrate the queen's journey to Hathor's country and thus to reinforce her own association with that goddess — thus strengthening her own grip on power.

Both Velikovsky and his critics may have been somewhat misled by their Bible-centered (and male-centered?) outlook. The Queen of Sheba's visit to Palestine must, they assumed, have been prompted by her desire to meet Solomon. No one imagined that that may have been of secondary importance: that the Queen's journey was primarily a pilgrimage to the 'home' of her tutelary deity.

Perhaps other monuments, or parts of the Deir el-Bahri monument, now lost, illustrated the meeting between Hatshepsut and the ruler of Israel/Punt. (There is much evidence, as we shall see, that she may have had a very personal interest in Punt and its king). But it would be quite unrealistic to suppose that any such structures could have survived. Upon Hatshepsut's death Israel became the target of Thutmose III's aggression, an aggression at least

---

1 Breasted, *History of Egypt*, op cit., p. 276

partly explainable by reason of Hatshepsut's friendship. Any illustrations of Hatshepsut and the Israelite king would certainly have aroused an especially destructive zeal on the part of Thutmose's henchmen. It is of course a great pity that no picture of the meeting between Hatshepsut and Solomon has survived, but bearing in mind the politics of the time such a survival would have been almost miraculous.

WAS THE "SPLENDOR OF SPLENDORS" A COPY OF THE JERUSALEM TEMPLE?

According to Velikovsky, Hatshepsut's wonderful temple was directly modeled on Solomon's fabulous temple in Jerusalem. She did, after all, say, that she had "built a Punt" in Egypt. If this structure were indeed a copy of the Jerusalem Temple, then we have before us the solution to one of history's most enduring conundrums.

Velikovsky noted that earlier Egyptologists had recognized the "striking foreign element" in the Splendor of Splendors, and he quoted Maspero, who remarked that "Mariette, struck by the strange appearance of the edifice, thought that it betrayed a foreign influence, and supposed that Queen Hatshopsitu had constructed it in the model of some buildings seen by her officers in the land of Puanit."[1] Again, Mariette had described the building as "an exception and an accident in the architectural life of Egypt." Now, it is widely accepted that the "Punt" built by Hatshepsut was indeed her splendid funerary temple. The last of the inscriptions describing the expedition to the region proudly proclaim, "It was done. ... I have made for him [Amon] a Punt in his garden, just as he commanded me. ... It is large enough for him to walk abroad in it."[2] Undoubtedly one of the propaganda coups of the Punt expedition was the bringing to Egypt of live incense bushes for transplanting in Amon's temple; and there is no doubt that the terraces of the Splendor of Splendors were once adorned with many of these plants. Egyptologists then accept that the Splendor of Splendors was the "Punt" raised by the queen; though they generally see the terraces as an architectural imitation of the "myrrh terraces" of God's Land, rather than a copy of a temple in God's Land. Velikovsky however called to mind the opinion of Mariette and conjectured that the Splendor of Splendors was a copy of some structure seen in Punt. Punt, he said, "being the area of Jerusalem, the temple at Deir el Bahari must have had features in common with the Temple of King Solomon."[3]

---

1 G. Maspero, *The Struggle of the Nations* (S. P. C. K., London, 1896), p. 241, note 2
2 Breasted, *Records*, Vol. 2, Sec. 295
3 Velikovsky, *Ages in Chaos*, op cit., p. 130

Since no portrayals of Solomon's Temple have ever been found, and the description in the Book of Kings not detailed enough to form the basis of an accurate reconstruction, scholars throughout the centuries have wondered about its appearance. From what little information we have, it is clear that the sanctuary was built upon terraces cut by an ascending causeway. Velikovsky notes that "the procession of the Levites started on the lowest terrace, and as they sang they mounted the path. This explains the fact that some of the Psalms are called *Shir ha-maaloth*, 'song of the ascent.'"[1] The terraces, we note, seem to have been planted with exotic trees.

The parallels here with the general outlay of the Splendor of Splendors need no stressing.

Velikovsky further noted that, "The Temple in Jerusalem contained a hall which was three times as long as it was wide; in front of the hall was a vestibule; behind the hall was a sanctuary." Every feature, as described in the Book of Kings, is closely paralleled at Deir el Bahri. "This temple," says Velikovsky, "was built upon terraces planted with trees brought from the Divine Land; the terraces were planted at progressively higher levels, and a path leading to the temple mounted from one level to another. Rows of pillars standing on a lower terrace supported the wall of the terrace above. The court of the temple was surmounted by a colonnade; the temple was divided into a vestibule, a hall, and a sanctuary. The ratio of the width to the length of the hall was almost one to three."[2]

According to Velikovsky, even the service of Solomon's Temple was copied by the Egyptians. "Not only the temple architecture but also the temple service in Egypt were given many new features." One of these was the idea of twelve priests, with a high priest heading them, officiating before the altar. Velikovsky notes that a relief on a fragment, now in the Louvre, shows twelve priests divided into four orders, three in each order, while a damaged inscription over their heads reads: "... in the temple of Amon, in Most Splendid of Splendors, by the high priest of Amon in Most Splendid of Splendors ..."[3] Breasted noted that, "The queen was conscious of the resemblance of the temple-gardens in Deir el Bahari and Punt. The service and equipment of the temple receive some light from the mention of its High Priest, with twelve

---

1 Ibid.
2 Ibid., p. 131
3 Quoted by Velikovsky, from Breasted, *Records*, Vol. 2, note to Sec. 679

subordinate priests in four orders."[1] He also claimed that the office of high priest was established in the Egyptian service only in the time of Hatshepsut.[2]

Was then Velikovsky right? Was the Splendor of Splendors a direct copy of Solomon's Temple? If true, this by itself is one of the most important archaeological and historical discoveries ever made.

The critics of course were quick to point out that Hatshepsut's temple, contrary to what Velikovsky claimed, did have an Egyptian antecedent: This was the funerary monument of Mentuhotep II, of the Eleventh Dynasty, which stands right next to Hatshepsut's own building at Deir el Bahri.[3] Now, Mentuhotep II's temple is much smaller and far less impressive than that of Hatshepsut, but the similarities between the two cannot be denied, and are obvious even to the casual observer. Velikovsky did in fact acknowledge Mentuhotep II's temple, but only in a footnote; and explained the resemblance to Hatshepsut's structure by suggesting that it too "probably represents ... a Phoenician influence."[4]

In order to get to the bottom of this issue, we need to take a closer look at Mentuhotep II and his temple.

There is, to begin with, no question that the Eleventh Dynasty monument does call to mind the architecture of Asia, but it is to Mesopotamia rather than Syria/Palestine that our minds are drawn. Reconstructions of the temple show that it was built upon terraces cut by an ascending causeway, and surmounted at the summit by a smallish pyramid. The overall impression is of a Mesopotamian ziggurat; a fact noted by more than one author.

In his 2007 book *The Pyramid Age*, Emmet Sweeney argued in some detail that the Mentuhotep pharaohs of the Eleventh Dynasty were actually contemporaries and adversaries of the Hyksos (who are normally placed six centuries later). In the same volume, he showed in great detail — following the lead of Gunnar Heinsohn — that the Hyksos were one and the same as the Old Assyrians, the Asiatic superpower overthrown by the Mitanni kings Parattarna and Shaushtatar. Since the Hyksos were Mesopotamians, it is not surprising that influences of various kinds, including architectural, from that region should spread throughout the territories they conquered in Syria/Palestine and in Egypt.

---

1 Ibid. Note to Sec. 291
2 Ibid. Sec. 388
3 The temple was actually begun by Mentuhotep II and completed by Mentuhotep III.
4 Velikovsky, *Ages in Chaos*, op cit., p. 130

It is clear then that by the time of the Eleventh Dynasty (which was actu-ally an alter-ego of the Seventeenth Dynasty), Mesopotamian-style building-forms had begun to appear in Syria and in Egypt. When the Hyksos were overthrown, the styles they had introduced continued to prevail through-out the region; and it follows that the temple built by Solomon in Jerusalem would have followed the same general pattern.

Importantly, it should be remarked that Mentuhotep II's temple, like that of its neighbor the Splendor of Splendors, was specially linked to the wor-ship of Hathor.[1] The whole of the crescent-shaped indent in which the two adjacent temples were situated was regarded as sacred to the goddess. Now Hathor, as we have stressed repeatedly, was specifically connected with Pal-estine/Lebanon and with Punt. This would in turn suggest that Mentuhotep II's monument, which, though superficially resembling a Mesopotamian zig-gurat, is otherwise unlike any other building known, was actually modeled on a Phoenician or Syrian temple of his own epoch.[2] However, in line with the chronology Sweeney has proposed in his Ages in Alignment series of books (and which the present author subscribes to), this was no more than forty or fifty years before Hatshepsut ascended the throne.

The temple of Mentuhotep II therefore certainly had an influence upon the Splendor of Splendors; but this does not preclude the possibility that both monuments were inspired by an Asiatic or Asiatic originals. And it would easy to exaggerate the debt owed by the architect of the Splendor of Splendors to the builders of the Mentuhotep monument. In the words of James Baikie: "Since the earlier temple [of Mentuhotep II] has been com-pletely excavated, it has been customary to deny to Hatshepsut's architect any claim to originality in the design which he evolved for the great temple. 'Hatshepsut's temple,' says Dr. H. R. Hall (*Cambridge Ancient History*, vol. of Plates, i. 88), 'was directly imitated from that of her predecessor, to whom, and not her or her architect Senenmut, any praise for its supposed (not real) originality of design is due.' This, however, is to carry purism to an extrava-gant extent. It is quite obvious that Hatshepsut and her architect took the suggestion of a terraced temple from the earlier building beside which they placed their own; but that is the beginning and the end of their indebtedness to the earlier architect. Senmut appreciated a good suggestion when he saw it — all the more credit to him for his commonsense; but to say that he must

1 "... the temple was for the worship of a deity other than the King; this deity was probably the goddess Hathor." Margaret A Murray, *Egyptian Temples* (Sampson Low, Martson and Co., London), p. 131
2 According to Margaret Murray, Mentuhotep's temple is "unique." Ibid., p. 129

therefore be denied any credit for originality is to set up a canon of criticism which would deprive Shakespeare of the credit for the creation of Hamlet, and Donatello of that for the creation of the Gattamelata statue."[1]

The whole question of Hatshepsut's temple and its relationship to that of Jerusalem could of course be answered immediately if we could find any trace of Solomon's great structure in Jerusalem. This would, following Velikovsky's revised chronology, be recognizably contemporary with the Hatshepsut and her epoch. Unfortunately however the Temple Mount, upon which Solomon's monument presumably stood, has been cleared down to the bedrock on many occasions and all trace of what previously existed used as fill in other areas of the city. Nonetheless, although no trace of a temple contemporary with Hatshepsut has been found at Jerusalem, we do know that Jerusalem in her time was a mighty citadel, perhaps the most important stronghold in the whole of contemporary Syria/Palestine.

In archaeological terms Hatshepsut's epoch, the early Eighteenth Dynasty, is designated as Late Bronze I. In Palestine/Syria, however, the settlements which are contemporary with the very beginning of Egypt's Eighteenth Dynasty are recognized as still belonging to the archaeological Middle Bronze Age. This is because the cities and towns of Syria/Palestine still maintained their Hyksos Age (i.e., Middle Bronze Age) culture until the coming of the Egyptians under Thutmose III. From this point onwards the region came heavily under the influence of Egypt and the subsequent culture is designated Late Bronze. In the words of Aaron A. Burke, the most important contemporary authority on the period: "It is generally agreed that it was Egypt's early Eighteenth Dynasty that was responsible for the demise of Canaan's defenses at the close of the Middle Bronze Age."[2]

It is clear then that if Solomon did build a temple and other impressive structures at Jerusalem, as the Bible claims, then we should be looking for signs of them in the strata designated as Middle Bronze, and more specifically the very end of the Middle Bronze Age, MB II or III.

What then does archaeology tell us?

It so happens that the final phase of the Middle Bronze Age saw massive building activity in Jerusalem: as recently as 2009 archaeologists in the city

1 James Baikie, *A History of Egypt* Vol. 2 (London, 1929), p. 67
2 Aaron A. Burke, "Canaan under Siege: The History and Archaeology of Egypt's War in Canaan during the Early Eighteenth Dynasty," in J. Vidal (ed.) *Studies on War in the Ancient Near East: Collected Essays on Military History* (Alter Orient und altes Testament, Ugarit Verlag, Munster, 2010), p. 47

reported the discovery of an enormous fortification wall close to the Temple Mount. An article from that year on CNN's website spoke of a " 'Massive' ancient wall" uncovered at the city and reported the following:

"An archaeological dig in Jerusalem has turned up a 3,700-year-old wall that is the largest and oldest of its kind found in the region, experts say.

"Standing 8 meters (26 feet) high, the wall of huge cut stones is a marvel to archaeologists."[1]

All of the boulders comprising this structure weigh between four and five tons, and the section uncovered was 24 meters (79 feet) long. "However, it is thought the fortification is much longer because it continues west beyond the part that was exposed," the Israel Antiquities Authority reported. A joint statement by the leaders of the dig announced that, "This is the most massive wall that has ever been uncovered in the City of David," and marks the first time that "such massive construction that predates the Herodian period has been discovered in Jerusalem." They also stated that "Despite the fact that so many have excavated on this hill, there is a very good chance that extremely large and well-preserved architectural elements are still hidden in it and waiting to be uncovered."

These latest discoveries only confirmed what archaeologists have known for some time: Namely that the latter part of the Middle Bronze Age marked a peak of power and prosperity at Jerusalem never again attained until the eighth century BC. In the words of Israel Finkelstein: "If one needs to summarize over a century of exploration in Jerusalem, the proper statement regarding the Bronze and Iron Ages would be that archaeology revealed evidence for major building activity in two periods only: The Middle Bronze II–III and the Late Iron II (the eighth–seventh centuries BCE). ... The interval between these periods, which covers the Late Bronze Age, the Iron I, and the Early Iron II (c. 1550–750 BCE) provides indication of habitation but almost no signs of monumental building operations."[2]

Since Middle Bronze III is right at the end of the Middle Bronze Age in Palestine, at which point the region was conquered by Thutmose III, it is clear that Jerusalem suffered a serious decline immediately after the time of Hatshepsut.[3] This is precisely what we would expect in Velikovsky's scheme,

---

1 "'Massive' ancient wall uncovered in Jerusalem," CNN News, September 4, 2009 www.cnn.com
2 Israel Finkelstein, "The Rise of Jerusalem and Judah: The Missing Link," in Andrew G. Vaughan and Ann E. Killebrew (eds.), *Jerusalem in Bible and Archaeology: The First Temple Period* (Atlanta, Georgia, 2003), p. 81
3 Aaron Burke has admitted that Jerusalem was probably one of Thutmose III's targets. Burke, loc. cit., p. 44

since it was just then that Solomon's kingdom was divided and Jerusalem was reduced to being the capital of a small and relatively impoverished kingdom of Judah.

Although no trace of the Middle Bronze Age temple at Jerusalem has survived (and there undoubtedly was one), we may perchance reconstruct how it would have looked by examining contemporary structures in the Palestine/Syria region. Several temples of the late Middle Bronze/early Late Bronze are known, and they all bear striking comparison with the Splendor of Splendors. They are typically composed of a sanctuary fronted by a pillared portico and approached by an ascending ramp. This is the case, for example, with the temples at Hazor, Tel el-Hayyat, Tel Kitan and Shechem and a great many other places.

There are, of course, important differences between these Canaanite temples and the Splendor of Splendors. The latter, for one thing, is on a far grander scale than the former and consists of three pillared porticos approached by three ascending ramps. Nonetheless, the resemblance in general concept is sufficient to indicate some influence. The Solomon Temple would presumably have been, like the Splendor of Splendors, on a much grander scale than the surviving Canaanite structures and there is every reason, from the descriptions provided in the Scriptures, to assume that it was composed of several ascending ramps and pillared porticos.

We may conclude therefore that the Splendor of Splendors was indeed probably inspired by Solomon's Temple. That the latter was itself partially of an earlier Mesopotamian inspiration is beside the point. The Jerusalem Temple had many unique features, and these were copied closely by Hatshepsut's architects at Deir el Bahri, who produced a monument which, though generally similar to Mentuhotep II's earlier structure, was significantly different in many ways, and on an altogether grander scale.

ECHOES OF HATSHEPSUT'S JOURNEY IN THE SONG OF SONGS?

Whether or not the Splendor of Splendors was a copy of the Temple in Jerusalem, there is no doubt that Hatshepsut was deeply affected by her experiences in Punt. The language used to describe the country is, as we saw, ecstatic. It is a "place of delight," and "a glorious region" of God's Land. Admittedly, there is no question that part of the reason for the Punt expedition and its reporting was to bolster Hatshepsut's association with Hathor, and therefore to secure her own position. And yet there is something about this language that seems to go beyond mere propaganda. The beauty of the

Queen herself is extolled on the temple walls; and we hear how "The best of myrrh is upon all her limbs, her fragrance is divine dew, her odor is mingled with Punt, her skin is electrum, shining as do the stars."[1]

Could it be, as the Ethiopian legend and some Jewish traditions suggest, that the Queen became Solomon's lover? As we saw, this notion is central to Abyssinian tradition, which not only insists upon it but claims that the fruit of the union, Menelik, was the ancestor of all Abyssinian kings. We have already seen that there is good reason to believe this tradition authentic, not least because it names the Queen Makeda (to Hatshepsut's Makera), whilst the son is named Menelik, or Menerik (to Hatshepsut's stepson Thutmose III/Menkheperre). Arab traditions about the Queen of Sheba also insist there was a love-affair with Solomon. Yet the Bible, we are told, is almost silent on the issue. There is but one somewhat dark hint, where we read in I Kings 10, "And King Solomon gave unto the Queen of Sheba all her desire."

There may however be another and far more extensive telling of the love-affair in the Scriptures. Much about the famous love poem, The Song of Songs (also known as The Song of Solomon, or The Canticle of Canticles) which the Scriptures claim was written by Solomon himself, seems to refer to the visit of the Queen of Sheba. So, for example, near the beginning, the female beloved states, "Black am I and beautiful, O Jerusalem girls, like the tents of Qedar, like the pavilions of Salmah. Stare not at me that I am swart, that the sun has blackened me." (1: 6) Again, we read, "Who is this that cometh out of the wilderness ... perfumed with myrrh and frankincense, with all the powders of the merchant?" (3: 6) (We note here that the beloved in the Song is described somewhat as Hatshepsut describes herself. This is something we shall return to.) Even more to the point, there is a direct reference to Egypt, with the female beloved compared, "To a mare among Pharaoh's cavalry." (1: 9)

What then of The Song of Songs: What do we know about it? Could it really be a paean to the love between Solomon and Sheba, or, as we believe, between Solomon and Hatshepsut?

This was a question examined in some detail by biblical scholar Hyam Maccoby in 1980 in an article titled, "The Queen of Sheba and the Song of Songs." "It is part of the legend of Solomon and Sheba," says Maccoby, "that they had a love-relationship. Can it be that the Song of Songs is an expression of that relationship?"[2]

---

1 Breasted, *Records*, Vol. 2 Sec. 274

2 Hyam Maccoby, "The Queen of Sheba and the Song of Songs," *Society for Interdisciplinary Studies, Review*, Vol. IV, No. 4 (Spring, 1980), p. 98

As it is, the Song of Songs presents many puzzles for commentators. As Maccoby notes, "despite the tenderness of the love expressed on both sides, there is no hint of a projected marriage. The love is consummated in the fields and has an atmosphere of romance untrammelled by human laws or conventions. There are evidently impediments to the love-affair, both in the side of the woman (her hostile 'brothers') and on the side of the man (the hostile 'guards')."[1] If the Song refers to an affair between Solomon and the Queen of Sheba, the ruler of an independent kingdom, then the impediments to it become very easy to understand. And if it was really an affair between Solomon and the Queen of Egypt, then the impediments become all too clear. Marriage between the King of Israel and the Queen of Egypt would have been impossible: The aristocracy of Egypt would certainly not have permitted it, for it would have delivered the country into the hands of a foreign ruler; whilst the religious authorities of Israel would have been no more welcoming of a union with an idolatrous foreign woman.

Even stranger (from the point of view of conventional history) than the impediments to the affair is the "frankness and boldness of erotic initiative on the part of the woman." So explicit are these verses that commentators throughout the centuries have felt it necessary to provide an allegorical interpretation, in terms of the love of God for his people Israel, or the love of the soul for God. Yet, as Maccoby notes, "Even modern academic commentators ... have felt very puzzled by this aspect of the Song. In a strongly patriarchal society, how could this love-song have arisen, in which the female expresses her desire so unashamedly and takes the sexual initiative so boldly?" Such verses as, "Let him kiss me with his mouth's kisses," and "His mouth is sweet, and all of him desirable. This is my love, this is my mate," are certainly explicit. Even more so is: "Come, my love, let us hie to the field, let us lie in the cypress, let us get to the vineyards. We will see if the vine sprouts, if the blossoms bud, if the pomegranate flowers. There I will give you my love. The mandrakes give scent, at our door is every delicacy; things both old and new, my love, I have stored for you." (7: 11-13)

Such expressions have prompted in recent times a "cultic" interpretation of the Song, which sees the two lovers not as human beings at all, but gods. Certainly many puzzling features of the Song can be explained by this hypothesis. The female and male beloved, for example, are described at times in ways that make them seem gigantic or inhuman. Of the female we hear, "Your neck is like an ivory tower ... your nose like towering Lebanon, over-

---

1 Ibid.

looking Damascus." (7: 4). Of the male we read, "His arms rods of gold, studded with gems; based on sockets of gold." (5: 14-15) Maccoby notes too that the encounter of the female with the guards, "who ill-use her, is reminiscent of the story of Ishtar, who encountered hostile guards during her descent into the underworld in search of the lost Tammuz." He also notes that numerous parallels have been found in the literature of Ugarit (contemporary with Egypt's Eighteenth Dynasty), where love between gods and goddesses is described.

"If the female beloved is a goddess," says Maccoby, "her sense of equality with the male in love-making is understandable. But if she was a queen, her sense of equality is just as understandable." Here Maccoby goes on to note that, "If she was indeed Queen Hatshepsut, an independent monarch of a kingdom greater than Solomon's, she might act with the pride of a goddess." Furthermore, "Queens were often described in terms appropriate to a goddess."[1] We have seen already that this was particularly the case with Hatshepsut, who associated herself with Hathor, deliberately even confusing the language of the inscriptions at Deir el Bahri so as to reinforce the identification.

Throughout the Song, the couple describe each other as "brother" and "sister." We know that Solomon was in fact married to an Egyptian princess and that, according to the reconstruction of history proposed by Velikovsky and supported in these pages, that princess was a sister of Hatshepsut. Thus Hatshepsut would in reality have been Solomon' sister-in-law.

The fact that both male and female lovers are described as shepherds and as owners of vineyards in no way detracts from this interpretation. Monarchs were habitually likened to shepherds of their peoples, and the pharaohs of Egypt carried (from the Hyksos period onwards) the shepherd's crook as part of their royal insignia. Again, in biblical usage the vineyard was a metaphor for the kingdom; and Israel is repeatedly described as the vineyard of the Lord.

Strikingly, Maccoby notes the astonishing parallels between the love-poetry of ancient Egypt, particularly Eighteenth Dynasty Egypt, and the Song of Songs; and he quotes John B. White, of Montana, who notes that, "Although the later Ramesside period saw the writing down of love lyrics, it is the 18th Dynasty ... which provides the most fertile ground within which the roots of love poetry could grow. The cultural development at the beginning of the New Kingdom [Hatshepsut's epoch] provides the atmosphere and the

---

1 Ibid., p. 98

background for many of the images which appear in the love poems."[1] To illustrate the point, consider the following example of Egyptian love-poetry of
the epoch in question:

> My brother, my beloved,
> my heart goes after your love ...
> I came from snaring,
> my traps are in my hand,
> in my other hand, my cage
> and my hunting instrument.
> As for all the birds of Punt,
> they alight upon Egypt, anointed with myrrh.
> The first to come seizes my bait.
> His odor is brought from Punt;
> his claws are filled with resin ...
> My ointment is good myrrh.
> You are there with me
> when I set a snare.
> The happiness is the going to the fields
> of the one who is loved.

The astonishing parallels here not only with the Song of Songs, but
with the material found upon the Splendor of Splendors, makes us wonder
whether the language of these inscriptions, plus Queen Hatshepsut's experiences in Punt/Israel, became the inspiration for the entire *genre* of love poetry
that was to flourish in Egypt from the first quarter of the Eighteenth Dynasty
onwards.

We may conclude by stating that the evidence from the Song of Songs
indicates the following:

That the poem originates during the time of the Egyptian Eighteenth
Dynasty.

That it celebrates a love affair between King Solomon and another monarch, who seems to be a foreigner, and connected to Egypt.

Whether or not Solomon and Hatshepsut became lovers in real life, we
can never be certain. That they were widely believed to have been so however seems beyond doubt, and that belief receives powerful circumstantial

---

1 John B. White, *A Study of the Language of Love in the Song of Songs and Ancient Egyptian
Poetry*, (SBL Dissertation Series 38, Scholars Press, Missoula, Montana, 1978). Cited
by Maccoby, loc. cit. This is the topic also of M. V. Fox's, *The Song of Songs and Ancient
Egyptian Love Songs* (Uni. Of Wisconsin Press, 1985)

support from the evidence outlined above. This is all the more probable when we consider the circumstances of their encounter and the unusual and strong personalities of each. In the months and years following their meeting the two might perchance have reminisced over the all too brief meeting. The impossibility of making their union permanent or even legal would likely have only increased the attraction. They must have corresponded (the Amarna Letters, written two or three generations after Hatshepsut, show that it was normal for the pharaohs to keep up a regular correspondence with the princes and kings of Syria/Palestine), and such communications might give free scope to their inmost desires and longings. How else to explain the precise repetition in the Song of Songs and other Hebrew works of expressions and phrases found at Deir el-Bahri and Egyptian love poetry of the same period?

Can we doubt that in her letters to Solomon Hatshepsut would have used many of the expressions found on the walls of the Splendor of Splendors? Did she not in these missives call his country her "place of delight," and did she not tell him that her odor was "mingled with the incense of Israel?"

CHAPTER 5: THE AFTERMATH

THUTMOSE III AND SHISHAK

Reducing the age of the Eighteenth Dynasty by just over five centuries makes Hatshepsut a contemporary of Solomon, and her successor on the Egyptian throne, Thutmose III, identical to pharaoh Shishak, whom the Book of Kings claims plundered the temple in Jerusalem. According to conventional history, there is no direct connection between the visit of the Queen of Sheba and the subsequent plundering of Solomon's Temple by a pharaoh; but in the scheme proposed by Velikovsky there is a direct causal link: Since the Queen of Sheba was an Egyptian monarch, it must have been her successor who attacked Israel.

It is worth recalling here that Abyssinian tradition seems to agree with Velikovsky. We remember that the Abyssinians described the Queen of Sheba as a ruler of Egypt and Ethiopia, and that her son by Solomon — Menelik — came to Jerusalem many years later with the object of plundering the temple; from which he took that sacred Ark of the Covenant. Solomon, we are told, pursued him as far as the borders of Egypt. If this story does not contain a germ of truth, then it is surprising that it concurs so well with the account outlined by Velikovsky. In his reconstruction, the king who returned to Jerusalem to plunder its temple was not indeed a son of the Queen of Sheba (Hatshepsut), but he was a stepson, and nephew. Furthermore, as we remarked, it seems strange that the Abyssinian Queen of Sheba should be called Makeda, and her son Menelik (or Menerik); whilst Hatshepsut's throne-name was Makera, and her stepson's throne-name Menkheperre.

Was it just coincidence that the Ethiopian legend agreed so well with the reconstruction of history proposed by Velikovsky; or did it agree because it was based on historical truth? We shall find that, if anything, the evidence linking Thutmose III with Shishak, the plunderer of Solomon's Temple, is even more compelling than that linking Hatshepsut to the Queen of Sheba.

Before looking at that evidence, however, I must emphasize that I do not intend simply to reiterate the evidence already garnered by Velikovsky. What I hope to do, as with the question of Hatshepsut, is bring forward new material, material either unknown to Velikovsky's critics or ignored by them.

The main points raised by Velikovsky in *Ages in Chaos* with regard to Thutmose III were:

(a) Archaeology demanded that Thutmose III be contemporary with Solomon's successors Rehoboam and Jeroboam I.

(b) Thutmose III was the greatest of all Egyptian conquerors, and his earliest campaigns involved the subjugation of the Palestine/Canaan region.

(c) This territory was known as Retjenu, or Rezenu, a name which is etymologically identical to one of the Hebrew names for Israel, Arzenu "our land." Many of the settlements of Retjenu had names identical to those mentioned in the Bible dating from the time of Solomon.

(d) The capital of Retjenu was known as Kadesh, the "holy" or "holy place," and Jerusalem too was called Kadesh or the kadesh mountain, the holy mountain in biblical times. Even today it is still known as Al Kuds, "the holy", in Arabic.

(e) Thutmose plundered the great temple of Kadesh and showed the material he took from it in Karnak.

(f) This was identical to the plunder taken from Solomon's temple by pharaoh Shishak.

Of all these statements only (a), i.e., the demand for a dramatic reduction in the date of Thutmose III's life, is really objectionable to orthodoxy. Of course, having rejected proposition (a) they then naturally also reject proposition (f), that the temple plundered by Thutmose III was the temple of Solomon. One rejection predicates the other. Nevertheless, no one denies that Thutmose III was the greatest warrior of all the pharaohs, that his first campaigns were directed against the natives of Canaan/Palestine, natives who spoke a dialect virtually identical to biblical Hebrew; and that the capital of this region, whose temple he plundered — Kadesh — has a name which was frequently used for Jerusalem.

There were other important issues raised by Velikovsky in the chapter on Thutmose III; one of the most significant being the fact that the Canaanite/Phoenician captives displayed on his victory stele at Karnak look exactly like Puntites, whilst his inscriptions showed that Retjenu (Palestine) was a source of incense (*anti*), as was Punt. But it was the things that Velikovsky left out that are of most interest to us here; and there were a great many of these.

THUTMOSE III DESTROYS HATSHEPSUT'S LEGACY

Thutmose III was the greatest warrior of all the pharaohs. In a series of seventeen campaigns, beginning in his first year and continuing throughout his reign, he extended Egypt's borders from the Euphrates in the north of Syria to the 4th cataract in Nubia. By the end of his life Egypt had reached the zenith of her power and prosperity, a peak she was never to see again. Egyptians of later epochs never tired of honoring the great soldier and there seems little doubt that the mighty king known to Herodotus as Sesostris, the conqueror of Asia, was one and the same as Thutmose III.[1] Echoing ancient tradition, modern historians dubbed him the "Napoleon of Egypt," and his exploits compared to those of Caesar or Alexander.[2]

The military achievements of Thutmose III represented a new departure for Egypt. Prior to his time the Egyptians had been remarkably unconcerned with foreign conquest. It is true that several pharaohs, at various times in history, had made brief expeditions into southern Palestine and the coastal regions of Philistia; yet these were minor operations, not in any way to be compared, either in concept or scale, with Thutmose III's program of conquest. What, historians have asked, could have been the driving force behind this aggression? What was it turned the previously inward-looking Egyptians into a nation of imperialists?

The answer is not difficult to find, though, having said that, it has hitherto been missed by Egyptologists. The clue to Thutmose's character seems to lie in his relationship with his stepmother Hatshepsut and in the true location of her "Holy Land," Punt. And I am indebted for this insight to Simon Miles of Sydney Australia, who first pointed it out to me. Scholars have long

---

1 George Rawlinson, *History of Ancient Egypt* Vol. 2 (London, 1881), p. 226. "Thothmes III is the nearest to the ideal Sesostris, the only Pharaoh who really penetrated with a hostile force deep into the heart of Assyria ..." The identity of Sesostris is examined more fully below.

2 Breasted, *A History of Egypt*, op cit., p. 320 "The genius which rose from an obscure priestly office to accomplish this [conquest] for the first time in history reminds us of an Alexander or a Napoleon."

suspected that Thutmose III had very personal reasons for his aggression; they came close to the truth, but never took things to their logical conclusion. The traditional view may be summarized as follows:

Fig. 15. Thutmose III, the "Napoleon of Egypt." Basalt staue in Luxor Museum.

For many years of his young life Thutmose III lived under the shadow of Hatshepsut, the woman who acted as regent in his minority, but who then, in defiance of all tradition and protocol, had the effrontery to mount the throne as a "pharaoh" — even going to the extent of having herself portrayed as a man.[1] This was an altogether unprecedented humiliation for any crown prince. It must have been doubly galling for a youth as vigorous and virile as Thutmose III. He must have burned with a desire simultaneously to prove himself a man and to exact vengeance against the woman who had so humiliated him. Both these desires were in fact satiated to the full. In the words of Breasted: "Thutmose III was not chivalrous in his treatment of her [Hatshepsut] when she was gone. He had suffered too much. Burning to lead his forces into Asia, he had been assigned to such puerile functions as offering incense to Amon on the return of the queen's expedition to Punt; and his restless energies had been allowed to expend themselves on building his mortuary temple of the western plain of Thebes."[2] With the queen's death or departure Thutmose exacted revenge; "Everywhere he had her name erased and in the terraced temple on all the walls both her figure and her name have been hacked out. Her partisans doubtless all fled. If not they must have met short shrift."[3]

The above was the view until comparatively recently, and when Breasted wrote these words just quoted, Egyptologists assumed, naturally enough, that Thutmose III had defaced Hatshepsut's monuments immediately after he assumed power. We now know, however, that this was not the case; in fact the destruction of her works — and those of her allies and confidants — appears to have been carried out only after the twentieth year of Thutmose III's sole rule. Why this should be so has proved a major puzzle to Egyptologists, and has led to all sorts of theorizing and speculating. In the words of Joyce Tyldesley: "... while it is possible to imagine and even empathize with Tuthmosis indulging in a sudden whim of hatred against his stepmother immediately after her death, it is far harder to imagine him overcome by such a whim some twenty years later. Indeed, if we can no longer be certain that Tuthmosis hated his stepmother as she lay on her deathbed, can we be certain that he ever hated her during her lifetime?"[4]

In search of an explanation Tyldesley notes that, "Tuthmosis III was clearly an intelligent and rational monarch. All that we know of his character suggests that he was not given to rash, impetuous acts and it seems logical to assume that throughout his life Tuthmosis was motivated less by uncon-

1 As Velikovsky and others have pointed out, this may explain several Jewish traditions which — inexplicably — described the Queen of Sheba as "masculine" and "hairy."
2 Breasted, *History of Egypt*, op cit., pp. 282-3
3 Ibid. p. 283
4 Tyldesley, *Hatchepsut: The Female Pharaoh* (Penguin Books, 1998), pp. 224-5

trollable urges than by calculated political expediency. We must therefore divorce his private emotions from his political actions, just as we must separate the person of Hatshepsut the woman from her role as Egypt's female pharaoh. Whatever his personal feelings towards his stepmother, Tuthmosis may well have found it advisable to remove all traces of the unconventional female king whose reign might possibly be interpreted by future generations as a grave offence against *maat* [divinely ordained order or truth], and whose unorthodox co-regency might well have cast serious doubt upon the legitimacy of his own right to rule."[1] This hardly sounds convincing reasoning, and Tyldesley herself seems to suspect it; for immediately afterwards she notes: "Wounded male pride may also have played apart in his [Thutmose III's] decision to act; the mighty warrior king may have balked at being recorded for posterity as the man who ruled for twenty years under the thumb of a mere woman."[2]

But the latter is merely a return to the traditional view — that Thutmose III felt humiliated by Hatshepsut's usurpation of the throne and destroyed her monuments out of sheer hatred. It also brings us back to the original problem: If he destroyed her monuments out of hatred, why wait twenty years to do so?

Notwithstanding the amount of ink spilt discussing this supposed enigma, I would contend that even a rudimentary understanding of human psychology would provide an easy answer. Let's consider again Thutmose III's situation: He had lived under the shadow of his aunt and stepmother for many years. He had been well treated and promised the crown in due course; and, in due course, when Hatshepsut died, he received it. At this stage, to begin a campaign against his predecessor's memory would have constituted an admission both to his contemporaries and to himself that he had been humiliated and that he had been too weak to remove his aunt. In such circumstances the only option open to him — from a psychological viewpoint — was to continue the fiction that all had been well and that Hatshepsut's situation had been normal. But living a lie like this has a price: The young pharaoh would have burned with a suppressed rage — a rage he could safely divert against his stepmother's foreign allies and friends. Many years later, having proved his own manhood repeatedly on the field of battle, he could, perhaps unobtrusively to begin with, commence the destruction of his hated aunt's monuments. And that, of course, is precisely what we do find.[3]

1 Ibid., p. 225
2 Ibid.
3 Breasted, *History of Egypt*, op cit., p. 283

We recall at this point that the identification of Hatshepsut with the Queen of Sheba means that she must have formed a particularly close and even intimate friendship with the ruler of Israel. If this were the case, then we would naturally expect the newly-crowned Thutmose III to have directed a great deal of his pent-up fury against the land of Israel, the ally of his hated stepmother.

Did this happen?

The facts speak for themselves: In his very first year on the throne, no more than a few months after he was crowned, Thutmose III led his armies against the land of Israel and reduced it to vassalage. That the campaign of this year was directed against the king of Kadesh and his Canaanite/Palestinian allies is not in doubt, though it is generally assumed that the Kadesh in question was the city of that name on the Orontes.[1] Yet this begs the question: Why would a king of northern Syria surround himself with Palestinian allies? As Velikovsky pointed out, the region of Israel (actually southern Israel, or Judah) was Thutmose III's prime target during his first campaign, and indeed a great number of cities and towns of Israel/Canaan can be identified on the list carved at Karnak: Gaza was taken; Joppa (Jaffa) was besieged; Megiddo was attacked; and Thutmose's list of towns conquered in his first year is full of the names of the towns of southern Palestine: Etam (Itmm) appears at number 36; Socoh (Sk) at 67, and Beth-Zur (Bt sir) at 110. And although not all settlements on the list can be positively identified as yet, it is clear that Thutmose claims to have either conquered or received the submission of everything between southern Palestine and Baalbek (Dan) and Byblos in the Lebanon. Indeed, the latter towns mark the northernmost limits of his conquests, though none of these settlements had to be taken by storm. No actual military action north of Megiddo is recorded, and it is presumed that all towns further north simply submitted.

Dozens of villages and towns to the south of Byblos and Baalbek, on both sides of the Jordan, figure in the pharaoh's catalogue. Many of these are small and can hardly have been more than hamlets. Towns in the Judaean and Samarian uplands are mentioned, as are settlements on the eastern side of the Jordan; yet Jerusalem is absent. Why?

Even before the conquest of Jerusalem by David we know it was an important city, commanding the very centre of Canaan. Why then is it not mentioned along with all the other (very often tiny settlements) that are listed?

1 See e.g., Joyce Tyldesley, op cit., p. 214

The answer, the only logical answer, is that Kadesh itself is Jerusalem. Once again, it is Velikovsky who has logic on his side, and his critics who defy it.

It should be remarked that the area covered by Thutmose III's catalogue corresponds very precisely with the combined territories of Judah and Israel as they would have been shortly after the breakup of Solomon's Empire. The latter polity stretched from Edom in the south to Dan (Baalbek) in Lebanon and as far as Tadmor (Palmyra) in north-east Syria. Damascus was firmly within Solomon's kingdom. All of these, with the exception of Tadmor, figure on Thutmose III's register; and indeed the northern limit of his conquests corresponds exactly (if we omit Tadmor) with the northern limit of the kingdom of Israel.

Yet Jerusalem, we are told, is not mentioned!

WHERE WAS THE LAND OF KADESH?

The identity of the city or country of Kadesh, against which Thutmose III launched his legions in the first year of his reign, has long posed a problem for historians. That it might be Jerusalem seemed never to have crossed the minds of numerous learned commentators. The names of towns and villages throughout Palestine, some of them tiny and obscure, were scrutinized by the historians, but Jerusalem was never considered.

We now know, of course (though Velikovsky, in his time, could only surmise), that Jerusalem in the time of Thutmose III was one of the most magnificent citadels in the whole of Syria/Palestine. Nothing between the Nile and the Euphrates has yet been found to match the mighty defensive walls, of the late Middle Bronze Age, uncovered at the city in 2009.[1] And as Aaron Burke noted, it was the Middle Bronze settlements of the region that Thutmose III overwhelmed. How then, we need to ask, could a conqueror marching through Palestine and Syria leave behind him, unsecured, the most important stronghold in the region? And how could he fail, apparently, even to notice the existence of such a citadel? Yet this is precisely what conventional scholarship would have the reading public believe.

In March 2012 I put the following question to two professors of archaeology specializing in the Bronze Age of Palestine. The first of these was the above-mentioned Aaron A. Burke, Professor of Middle Eastern archaeology at University of California, Los Angeles. Professor Burke has written numerous

---

1 It is highly likely that the great Middle Bronze walls were constructed by Solomon and no one else. We are told (2 Samuel 5:9-12) that David built at Jerusalem after taking the city from the Jebusites, but the Scriptures make it clear that the great defensive walls were the work of Solomon. See (1 Kings 3:1).

articles on the decline and fall of Canaan's Middle Bronze Age strongholds,[1] and has stressed the role of Thutmose III in that process. I wrote:

> "I understand that during the final phases of the Middle Bronze Age many settlements in Palestine were heavily fortified, and this seems also to have been the case with Jerusalem, which has now revealed massive 'cyclopean' walls dating from Middle Bronze III. In view of the apparent importance of the city at this time, is it possible that Thutmose III did not mention it on his register of conquered Palestinian cities? I am aware that this list displays the names of 119 Palestinian and south Syrian sites, some of them rather insignificant, to put it mildly. My question is: Do Egyptologists currently consider Jerusalem to be present?"

I received no response from Professor Burke, so then put the same question to Professor Gabriel Barkay, of Bar-Ilan University in Tel Aviv, another authority on the archaeology of the region and Jerusalem in particular. He too failed to respond.

According to conventional ideas, to which presumably Professors Burke and Barkay subscribe, Kadesh, which leads Thutmose III's register, stood on the Orontes, perhaps 100 miles to the north of the other cities mentioned. This Kadesh of the Orontes has never been identified. Kenneth Kitchen has attempted to link it with Tell Nebi Mend, about 15 miles southwest of Homs in central Syria, but offers no convincing proof.[2] A great city of Kadesh was the scene of the famous battle fought by Ramses II against the Hittites, around a century after the death of Thutmose III, and he clearly locates the stronghold in the vicinity of Tunip, in northern Syria. Whether Kadesh be located at Tell Nebi Mend, however, or further north, it is agreed that Thutmose III *did not actually conquer it* in his first year. This is apparently illustrated by the fact that Thutmose claims to have conquered this northern Kadesh much later in his career. Yet here the subjugation of this supposedly powerful and prestigious city is passed over in a single sentence. We read: "His majesty arrived at the city of Kadesh, overthrew it, cut down its groves, harvested its grain" (Breasted, *Records* 2, 465). Breasted notes that "it is with peculiar regret" that the taking of such an immensely important city is recorded in these "laconic words."[3]

---

1 Articles include, "Canaan Under Siege: The History and Archaeology of Egypt's War in Canaan during the Early Eighteenth Dynasty," loc. cit., and "More Light on Old Reliefs: new Kingdom Egyptian Siege Tactics and Asiatic Resistance," in (J. D. Schloen, ed.) *Exploring the Longue Durée: Essays in Honor of Lawrence E. Stager* (Eisenbrauns, Winona Lake, IN, 2009).

2 Kenneth Kitchen, *Ramesside Inscriptions*, Vol. 2 (Blackwell Publishing Limited, 1996), pp. 16-7

3 Breasted, *A History of Egypt*, op cit., p. 301

Let's consider this carefully: The Kadesh which Thutmose III claims to have conquered in his first year (but did not!) stood at the head of a mighty coalition, a coalition which included everything between Edom in the south and Damascus in the north. After defeating this coalition and falsely claiming to have conquered it, the city diminishes in importance. The king of an Orontes Kadesh, at the head of a coalition of warlike states, should still have posed a threat to Thutmose III's conquests in Palestine, yet in the campaigns waged by Thutmose III to the north in subsequent years, Kadesh hardly figures at all. And when he finally takes the city, the event merits no more than a line in his annals.

None of this — the scenario accepted in all textbooks — makes any sense at all.

If however Jerusalem occurs in Thutmose III's lists as Kadesh — its alternative name throughout the Scriptures, then all is explained. Kadesh is the great power of the region, the stronghold which commands a host of lesser Canaanite cities and towns: it is Jerusalem.

At this point it is perhaps worth repeating what Velikovsky said on this topic sixty years ago and which was ignored by the scholarly establishment:

"The historians claim to know one famous Kadesh, located by them on the Orontes River in northern Syria. But in the list of Thutmose III the city of Kadesh is named as the first among one hundred and nineteen Palestinian (not Syrian) cities; in second place comes Megiddo, the scene of the battle; and one hundred and seventeen other cities follow them. This Kadesh could not be a city in Syria, for in the Palestine campaign Thutmose did not reach the Orontes. There was a Kadesh in Galilee, Kadesh Naphtali, mentioned a few times in the Scriptures; but what would be the purpose in placing this unimportant city at the top of the list just before Megiddo? It became a matter of conjecture.

"According to one hypothesis, the city was Kadesh Naphtali; according to another, Kadesh on the Orontes; and each theory had to be supported by some explanation as to why a city outside Palestine or an insignificant city in Palestine was placed at the head of a list of Palestinian cities where one would expect to find the capital of the land.

"The suggestion was advanced that the first name on the Palestine list did not belong to the register and had been added later. This is highly improbable, especially since the interpolation (if it be such) was made on all three copies. Or, it was said, the Galilean city might have been intended, but the sculptor mistook it for the famous Kadesh on the Orontes and for this erroneous reason put it in first place.

"These theories met opposition. The Palestinian lists were executed shortly after the return from the Palestinian campaign and prior to the Syrian campaign; at that time there was no reason to confuse the cities; beyond doubt the list was executed with the personal knowledge of Thutmose III and was checked by his officials.

"The coeval history of Judah, short yet clear, records:

> II CHRONICLES 12:2-4 And it came to pass, that in the fifth year of king Rehoboam, Shishak king of Egypt came up against Jerusalem. ...

> With twelve hundred chariots, and threescore thousand horsemen: and the people were without number that came with him out of Egypt; the Lubim [Libyans], the Sukkiim, and the Ethiopians.

> And he took the fenced cities which pertained to Judah, and came to Jerusalem.

"The conquest of the walled cities is the phase of the war related in the beginning of the annals of Thutmose III which have been preserved. The second phase is the move on the capital.

"Jerusalem, against which the pharaoh advanced, must have been the city of Kadesh. This one answer serves two questions: Why was Jerusalem not on the list of Thutmose III, and Where was the king-city of Kadesh?

"Is Jerusalem anywhere else called Kadesh? In many places all though the Scriptures. 'Solomon brought up the daughter of Pharaoh out of the city of David ... because the places are *kadesh* [holy].' In the Psalms the Lord says: 'Yet have I set my king upon Zion, my mount *kadesh*.' Joel called on the people: 'Blow ye the trumpet in Zion, and sound an alarm in my mountain *kadesh*.' He also said: 'So shall ye know that I am the Lord your God dwelling in Zion, my *kadesh* [holy] mountain: then shall Jerusalem be [really] holy [*kadesh*]. Isaiah said of the people of Jerusalem: '... for they call themselves of the city Kadesh.' He prophesied about the day when the Lord 'will gather all nations and tongues. ... And they shall bring all your brethrens ... out of all nations ... to my *kadesh* mountain Jerusalem.' Daniel prayed: '... let thine anger and thy fury be turned away from thy city Jerusalem, thy *kadesh* mountain,' 'thy city *kadesh*.' And Nehemiah wrote: '... the rest of the people also cast lots, to bring one of ten to dwell in Jerusalem, the city *kadesh*.'

"The 'Holy Land' and the 'Holy City' are names given to Palestine and Jerusalem in early times, as not only the Scriptures but also the Egyptian inscriptions ('God's Land,' 'Kadesh') bear witness.

"The name Kadesh is used for Jerusalem not in Hebrew texts alone. The names of the most obscure Arab villages in Palestine were scrutinized by the scholars in biblical lore in an endeavor to locate the ancient cities, but the Arab name for Jerusalem was overlooked: it is el-Kuds (the Holy, or the Holiness)."[1]

Fig. 16. Map showing Thutmose III's conquests in Palestine. The regions submitting to Thutmose III in his first year correspond rather precisely with the territory of the ancient kingdom of Solomon. Only Tadmor (Palmyra), in north-eastern Syria is missing. We should note too that although Thutmose III names Kadesh at the very beginning of his list, Egyptologists insist that he never actually conquered the latter city in his first year — a city which they claim was in the Syrian region of Homs, or even further north. If Kadesh was however Jerusalem, the mightiest fortress-citadel in Syria/Palestine at the time, then Thutmose III's list makes perfect sense.

We recall here that as well as attacking Canaan/Palestine, Thutmose III also made Punt, "all the regions of Punt," the subject of his army's attention in his first year. It has already been shown above that the Karnak lists nam-

1 Velikovsky, *Ages in Chaos*, op cit., pp. 151-3

ing Punt in this context do not in any way imply a southern location for the territory. Rather they emphasize the region's location in the Canaan/Palestine locality and prove further that Thutmose III was motivated by desire for revenge against the allies of his stepmother. It should be noted too, as Simon Miles pointed out to me, that one of the walls of the temple in Karnak, upon which he boasted of subjugating "all the regions" of Punt, was constructed around Hatshepsut's obelisk, thereby completely concealing it! This looks like a deliberate and vindictive piece of irony.

THE PEOPLE OF PALESTINE FALL INTO DISAGREEMENT

Chapter 4 of *Ages in Chaos* contains a section entitled "Thutmose III prepares the disintegration of the empire of Solomon." In these pages Velikovsky argued that the division of Solomon's kingdom into two warring factions had been the direct result of the pharaoh's own actions. He quotes a well-known line in Thutmose's annals,

> Now at that time of Asiatics had fallen into disagreement each man fighting against his neighbor.

This sentence, usually regarded as Thutmose's statement of justification for his invasion, elicits this comment from Velikovsky, "A victory over a foe weakened by internal discord is a diluted triumph. Why, then, do the annals mention this discord in the land of Pharaoh's foes? It was the work of Thutmose III himself to prepare the disunity by setting one part of the population against the other; hence this record does not detract from his right to laurels."[1]

There is no doubt that the biblical account of events leading up to the division of the kingdom lends itself to this interpretation. We are told that pharaoh Shishak sheltered the rebel Jeroboam after he had plotted against Solomon. "And Jeroboam arose, and fled into Egypt, unto Shishak king of Egypt, and was in Egypt until the death of Solomon" (I Kings 11:40). Upon Solomon's death, Jeroboam returned to Israel with the obvious intention of fighting for the throne.

Egypt, under Shishak, appears to have been deeply involved.

Yet here we encounter a problem not mentioned by Velikovsky. If Thutmose III is the same person as Shishak, he cannot have been the ruler of Egypt who sheltered the fugitive Jeroboam. Thutmose III's attack on Palestine took place in his first year as sole ruler; in other words, as soon as Hatshepsut was dead. Hatshepsut, as a friend of Solomon, would not have sheltered one

1 Ibid., p. 141

of his enemies; yet we are told that Jeroboam had fled to Egypt well before Solomon's death and that Shishak's attack on Israel took place five years after that event (I Kings 14:25). Assuming the biblical record to be accurate, this means that Jeroboam fled to Egypt during the lifetime of Hatshepsut.

One possible solution to the problem is that Jeroboam's sojourn in Egypt was with the tacit approval of Solomon; his stay in that country more of a banishment than a flight. And although the Egyptians under Hatshepsut could not have harbored an enemy of Israel with the intention of destroying what was at that time a friend and ally, it is nevertheless entirely possible that, before he became pharaoh, Thutmose III conspired with the exiled Jeroboam to rebel against Solomon's successor; a revolt scheduled to begin as soon as Hatshepsut and Solomon were dead. The fact that the northern kingdom under Jeroboam became a close ally of Egypt and was to remain such for the entire period of the state's existence certainly supports this view.

Taking everything into account then it seems that Thutmose's statement about the Asiatics falling into disagreement is not conclusive proof that he had engineered the disagreement. It almost certainly does refer to the ongoing strife between Rehoboam and Jeroboam which, by that time, was already about five years old. But it was not necessarily put there as a boast, as Velikovsky believed. Rather, it represents the standard, stock-in-trade excuse of the conqueror throughout history. He came there to "restore order." It may have been Jeroboam who requested Thutmose's assistance, and if this is the case, then all the cities and territories north of Jerusalem, which Thutmose III put under tribute during his first campaign, did not need to be conquered: they were allied and tributary regions even before the pharaoh marched out of Egypt.

THE ROAD TO KADESH

Thutmose III's records leave us in no doubt that the main foe against whom he waged war was the king of Kadesh. He is described repeatedly as the "wretched foe of Kadesh." All of the action against this enemy took place in Palestine. In actual fact, only two military engagements are mentioned. One was the taking of Joppa (Jaffa), which fell after a long siege; the other was an engagement at the fortress of *Mykty* (normally interpreted as Megiddo, in northern Palestine), which was followed by the siege and eventual surrender of that city.

The approach to Mykty and the battle that followed is described in great detail by the Egyptian chroniclers. Thutmose's generals feared to approach

Mykty by the most direct route, the Aruna road. It was narrow and treacherous and their line would be dangerously drawn out. The pharaoh replied that he would go by the Aruna road even if he went alone. Gaining courage from such decisive leadership, the army advanced by the direct route, approached Mykty and won a decisive victory:

> ... When they saw his majesty prevailing against them they fled headlong to Megiddo, in fear, abandoning their horses and their chariots of gold and silver.

> ... Now, if only the army of his majesty had not given their heart to plundering the things of the enemy, they would have [captured] Megiddo at this moment, when the wretched foe of Kadesh and the wretched foe of this city were hauled up in haste to bring them into this city. The fear of his majesty had entered their hearts.[1]

A short time later the city surrendered. "Behold, the chiefs of this country came to render their portions." The description of the campaign's termination has not been preserved, but it can be reconstructed. The campaign ended with the submission of the entire land of Retjenu, with its one hundred and nineteen walled cities. The city or country of Kadesh appears first on the list.

It is generally believed that, notwithstanding the earlier mention of Gaza and Joppa, which point to central/southern Palestine, the above events took place in the vicinity of the biblical Megiddo, located to the north of the Carmel Ridge in the Jezreel Valley. Yet such a location causes immense problems, both for the conventional view and for Velikovsky's. To begin with, Velikovsky claimed that this campaign of Thutmose III was directed primarily against the kingdom of Judah. Rehoboam was the "wretched foe of Kadesh." Yet Megiddo in the Jezreel Valley is far to the north of Rehoboam's kingdom. The Jezreel Valley and Plain of Esdraelon was right in the middle of the kingdom of Israel, ruled at that time by Rehoboam's arch enemy Jeroboam I. It is extremely unlikely that Jeroboam, as a long-time friend of Egypt, would have allowed his territory to be used as a rallying-point against the pharaoh.

But locating Thutmose III's Mykty in the Jezreel Valley causes great problems also for conventional history.

The description of the campaign preserved at Karnak makes it perfectly clear that Thutmose's officers were in great fear of approaching the fortress of Mykty by the most direct route, the road of Aruna. This highway is described by them as a narrow and dangerous passageway; "Will the vanguard of us be fighting while the [rear guard] is waiting here in Aruna, unable to

---

1 Breasted, *Records*, Vol. 2, Sec. 430

fight?" Two other roads, they say, offer a safer alternative; one goes by way of Taanach; the other to the north of Djefti, or Zefti. This latter comes out "to the north of Megiddo." Clearly Thutmose III's battle-hardened officers were terrified of traversing this route; so afraid indeed that they seemed almost on the point of mutiny. Yet according to accepted ideas the "Aruna Road" was the gently inclining and broad road through the Wadi Ara, which to this day climbs from the Plain of Sharon northwards over Carmel to the Plain of Esdraelon.

Why would the Egyptian strategists have been afraid of passing such a barrier?

The answer, I believe, was provided by Eva Danelius, who possessed a great knowledge of the region's topography. According to Danelius, the Aruna Road was not the path of the Wadi Ara but the steep and treacherous path of Araunah (or Beth Horon) which led from Joppa to Jerusalem. (We remember at this point that immediately before setting out for Mykty and the Aruna Road Thutmose III invested the city of Joppa). Before its conquest by David, the hill upon which Jerusalem stood was known as the threshing floor of Araun or Horon, the Jebusite.[1] Evidently the region, said Danelius, kept this name well after its incorporation into the kingdom of Israel. The road between Lower and Upper Beth Horon is a treacherous defile, rising 225 meters over a distance of 2.8 kilometers. "Due to its special topography, the Beth Horon Ascent ... was always a focal point of battles and attempts to stop troops trying to reach Jerusalem or to descend from the Judean Hills to the coastal plain," according to the opinion of a modern historian.[2] Danelius quotes, as one example of many, the experience of the Roman general Gaius Cestius Gallus, during the Jewish War in AD 66. The Roman troops suffered many casualties on their way up the Beth Horon ascent, but on their retreat they suffered disaster:

> While even the infantry were hard put to it to defend themselves, the cavalry were in still greater jeopardy; to advance in order down the road under the hail of darts was impossible, to charge up the slopes was impracticable for horses; on either side were precipices and ravines, down which they slipped and were hurled to destruction; there was no room for flight, no conceivable means of defense; in their utter helplessness the troops were reduced to groans and the wailings of despair.[3]

---

1   2 Samuel, 24:16

2   B. Bar-Kochva, quoted by Eva Danelius, "Did Thutmose III Despoil the Temple in Jerusalem?" *Society for Interdisciplinary Studies; Review* Vol. 2 (1977/78), p. 71

3   Josephus, *Jewish War* II, xix, 1-9 Josephus gives the number of killed Roman soldiers as 5,300 infantry and 480 cavalry.

Only night prevented the complete destruction of the Roman army.

The Beth Horon or Araunah road, leading to Jerusalem, seems a far better candidate for the Aruna road of Thutmose III than the thoroughly safe and unremarkable road that passes through the Wadi Ara; and there is other evidence pointing in the same direction. It will be remembered, for example, that Thutmose III's annals at Karnak refer to two other roads, safer than the Aruna passageway, by which the Egyptian army could reach the stronghold of Mykty. One of these was to the north of Djefti, or Zefti. Commentators throughout the years have wondered about the latter's location. According to Danelius, it must be identical to Zephathah, the spot near Mareshah, where Asa met and defeated the Ethiopian invader Zerah (2 Chronicles 14:10). There is no linguistic objection to this identification, but, if it is correct, it means without question that the Road of Aruna cannot have been the route that leads over Carmel but must have been precisely where Danelius said it was. The site of Mareshah (adjacent to Zephathah) has never been lost. It was the Judean border-fortress guarding against Philistia, located just to the east of Lachish and south-west of Jerusalem.

The eastern opening of the Beth-Horon road lies in a district called Jebel el Kuds, or, in Hebrew Har Kodsho, "the Holy Mountain." In other words, as Danelius puts it, *Kd-sw* of the Egyptian inscriptions, "was not the name of a city, but of a land." And indeed throughout the Scriptures the region around Jerusalem, the territory of the Tribe of Benjamin, is named the "Holy Mountain." This is a crucial point, and explains why "Kadesh" always heads the Egyptian lists referring to campaigns in the region. But if Kadesh was a region and not a city, we are also presented with an explanation as to why the king of Kadesh was in Mykty, rather than a city of Kadesh. Evidently Mykty, a name derived from the Semitic *migdol*, or "fortress," was the name of the actual capital of the country Kadesh. We ask ourselves: Was the city of Jerusalem ever known as migdol, or any name equivalent to it? The answer is provided by Danelius: "Among the names enumerated as designating Jerusalem is Bait-al-Makdis, or in brief, Makdis, corresponding to Beith-ha-Miqdash in modern Hebrew pronunciation. The 10th century Arab writer who mentions this name calls himself Mukadassi = the Jerusalemite. The name Makdes was still used by the Samaritans (a Jewish sect who never left the country, who trace their ancestors to three of the northern tribes of Israel) at the beginning of this century, when discussing with Rabbi Moshe Gaster their attitude towards Jerusalem, and a local shop outside Damascus Gate still bears the inscription: Baith el-Makdis."[1]

According to Danelius, the name Miqdash was originally confined to the holy precinct north of the Jebusite city, the area which had once been the threshing-floor of Araunah the Jebusite. In the time of Rehoboam this region contained the temple and its precincts, as well as the royal palace. It was these which had to be taken; the Jebusite city down the hill apparently having been of no interest to the pharaoh. "Thus," says Danelius, "it was that his officers laid special stress on the fact that the Zaphata defile, too, reached the ridge north of the Temple mount, and that there was no necessity to use the Aruna road for an approach from the north."[2]

According to Breasted, a vast treasure was taken by Thutmose III from Mykty. The plunder included, "Nine hundred and twenty four chariots, including those of the kings of Kadesh and Megiddo, two thousand two hundred and thirty eight horses, two hundred suits of armour, again including those of the same two kings, the gorgeous tent of the king of Kadesh ... the magnificent household furniture of the king of Kadesh, and among it his royal sceptre, a silver statue ... and an ebony statue of himself, wrought with gold and lapis-lazuli."[3] We might not be surprised by the king of Kadesh storing his tent at Megiddo/Mykty, but why, if he were the king of a city hundreds of miles to the north, would he have his "household furniture" in Palestine? Breasted notes that, "Immense quantities of gold and silver were also taken from the city, but they are combined with the spoil of other cities in Thutmose's account of the plunder, and we cannot determine how much came out of Megiddo alone."[4]

We shall have more to say on the gold and silver taken from the city, for most of it came from a great temple, and Thutmose III offered it to Amon in Thebes, were he caused a record of it to be carved on the temple wall.

Another point. According to the pharaoh's annals, Mykty could also be reached by way of *Ta-'a-na-ka* (interpreted as Taanach). There is of course a well-known fortress by this name on the Plain of Esdraelon, north of Carmel, but, as Danelius notes, there is also a ridge on the western approaches to Jerusalem known as the Tahhunah Ridge; and there is a wadi Tahhunah in the same district. The name appears a third time in that of Khirbet at-Tahuna, which overlooks the exit of the defile from the mountains, opposite

---

1 Danelius, "Did Thutmose III Despoil the Temple in Jerusalem?" loc. cit., pp. 73-4
2 Ibid., p. 74
3 Breasted, *A History of Egypt*, op cit., p. 292
4 Ibid.

Zorah, one of the border-fortresses against the Philistines strengthened by Rehoboam (2 Chronicles 11:10).

THE CONQUEST OF GOD'S LAND

Although in later years Thutmose III campaigned as far north as the Euphrates and scored some astonishing military successes — against the Mitannians, for example — none of these later achievements were commemorated in anything like the fashion of his first-year conquest of Palestine. Yet it is doubtful if the latter campaign saw even a single pitched battle. After advancing towards Mykty and Kadesh along the Aruna Road, the Egyptian army lined up against the Asiatics, who simply melted away, apparently. Certainly no record, either at Karnak or anywhere else, mentions a real battle outside the walls of Mykty. The king of Kadesh had to be hauled up the walls of the fortress by the defenders, who had locked the city gates in fear. Why the extraordinary prominence given to such a victory? The pharaoh ordered a list of the 119 "cities" of Palestine taken during the campaign to be copied three times upon the walls of his temple at Karnak. Most of these, it should be remembered, were not cities, but small walled settlements. In addition to this, he devoted an enormous bas-relief at Karnak to an illustration of the treasures he took in that campaign. These certainly came from Kadesh and were seen by Velikovsky as the plunder taken from Solomon's temple by Shishak; a proposition entirely supported by the present writer.

For those not convinced by Velikovsky's arguments however, the question remains: Why would such an apparently small success be so commemorated? The answer, the only possible one, is that proposed by Velikovsky. Thutmose III reveled in his conquest of Palestine because this was formerly the greatest power in the region and moreover the kingdom beloved by his hated stepmother Hatshepsut. We recall that the list of conquered Palestinian cities is carved on a wall whose construction involved the building around and concealing of Hatshepsut's great obelisk.

The actual defeat and capitulation of the king of Kadesh, Rehoboam, is best described by Eva Danelius:

"Though Rehoboam had fortified the cities guarding the roads to Jerusalem, he lacked any war experience, and so did his subjects, who like himself were thoroughly demoralized, according to Josephus. These soldiers were in no way prepared to stand up against the sudden attack of the Egyptians, led by the Pharaoh who stood 'in a chariot of electrum, arrayed in his weapons of war, like Horus, the Smiter, lord of power; like Montu of Thebes....' In an instant, the country was covered with Egyptian chariots and horsemen. Panic seized the Asiatics. Officers and men threw away their weapons and fled, be it in the direction of Jerusalem (Makdis), or down the valley and across the fords of the Jordan. From the walls of the Holy City, the watchmen saw the wild chase. Rehoboam and the princes galloping for their lives, closely followed by the Egyptian horsemen. The capital hastily closed its gates before the approaching foe; as to the fugitives: 'The people hauled them (up) pulling by their clothing ... (and dangled) clothing to pull them up into the city,' as so vividly described in the *Annals*. And the long siege of Jerusalem began. 'Then came Shemaiah the prophet to Rehoboam, and to the princes of Judah, that were gathered together in Jerusalem because of Shishak, and said unto them, "Thus saith the Lord, Ye have forsaken me, and therefore have I also left you in the hand of Shishak." Whereupon the princes of Israel and the king humbled themselves....'" Therefore 'they shall be his [the Pharaoh's] servants; that they may know my service, and the service of the kingdoms of the countries,' reports the Chronicler (II Chron. 12:5-6, 8). They opened the gates of the city: 'The chiefs of this country came to render their portions, to smell the earth (do obeisance) to the fame of his majesty, to crave breath for their nostrils,' writes the Pharaoh."[1]

Crucially, both the biblical and the Egyptian accounts tell us that the city was not stormed. After a siege, the defenders opened the gates, thus saving their lives. Nevertheless, the pharaoh "took away the treasures of the house of the Lord, and the treasures of the king's house; he took all: he carried away also the shields of gold which Solomon had made." (II Chron. 12:9).

Danelius ends by quoting Velikovsky, who said: "In the bas-reliefs of Karnak we have a very excellent and detailed account of the vessels and furniture of the Temple of Solomon." "It seems," says Danelius, "that Velikovsky is right. There is nothing in the *Annals* to contradict his statement."[2] We shall shortly take a closer look at the plunder of Kadesh displayed by Thutmose III at Karnak.

THE PEOPLE, FLORA AND FAUNA OF CANAAN

The towns and cities conquered by Thutmose III were shown by him at Karnak. Each town was represented by a kneeling and bound prisoner, in front of whom was shown a shield with the name of the city. These apparently are accurate representations of the inhabitants of Palestine and Syria at the time. The prisoners of Palestine and southern Syria (Lebanon) look exactly like the inhabitants of Punt, portrayed on the Deir el-Bahri temple.

1 Danelius, loc. cit., pp. 76-7
2 Ibid.

There we see the same long hair tied with a headband, and, most importantly, the same peculiar long and pointed beard; the beard which, in Egypt, was the symbol of royalty and divinity.

During Thutmose III's reign Egyptian contacts with Asia opened up as never before. Almost every year of the first half of his reign, Thutmose undertook a campaign in Asia. Mostly this was concerned simply with collecting tribute, though occasionally there was real military action. These campaigns were extensively reported and depicted throughout the pharaoh's lifetime; and what they tell us about Syria/Palestine at the time is revealing. In his third year, which he enumerated as "year 25," Thutmose III returned to Palestine for inspection. In Upper Retjenu (the central uplands) he found gardens rich in color, form and fragrance. Many of the plants, great quantities in fact, were transplanted to Egypt.

> All the plants that grow, all flowers that are in God's Land which were found by his majesty, when his majesty proceeded to Upper Retenu.

The transplanted collections were reproduced on the walls of the Karnak temple, showing the peculiar and exotic shapes of the Palestinian flora. A zoological collection was also taken along. No inscription mentions it, but the figures of animals appear among the plants on the bas-relief. Many were decidedly exotic, and not what is normally, nowadays, regarded as typical of Palestine. Some of them, particularly the birds, could not even be identified, and seemed to one eminent zoologist to be fantastic inventions of the sculptor.[1]

Among the plants, botanists recognized various rare species, such as the blue lotus, the vine date tree, the pomegranate, the dragon plant, the arum, the iris, the chrysanthemum, as well as the cornflower and the mandragora, along with a variety of pine tree and some sort of "melon tree." Many of the plants too however, just like the birds, could not be identified at all. It seemed clear that several of the various specimens of flora were not indigenous to Palestine. How then was their presence to be explained among those brought by Thutmose III from Palestine? According to one authority, "Possibly, the twofold geographical designation, Palestine and God's Land, could be explained by the fact that a number of plants actually came from God's Land. Still another conjecture to explain the presence of these plants may be made, namely that princes of distant countries sent messengers with gifts to the pharaoh while on his war expedition."[2]

---

1 M. Hilzheimer, quoted by Wreszinski, *Atlas* Pt. II text to Plate 33
2 Wreszinski, *Atlas* Pt. II text to Plate 33

The second surmise, as Velikovsky notes, is strange; given the fact that it is unusual for remote countries to send plants and birds to warriors on a march of conquest. The first surmise, he notes, "merely illustrates the type of conjecture necessary in order to evade the identification of Palestine with God's Land."

There seems little doubt, as Velikovsky believed, that many of the ex-otic plants and animals depicted at Karnak were indeed from the famous collections of Solomon, whose interest in such things is celebrated in the Scriptures:

> And he spake of trees, from the cedar tree that is in Lebanon even unto the hyssop that springeth out of the wall: he spake also of beasts, and of fowl, and of creeping things, and of fishes" (1 Kings 4:33).

Yet we must also bear in mind what we discovered in the previous chap-ter: Palestine/Syria in the days of Hatshepsut and Thutmose III was a very different land from the one we now know. Species of animals and plants found nowadays only in Africa or southern Arabia roamed freely through-out the region. Perhaps the most spectacular illustration of this comes from the tomb of an official under Thutmose III named Rekhmire. This is a wall-painting depicting Syrians bringing tribute, amongst which is a young el-ephant and a bear. The Syrian leading the bear carries large tusks of elephant ivory.[1] It was of course such materials as ivory, as well as the ebony and in-cense, products of Punt, which helped to convince many experts that this re-gion be located in Africa. Yet the monuments of Thutmose III show that they all occurred in Palestine/Syria. Another official of the time, one Amenemhab, writes in his biography;

> Again [I saw] another successful deed which the Lord of the Two Lands accomplished in Ni. He hunted 120 elephants at their mudhole. Then the biggest elephant which was among them began to fight be-fore the face of his majesty.[2]

This encounter with the elephant herd, enormous by modern standards, took place in northern Syria.

THE PLUNDER OF SOLOMON'S TEMPLE

The looting of Solomon's Temple is as central to the story of Shishak as the visit to Jerusalem is to the story of the Queen of Sheba. Just as an ac-count of the Queen's visit to that region would almost be required in any attempted identification of her, so an account of the plunder taken from the

---

1 See G. Maspero, *History of Egypt* Vol. 5 (London, 1906), p. 34
2 J. Pritchard, *Ancient Near Eastern Texts* (Princeton, 1950), p. 240

Temple would be required in any identification of Shishak. The looting of this building, we have noted, is viewed as a major event in Jewish tradition, where it is seen as divine punishment for Solomon's infidelity to the Lord:

> So Shishak king of Egypt came up against Jerusalem and took away the treasures of the house of the Lord, and the treasures of the king's house; he took all: he carried away also the shields of gold which Solomon had made. (2 Chronicles 12:9)

Abyssinian tradition too makes the robbing of the Temple an event of central importance: By bringing the Ark of the Covenant to Ethiopia, Menelik conferred upon that region and its people the favor of God.[1]

The Book of Kings and Chronicles emphasize again and again the wealth and power of Solomon's kingdom; and they recount in detail the treasures accumulated by him and placed in the House of the Lord. In Velikovsky's words, Solomon's kingdom was the repository of, "Wealth accumulated by a nation during hundreds of years of industrious work and settled life in Palestine, spoils gathered by Saul and David in their military expeditions, look of the Amalekite Auaris, earnings from the trade between Asia and Africa, gold from Ophir, the gifts of the queen Sheba-Hatshepsut ..."[2] By all accounts, the precious things deposited in the Temple by Solomon were truly fabulous in their quantity. Irrespective of whatever pharaoh we identify with Shishak, he must surely have left some record of the plundering of such a treasure-house. Sosenk I, of the so-called Twenty-Second Dynasty, the pharaoh normally identified with Shishak, left no such record; but Thutmose III did. This is shown in a great bas-relief in the temple of Amon at Karnak. According to Velikovsky, "The bas-relief displays in ten rows the legendary wealth of Solomon. There are pictures of various precious objects, furnishings, vessels, and utensils of the Temple, of the palace, probably also of the shrines of foreign deities ..."[3]

The critics, naturally, rejected such an interpretation. They argued that nowhere did Thutmose III specifically claim that the treasures came from a temple in Kadesh. Yet such an objection is without merit. The material shown by the pharaoh is clearly described as spoil taken from Retjenu — i.e., Palestine — and is of such value that it could only have been taken from a religious shrine of some sort. Furthermore, since Kadesh (which means "the

---

1 Notwithstanding the Abyssinian tradition however, it should be pointed out that Jewish tradition (as in Seder Olam 25, and various references in Ginzberg's *Legends of the Jews*, Vol. 4), held that Shishak did not remove the Ark of the Covenant from the Temple, and that it remained there until the Babylonian exile.

2 Velikovsky, *Ages in Chaos*, op cit., p. 156

3 Ibid. p. 155

Holy") headed the list of Palestinian cities, it seems beyond question that the loot was taken from a temple in Kadesh itself. Velikovsky stressed that of the items shown at Karnak there are no idols, or images of gods. "Idols were and still are used in all pagan worship. The hundreds of sacred objects appearing in the mural [at Karnak] were obviously not of an idolatrous cult; they suggest, rather, a cult in which offerings of animals, incense, and showbread were brought, but in which no idols were worshiped. The Temple of Kadesh-Jerusalem, sacked by Thutmose III, was rich in utensils for religious services but devoid of any image of a god."[1] There are, it is true, among the objects displayed by Thutmose III, two human figures or figurines, holding a kind of lotus-shaped staff and wearing a strange kind of headdress. These cannot have been deities or idols, and look far more like stylized lamp-stands. Several animal forms also appear in the relief, and "the head of an ox is recognizable as an ornament on a drinking vessel."[2] This accords with what we know of the Temple in Jerusalem, where lions and oxen are mentioned as decorative motifs (1 Kings 7:29 and 36).

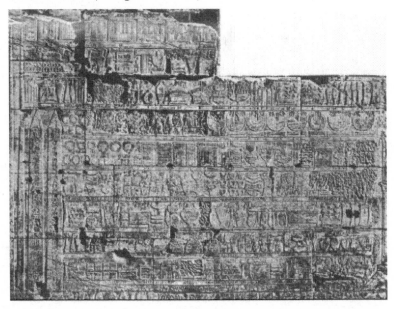

Fig. 17. Thutmose III's pylon at Karnak, showing treasures from Kadesh.

The wealth of this temple was obviously enormous. Thutmose III shows artifacts of gold, silver, bronze, and precious stones. There were altars for

---

1 Ibid., p. 159
2 Ibid., p. 159

burnt offerings and incense, tables for sacrifice, lavers for liquid offerings, vessels for sacred oil, tables for showbread, and the like. Their quantities are indicated by numerical symbols: a single stroke meant one, an arch meant ten, and a spiral a hundred. If Thutmose III had wanted to display all his spoils from Kadesh by showing each object separately, he would have needed a wall more than a mile long. The upper five rows of the bas-relief depict objects of gold; in the next row silver artifacts are mingled with those of gold and precious stones; and objects of bronze and semi-precious stones are placed in the lower rows. The latter are the most numerous; but those in the upper rows, in gold, silver and precious stones, were also of a vast quantity.

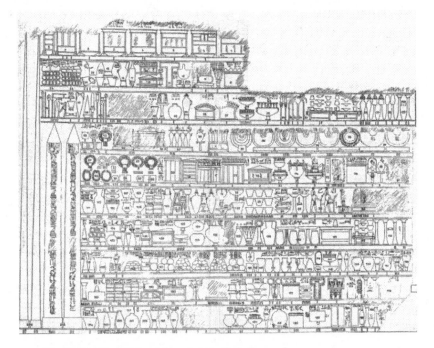

Fig. 18. Vessels and furnishings of the Kadesh temple.

Velikovsky himself provided a fairly comprehensive evaluation of the objects displayed by Thutmose III, and it is his lead we shall follow here. The research he did was not exhaustive; yet it was the best done as yet. And nothing of what he said has ever been disproved.

As Velikovsky says, "Often an article is represented on the wall [of Thutmose III's temple] in gold and another of the same shape in brass [bronze]. The fashioning of identical objects in gold as well as in bronze (brass) for the Temple of Solomon is repeatedly referred to in the Books of Kings and Chronicles."[1]

"A crown of gold round about," says Velikovsky, "was an ancient Judean ornament of sacred tables and altars." Such ornamentation, he says, is seen on the golden altar in the second row of Thutmose III's mural, as well as on the bronze altar in the ninth row.[2] Velikovsky stresses that this golden altar was the only one of its kind. (1 Kings 7:48; 2 Chronicles 4:19). An identical altar of bronze, shown in the ninth row of the Karnak relief, seems to be a reference to the altar of bronze mentioned in 2 Chronicles 4:1. However, "Inasmuch as its height is equal to its width, the altar [at Karnak] does not fit the description of the altar mentioned in the Second Book of Chronicles, which was half as high as it was wide. However, from the first chapter of the Second Book of Chronicles we know that another brazen altar made by Bezaleel was among the holy objects of the Temple at Jerusalem."[3]

Next to the altar, notes Velikovsky, was the table "whereupon the show-bread was" (1 Kings 7:48, and 2 Chronicles 4:19). This showbread was obviously not of flour, but of silver or gold. Velikovsky notes that in the Book of Exodus (25:30; 35:13, and 39:36) it is said that showbread was made by Bezaleel, who was a goldsmith. Now showbread is pictured on the bas-relief of Karnak in the form of a cone. "The cone in the seventh row bears the explanation: 'White bread.' This bread was of silver. The thirty cones of gold and the twenty-four cones of colored stone (malachite), identical in form with the silver cone, also represent showbread."[4]

From the Bible, we know that the "candlestick with lamps" (2 Chronicles 4:20) was an illuminating device with lamps shaped like flowers. "Figures 35, 36, 37, and 38 of the [Karnak] mural are candlesticks with lamps." One of these (number 35) "has three lily lamps on the left and three on the right. The other candlesticks (37, 38) have eight lamps to the left and eight to the right. The candlestick with lamps wrought by Bezaleel for the tabernacle had three lamps to the left and three to the right. There were almonds, a knop, and a flower on the arms. A later form showed a preference for seven lamps on both sides of the stem."[5]

The preferred ornament on Temple vessels, he notes, was the *shoshana*, translated as "lily," or "lotus." In 1 Kings 7:26, we read, "… the brim thereof

---

1 Ibid., p. 157
2 Ibid., p. 158
3 Ibid., pp. 159-60
4 Ibid., p. 160
5 Ibid., p. 160

[of the molten sea] was wrought like the brim of a cup, with flowers of lilies." Velikovsky notes that the lotus motif is repeated on the vessels depicted on the wall of Karnak. "A lotus vial is shown in gold, in silver, and in colored stone (malachite?). A rim of lily work may be seen on various vessels, a very unusual type of rim ornament, found only in the scriptural account and on the bas-reliefs of Thutmose III.[1]

The "candlestick with the lamps" mentioned in 2 Chronicles 4:20 had lamps shaped like flowers. "Figures 35, 36, 37, and 38 of the mural [at Karnak] are candlesticks with lamps."[2] One of these, number 35, "has three lily lamps on the left and three on the rights. The other candlesticks ... have eight lamps to the left and eight to the right. The candlestick with lamps wrought by Bezaleel for the tabernacle had three lamps to the left and three to the right." Velikovsky also notes that "A later form showed a preference for seven lamps on both sides of the stem [ie the Menorah]."[3]

In the Book of Kings we hear of other candlesticks in addition to those with lamps. In 1 Kings 7:49 these are described as bearing flowers. "This form is seen in the third row of the bas-relief. ... The candlestick is in the shape of a stem with a lotus blossom."

Next to the altar in Solomon's Temple were the tables for offerings. This table, like the vessels which sat upon it, was of gold. "The 'tables of sacrifice' in the third row (of gold) and in the seventh row (of silver) of the mural have sets of vessels on them: three flat dishes, three large cups, three pots (or bowls), one shovel." In fact, "Many tables of gold and silver and bronze are reproduced on the bas-relief."[4]

We know that the paraphernalia of the Temple contained "hooks and other instruments" (2 Chronicles 4:16). "In the third row of the Karnak mural," says Velikovsky, "near the table of offerings, and in the same row at the left end, there are hooks, spoons, and other implements .... bowls appear in most of the rows, but especially in the second and sixth (of gold)."[5]

Velikovsky notes that "The incense altar, and his staves, and the anointing oil" were in the Temple of Jerusalem. However, as no detailed description of what this altar looked like has been preserved, we may guess that some of the objects displayed at Karnak may add light on the subject. "Was the incense burned in a dish set on a base [as in two of the objects at Karnak]?"

---

1 Ibid., p. 158
2 Ibid., p. 160
3 Ibid.
4 Ibid., p. 161
5 Ibid., p. 161

Also, "Vessels containing anointing oil are shown on pedestal altars (41); over the figures in the lower row (197-99) is written: 'Alabaster, filled with holy anointing oil for the sacrifice.'"[1]

During services in the Temple of Solomon golden snuffers were used fro spreading fragrance (2 Chronicles 4:22, and 1 Kings 7:50). As Velikovsky notes, "Masrek in Hebrew means a fountain or vessel that ejects a fluid. Such fountains are mentioned as having been in the Temple of Solomon. ... Among the vessels shown on the wall at Karnak there are one or two whose form is peculiar. The vessel in the fifth row (73) has two side spouts and is adorned with figures of animals. The spouts are connected with the basin by two animals (lions?) stretching toward them; rodents run along the spouts, one pair up and one pair down; amphibians (frogs) sit on top of the vessel. It is not unusual to decorate modern fountains in a like manner. The figures of frogs are especially appropriate for this purpose. The tubes and the mouths of the animals on the vessel could be used to spout perfume or water."[2]

Velikovsky notes that "One hundred basins of gold were made by Solomon for the Temple (2 Chronicles 4:8). Ninety-five basins of gold are shown in the sixth row of the mural; six larger basins are shown apart."[3]

Again, "Thirty-three doors are represented in the lower row of the bas-relief and the inscription says they are 'of beaten copper.'"[4] This finds a striking echo in the Second Book of Chronicles, where we read that Solomon "made the court of the priests, and the great court, and the doors of the court, and overlaid the doors of them with copper." (2 Chronicles 4:9)

Shields of "beaten gold" are listed in Chronicles among the booty taken by Shishak. "These three hundred shields, together with two hundred targets of gold (2 Chronicles 9:15, 16), were not part of the furnishings of the Temple; they adorned 'the house of the forest of Lebanon.' In the seventh row of the mural [at Karnak] there are three disks marked with the number 300, which means that they represent three hundred pieces. The metal of which they are made is not mentioned; some objects in this row are of silver, but the next figure has a legend indicating that it was of gold."[5]

Finally, the "ephod of the high priest (a collar with a breastplate) was not mentioned in the Scriptures among the booty of the pharaoh and might not have been taken. But precious garments of the priests were carried off. The

---

1 Ibid.
2 Ibid.
3 Ibid.
4 Ibid., p. 162
5 Ibid., p. 162

fourth row displays rich collars, some with breastplates; they were destined to be gifts for the priests of Amon." The conclusion, which the presently writer fully supports, is that, "In the bas-reliefs of Karnak we have a very excellent and detailed account of the vessels and furniture of the Temple of Solomon, much more detailed than the single bas-relief of the Titus Arch in Rome, showing the candlestick and a few other vessels of the Second Temple, brought to the Roman capital just one thousand years after the sack of the First Temple by the Egyptians."[1]

Thutmose III did not destroy the Temple of Kadesh/Jerusalem: he merely robbed it of its treasures. In future years the shrine was refurbished and re-endowed with precious artifacts; and it continued to be the focus of Hebrew worship for many centuries.

Two generations after Thutmose III, in the time of Amenhotep III, the king of Jerusalem (Urusalim), still a vassal of Egypt, wrote several letters to the pharaoh. These documents, part of the Amarna archive, give the name of the king as Abdi-Hiba, or more probably Abdi-Tibbi (the "Good Servant"). In one of his addresses to the pharaoh — letter 290 — Abdi-Hiba refers to a place read as Bet-NIN.IB. Originally, this was believed to be a reference to Assyria ("House of Nineveh"). However, in 1940, the eminent Assyriologist Professor Jules Lewy suggested that Bet-NIN.IB be translated as "Temple of Shulman" and that this was an alternative name for Jerusalem at the time.[2] In the letter in question, Abdi-Hiba complained that the land was falling into the hands of bandits, "and now, in addition, the capital of the country of Jerusalem — its name is Bit Sulmani — the king's city, has broken away." Beth Sulman in Hebrew, as Professor Lewy correctly translated, is Temple of Sulman. Believing the Amarna Letters to date from the fourteenth century BC, Lewy could not, of course, surmise that the edifice was the Temple of Solomon and therefore supposed it to be a Canaanite place of worship of a god found in Akkadian sources as Shelmi, Shulmanu, or Salamu. He wrote; "Aside from proving the existence of a Sulman temple in Jerusalem in the first part of the 14th century BC, this statement of the ruler of the region leaves us in no doubt that the city was then known not only as Jerusalem, but also as Bet Sulman." He saw it as "significant" that it was only the name Jerusalem that "reappears after the end of the occupation of the city by the Jebusites, which the Sulman temple, in all probability, did not survive."

---

1 Ibid., p. 163
2 Jules Lewy, "The Sulman Temple in Jerusalem," *The Journal of Biblical Archaeology*, 59 (1940) pp. 519 ff.

A god named Shulman was indeed worshipped throughout Syria and Assyria during this period, and several Assyrian kings were named Shalmaneser ("Shulman is pre-eminent") in his honor. Images of the deity have been found throughout Syria and Assyria; yet none have been found in Jerusalem or anywhere in Palestine. Indeed, although during the time of the Eighteenth Dynasty southern Palestine was an extremely prosperous and heavily-populated region harboring many great cities, almost no examples of deities or idols of any kind have been found in the territory from this period. If the inhabitants of the country during this period were the idol-worshipping Canaanites, this is very difficult to explain. But if they were the idol-rejecting Hebrews, it makes perfect sense.

The Bit Sulmani of Jerusalem was the House of Solomon; and Abdi-Tibbi the king was Asa, Solomon's own grandson.[1]

SHISHAK AND SESOSTRIS

During his stay in Egypt, the historian Herodotus was told about a mighty king named Sesostris (called Sesoosis by Diodorus Siculus) who had conquered most of Asia and whose military exploits, the Egyptians boasted, were unparalleled in history. The account given by Herodotus is clearly fabulous and grossly exaggerates the extent of his empire, an empire well beyond anything achieved by any pharaoh:

> ...he [Sesostris] collected a vast armament, and made a progress by land across the continent [of Asia], conquering every people which fell in his way. In the countries where the natives withstood his attack, and fought gallantly for their liberties, he erected pillars, on which he inscribed his own name and country, and how that he had here reduced the inhabitants to subjection by the might of his arms: where, on the contrary, they submitted readily and without a struggle, he inscribed on the pillars, in addition to these particulars, an emblem to mark that they were a nation of women, that is, unwarlike and effeminate.
>
> In this way he traversed the whole continent of Asia, whence he passed on into Europe, and made himself master of Scythia and of Thrace, beyond which countries I do not think that his army extended its march. For thus far the pillars which he erected are still visible, but in the remoter regions they are no longer found.[2]

Identifying this man from the hieroglyphic records has always been problematic, since neither this name nor anything closely resembling it, has

---

1 As Sweeney demonstrates in some detail in his *Empire of Thebes*, op cit., the "bandits" whom Abdi-Tibbi says threatened Jerusalem can only have been the forces of Baasha, the king of Israel, who besieged the city.

2 Herodotus, ii, 102-110 (trans. Rawlinson)

been found in the king-lists and monuments. Nevertheless, it is now generally assumed that Sesostris is a corrupted form of the hieroglyphic Senwosret (a name actually written as *Wsr.t.sn* or Usertasen); and indeed kings of the latter name are now routinely called "Sesostris" in the textbooks. Nevertheless, none of these pharaohs were military men of any stature and it is admitted that whilst the *name* Sesostris is derived from them, the *character* of the great conqueror owes much more to the imperialist pharaohs of the New Kingdom — most especially to Thutmose III. Thus in the words of George Rawlinson, "The name Sesostris no doubt comes from Sesortosis, a Grecised form of Usurtasen," but "the figure [of Sesostris] was composed by uniting in one the actions of all the chief Egyptian conquerors. As the greatest of these Thothmes III furnished the most traits."[1]

But why, it may reasonably be asked, should the non-military Senwosret/Usertasen kings furnish the name of a great conqueror at all? The implausibility of such a circumstance, especially in view of the fact that the Egyptians had other, real military men, whose name or names they could have used instead, makes us wonder whether the word "Sesostris" has anything to do with the Senwosret/Usertasen kings at all.

If the outline of history proposed by Velikovsky is right, then Thutmose III (the admitted model for the *character* of Sesostris) must also have been called Shishak, or Sesak. This word of course shares its first syllable with Sesostris, which would naturally lead us to suspect a connection. But this then begs the question: Is Thutmose III actually called Shishak or anything like it, on the monuments?

He is indeed.

Thutmose III, like all New Kingdom pharaohs, possessed a multitude of royal titles. In documents of the time he is in fact more commonly known by the so-called prenomen ("Suten Bat") name Menkheperre (also transcribed into cuneiform as Manakhibiria or something like it). He was also known by the Golden Horus name of Djeser-kau. As early as 1987 Kenneth Birch of South Africa suggested this as the origin of the word Shishak. The name now transcribed as Djeser-kau was previously rendered variously as Cheser-kau, Tscheser-kau etc., and was probably pronounced something like Djesey-ka or Sheshy-ka (the best guess is that the consonant *dj* was pronounced something like the French *j*).[2]

---

1   G. Rawlinson, *History of Ancient Egypt* Vol. 2 (London, 1881), p. 226n.
2   K. Birch, *Society for Interdisciplinary Studies: Catastrophism and Chronology Workshop* No. 2 (1987), p. 35

Admitting that Djeser-kau could quite easily be transliterated into Shishak in Hebrew ears, it may however be argued that the Golden Horus name of a pharaoh was not one commonly used, especially by foreigners. But this was not always the case; and at least one prominent pharaoh of the Nineteenth Dynasty was known to the Greek authors by his Golden Horus name, or by an abbreviation of it.[1] Furthermore, there is abundant evidence to suggest that pharaohs were often known by nicknames and abbreviations. So for example David Rohl has shown that Ramses II at least was sometimes called "Sheshy" — derived from the *ses* part of his son of Ra title. In addition, it has been pointed out that Shishak sounds very much like the Hebrew *shashak*, (variously "attacker," "assaulter," or "the one who crushes"), so that this at least may have been a nickname given to the pharaoh by his Hebrew victims. I would suggest that Djeser-kau/Sheshy-ka reminded the Hebrews of their own word for attacker, *shashak*, which name was then accorded him in the Book of Kings.

---

1 In his 2008 book *Ramessides, Medes and Persians* op cit., Sweeney demonstrates in great detail that Seti II, of the Nineteenth Dynasty, can only have been the same person as Inaros, the Egyptian leader who battled for a decade against the Persians during the 480s and 470s BC. Seti II's Golden Horus name was Ineruemtawnebu, a title evidently abbreviated as Inaros by Herodotus.

EPILOGUE

As Velikovsky remarked many years ago, we cannot make Hatshepsut a contemporary of Solomon without rewriting the whole of ancient history. Not only
Hatshepsut, but the dynasty and empire associated with her must be moved
down the timescale by over five centuries. But such a move cannot leave the rest
of ancient history untouched: whole empires and civilizations must find new
places in the succession of events which preceded the coming of Alexander the
Great. Indeed, ancient history would need to be rewritten in its entirety, and this
was a task Velikovsky set himself after the appearance of *Ages in Chaos* in 1952.

A series of books, known collectively as "Ages in Chaos," was to follow, and
the next installment came in 1977 with the publication of *Peoples of the Sea*. The
final (published) volume came the following year, *with Ramses II and his Time*. These
two works dated Egypt's Nineteenth and Twentieth Dynasties to the seventh,
sixth, fifth and fourth centuries BC. Thus in *Ramses II and his Time* Velikovsky argued that Ramses II had reigned in the sixth century BC, and that his line of succession came to an end with the Persian Invasion of Egypt in 525 BC. In *Peoples of
the Sea* he argued that the Twentieth Dynasty only rose to power around 400 BC,
and that its greatest pharaoh, Ramses III, who saved Egypt from an invasion of
the mysterious "Sea Peoples," was none other than pharaoh Nectanebo I of the
Thirtieth Dynasty, who saved Egypt from a second Persian invasion in the early
fourth century.

It was clear then that the scheme outlined by Velikovsky proposed opening
an enormous gap between the end of the Eighteenth Dynasty (around 840 BC,
according to *Ages in Chaos*, Vol. 1) and the start of the Nineteenth (around 660

BC in *Ramses II and his Time*). His critics, of course, were quick to point out that neither archaeology nor written history could support such a separation, and the entire "Ages in Chaos" project floundered.

What had gone wrong? *Ages in Chaos*, Volume 1, was an excellent piece of research, and had been hailed by many at the time as marking a major paradigm shift. Yet any examination of *Ramses II and his Time* and *Peoples of the Sea* will show that these too represented first-class research and thinking, providing their own powerful testimony for down-dating the Nineteenth and Twentieth Dynasties into the period between the sixth and fourth centuries BC. Argument raged back and forth. One group, mainly composed of British researchers, briefly proposed that the Nineteenth Dynasty should follow directly from the Eighteenth, where Velikovsky had placed the latter — in around 840 BC. This chronology, known as the "Glasgow Chronology," thus had Hormeheb and Seti I of the early Nineteenth Dynasty reigning roughly between 840 and 810 BC, and made them contemporaries of Kings Jehu of Israel and Shamshi-Adad IV of Assyria. Ramses II was placed by the Glasgow Chronologists between about 810 and 760 BC, and had him contemporary with Azariah (Uzziah) of Judah and Adad-Nirari III of Assyria. For the Glasgow Chronologists, the Nineteenth Dynasty came to an end in around 730 BC, roughly corresponding with the start of the unsettled period which saw the Ethiopian and Assyrian invasions, and may be schematically represented thus:

Date BC	EGYPT	ISRAEL/JUDAH	ASSYRIA
1020	Ahmose	David	
	Thutmose I		
960	Hatshepsut	Solomon	
	Thutmose III	Rehoboam	
900	Amenhotep II	Asa	Tukulti-Ninurta II
	Amenhotep III	Asa	Ashurnasirpal II
850	Akhnaton	Jehoshaphat	Shalmaneser III
	Horemheb	Jehoram	
800	Seti I	Ahaziah	Shamshi-Adad IV
	Ramses II	Uzziah	Adad-Nirari III
750	Ramses II		
	Merneptah	Jotham	Tiglath-Pileser III

The above chronology, essentially a modification of Velikovsky's Ages in Chaos, had some currency for a time but was eventually abandoned as un-workable, partly because of difficulties involved in making the reign of Akh-naton contemporary with Shalmaneser III and partly because of a perceived inability to "fit" the Twentieth Dynasty (of Ramses III) into the period of the Ethiopian and Assyrian Invasions, in the late eighth and early seventh centuries.

With the abandonment of the "Glasgow Chronology" there was what can only be described as a free for all. Countless independent researchers threw their hats into the ring, with dynasties and kings moved backwards and forwards like historical playing cards. The best-known and perhaps most successful of these revisions was that of David Rohl, who, beginning in the early 1990s, published a series of volumes which took just over three centuries from Egyptian New Kingdom dates, and which placed the Amarna Age — and Akhnaton — around the time of King Saul of Israel, i.e., roughly between 1020 and 1000 BC.

Yet for all the publicity it garnered Rohl's chronology failed to gain aca-demic approval and was severely criticized both by mainstream and revi-sionist scholars. Perhaps the most glaring problem encountered by his sys-tem was the complete disconnection of biblical and Egyptian history in the time of the Eighteenth Dynasty. For Rohl, the very end of the Eighteenth Dynasty, as reflected in the Amarna Letters, was contemporary with the rise of the first Israelite monarchy, under King Saul. For Rohl, Saul was the trou-blesome freebooter named Labayu encountered in the Amarna documents. Yet in the relevant biblical texts Egypt and/or Egyptians are mentioned only once at this time: when an Egyptian slave of an Amalekite soldier defects to the side of the Israelites.[1] In all the period of the Judges, which precedes this, Egypt is not mentioned at all; which of course is astonishing if this was the epoch of the mighty Eighteenth Dynasty, a line of pharaohs which controlled the whole of Syria/Palestine as far as the Euphrates. And the one mention the Egyptians do get, right at the end, is as a slave of a nomad desert warrior!

Contrast Rohl's disconnected Eighteenth Dynasty with the Velikovsky scheme, which bristles with precise synchronisms and connections between Egypt and Israel at this crucial historical juncture.

---

1 1 Samuel 30, 11-13

So, if Rohl and the other alternative theories were wrong, and if Velikovsky, for all his ingenuity, could not fit all the pieces together properly, what was the solution, and even more to the point, what was the problem?

The solution, I believe, finally appeared in 1989, when German writer Gunnar Heinsohn proposed that the Eighteenth Dynasty should be brought forward into the seventh century BC, with the Nineteenth Dynasty following on directly in the sixth and the Twentieth Dynasty in the fifth and fourth centuries, just as Velikovsky had argued (for the latter two dynasties) in *Ramses II and his Time* and *Peoples of the Sea.*

Heinsohn's reasons for this adjustment were primarily stratigraphic, but a brief look at the documentary evidence shows that he had a very powerful case: major events of the seventh century BC, mentioned in the Greek authors, seem to find echoes in the texts and inscriptions of the Eighteenth Dynasty and their Mesopotamian contemporaries. Thus for example during this period of history northern Syria, as well as the land of Assyria, was controlled by a group or nation known as the Mita or Mitanni. The monarchs of this mysterious people bore Indo-Iranian (Old Persian) names and there is strong evidence to suggest they worshipped the Persian gods Mithra, Indra and Varuna.[1] Around the time of the first pharaohs of the Eighteenth Dynasty the Mitanni king Parsatatar (or Parsatra) had waged a great war against the Old Assyrian kingdom. He apparently succeeded in stripping the Assyrians of their possessions outside of Assyria proper, though he could not conquer their heartland, in northern Mesopotamia. Nevertheless, from the time of Parsatatar princes with Indo-Iranian names are found throughout Syria, as far as the region of the Euphrates. A generation or so later the Mitannians seem to have renewed the war against Assyria, and king Shaushtatar (or Shaushattra) was ever afterwards credited with the conquest of all the cities of Assyria, including Ashur and Nineveh. Heinsohn equated these Mitanni with the "Mighty Medes," whom the Greeks had claimed conquered the Assyrian Empire in the seventh century. Even the names of the Mitannian monarchs seem to have echoes in the writings of the classical authors. Thus Parsatatar/Parsattra, who waged the earlier inconclusive war against the Assyrians, would have been Herodotus' Phraortes, who was also said to have waged an inconclusive war against the Assyrians, whilst his son Shaushtatar/Shaushattra, who finally destroyed Assyrian power, would

---

1 The text of a treaty between Mitanni and the Hittites invokes the names of Mithra, Indra and Varuna, and is widely hailed as the first documented mention of these important Indo-Iranian deities.

be identical to Phraortes' son Cyaxares (Hvakhshatra), who also finally destroyed Assyrian power.

There are other clues.

According to the Greeks, the entire Near East had been overrun in the
early seventh century by Scythian nomads from the steppes of Russia, who
then participated in the battle for Assyria. And sure enough, texts from the
time of the Eighteenth Dynasty refer repeatedly to groups of barbarians who
could well be identical to the Scythians. Thus for example the Amarna Letters, from the time of Amenhotep III and Akhnaton, refer repeatedly to the
depredations of a group of nomads named the SA.GAZ, who caused havoc
throughout the region and were greatly feared by the settled communities
amongst whom they operated. Although the pronunciation of the Sumerian
logograms which give us SA.GAZ is uncertain (a logogram can represent a
sound, but it can also represent an idea), it seems strange that this group of
brigands and marauders should bear a name which look suspiciously like
Ashguzai or Ashguza, the Akkadian word for "Scythian."[1] Compare also with
the Persian word Saka.

Contemporary with the composition of the earliest Amarna Letters
the Hittite kingdom was very nearly destroyed by the inroads of barbarian
tribes variously named Ga-as-ga or Ga-as-ga-as. That the latter groups were
nomads probably issuing from north of the Caucasus is generally agreed.[2]
The biography of Suppiluliumas I, written by his son Muwatallis, describes
how Suppiluliumas spent the first twenty years of his reign in a desperate
struggle against the barbarians, who laid waste to a large part of Anatolia
and sacked the Hittite capital.[3] If the Ga-as-ga-as and SA.GAZ (also written
as GAZ) are identical, and if they are both Scythians (Ashguza), then we
would expect them to have devastated the Hittite realms, which are much
closer to the Scythian homelands. Indeed, the Hittites would have borne the
brunt of Scythian inroads — which seems in fact to have been the case.

So, the Eighteenth Dynasty was contemporary with two peoples, the
SA.GAZ and the Mitanni, who stand every chance of being identical to the
Scythians and the Medes, two nations which rose to prominence in the seventh century BC. And a whole plethora of linguistic, cultural, artistic and
stratigraphic evidence points in the same direction. Consider for example
the fact that some of the Ugarit texts, also dating from the same general pe-

---

1 H. W. F. Saggs, *The Greatness that was Babylon* (London, 1962), p. 117

2 A. Goetze, "Anatolia from Shuppiluliumash to the Egyptian War of Muwatallish,"
in *The Cambridge Ancient History*, Vol. 2, part 2 (3rd ed.), p. 118

3 Ibid., p. 117

riod as the Amarna Letters, were written entirely in a Hebrew/Phoenician dialect strikingly similar to that of the Books of Kings — as well as to the language used in Phoenician inscriptions of recognizably seventh and sixth centuries dates.[1] A few rare expressions or names found on Ras Shamra tablets occur also on monuments of the seventh century.[2] Again, innumerable cultural and linguistic details in the Ugarit documents called to mind the Aegean world of the seventh and sixth centuries. Thus for example Claude Schaeffer was struck by an Ugarit catalogue of ships strangely reminiscent of Homer's catalogue of ships in the Iliad.[3] Yet few experts would now date the composition of the Iliad before the seventh century. And what about the fact that some of the Ugarit texts were written in an alphabetic script; though no one now would place the invention of the alphabet much before the eighth century? Yet certain features of the Ugarit alphabet made it clear that it was a system that clearly had reached an advanced stage of development.[4] These documents used a characteristic stroke to separate words — a stroke also found in Cypriote scripts of the sixth and seventh centuries.[5] What about the tombs of Ugarit, with their distinctive design features reminiscent of Cypriote tombs of the seventh and sixth centuries?[6] And speaking of Cyprus, we should remember that the burials at Enkomi, which were dated to the Amarna Age, contained pottery and objets d'art of every kind strikingly reminiscent of Greek work of the seventh and sixth centuries.[7] We might mention too the art of glass production in Eighteenth Dynasty Egypt, which finds its strongest parallels in glasswork of the Twenty-Sixth Dynasty (sixth century) and of the Persian Age.[8]

So much for the Eighteenth Dynasty. In *Ramses II and his Time* (1978) Velikovsky presented a great deal of evidence for placing the Nineteenth Dynasty in the sixth century, just before the Persian Invasion. There was for example the burial of King Ahiram of Byblos, whose sarcophagus bore a

---

1 Claude Schaeffer, *The Cuneiform Texts of Ras Shamra-Ugarit*, op cit., p. 40
2 J. W. Jack, *The Ras Shamra Tablets* op cit., p. 9. "A word of uncertain meaning, *mphrt* (community or family), which is found on two of the Ras Shamra tablets, occurs on the stele of Yehawmilk, king of Byblos (circa 650 BC). Strange to say, the name Yehawmilk also appears on the Ras Shamra tablets."
3 Schaeffer, *Cuneiform Texts*, op cit..
4 Ibid., p. 36. "The Ras Shamra alphabet is already so advanced that it implies the existence of a still earlier alphabet yet to be found."
5 Charles Virolleaud, "Les Inscriptions cunéiformes," *Syria*, X (1929), p. 309
6 Schaeffer, *Cuneiform Texts*, op cit., p. 29
7 See A. S. Murray, "Excavations at Enkomi," in A. S. Murray, A. H. Smith, and H. B. Walters, *Excavations in Cyprus* (London, British Museum Press, 1900)
8 See P. Fossing, *Glass Vessels before Glass Blowing* (Copenhagen, 1940), p. 134

seventh-sixth century Phoenician inscription, yet who was interred with artifacts of Ramses II. And there was the letter from the scribe Hori to his rival Amenemope, who revealed an astonishing familiarity with what can only be described as biblical Hebrew, and who wrote an entire sentence in perfect sixth century Hebrew — even using the word *mahir*, a term found in various biblical books indicating a "speedy" or shorthand scribe.[1] We might also consider the fact that Ramses II's opponents at the Battle of Kadesh spoke a language (Neshili) which was basically a slightly archaic version of Classical Age Lydian and who were led by a king whose name Hattus-ili (or Ili-hattus/ Ali-hattus) is strangely reminiscent of the Lydian Alyattes.[2] Indeed several Hittite emperors bore the name Mursilis — identical to that of one of Lydia's greatest kings (Myrsilos), whilst the Hittite goddess Kubabu is recognized as identical to the Lydian Cybele (Greek, Kubele).

In the same way, *Peoples of the Sea* (1977) presented an enormous quantity of evidence of the same type indicating that the Twentieth and Twenty-First Dynasties should be placed in the Persian epoch — the fifth and fourth centuries. Whilst this material is far too voluminous to consider here, it should be noted, for example, that Twentieth Dynasty burials at Tell el-Yahudiya displayed countless features strongly reminiscent of the Ptolemaic Age.[3] Again, Pierre Montet found that the word "king," from a bracelet of the Twenty-First Dynasty ruler Psusennes I, was "written as in the Ptolemaic period,"[4] whilst the word "god," on the same bracelet, "is written with a hawk as often found in the Ptolemaic period."[5] Si-Amon, the Twenty-First Dynasty prince who rewrapped the royal mummies found at Deir el-Medinah, built himself a tomb in the Siwa Oasis where we find an illustration of his son wearing "a short cloak of Greek style."[6]

On the strength of the archaeological evidence, then, it seems that the Egyptian New Kingdom, from the Eighteenth Dynasty through to the Twenty-First, needs to be placed between the last quarter of the eighth and the start of the third centuries BC. Such a placement brings Egyptian history

---

1 See Velikovsky's comments in *Ramses II and his Time* (1978)

2 For Lydian parallels with Neshili see J. G. MacQueen, *The Hittites and their Contemporaries in Asia Minor* (Westview Press, London, 1975), p. 59

3 See E. Naville, *The Mound of the Jew and the City of Onias*: Egyptian Exploration Fund, 1887 (Kegan Paul, London 1890)

4 P. Montet, *Tanis, douze années de fouilles dans une capitale oubliée du delta égyptien* (Payot, Paris, 1942), p. 149

5 Ibid.

6 Ahmed Fakhri, *Siwa Oasis* (American University in Cairo Press, 1992)

into line with the history of the ancient Near East as outlined by the Greek and Hellenistic authors. But if this be the case, how is it that *Ages in Chaos*, Volume 1, which appears to synchronize Eighteenth Dynasty history with that of the early Hebrew Monarchy in the tenth and ninth centuries, is separated from the Nineteenth Dynasty by almost two centuries?

This is the whole nub of the problem and it was Gunnar Heinsohn who first identified it. For the fact is, Bible chronology is not accurately aligned with that of the Classical world. Until Heinsohn's breakthrough, it was universally assumed that the sequence of events described in the Old Testament matched the sequence of events described in Herodotus, Diodorus and other historians of the Greek- and Latin-speaking worlds. It was taken as self-evident, for example, that the "Neo-Assyrian" kings mentioned in the biblical books were the same as the Imperial Assyrians whom the Greek writers had described being conquered by the Medes in the seventh century. Detailed examination of the evidence of stratigraphy, from dozens of sites in the Middle East, finally convinced Heinsohn that this was *not* the case; and by 1989 he came to the startling conclusion that the Neo-Assyrian kings mentioned in the Bible were in fact Persians, who rightfully belonged in a period much more recent than that to which they had been assigned.[1] Heinsohn reached this conclusion primarily because of the fact that throughout Mesopotamia there is virtually no recognizable Persian strata or remains of any kind. This is all the more remarkable considering the fact that Mesopotamia was, according to Herodotus and other classical authors, the wealthiest satrapy of the Achaemenid state. How could it be then there are no Achaemenid remains? What is found, directly beneath the Hellenistic remains, are the material detritus of the Neo-Assyrian and Neo-Babylonian epochs. After having considered all the options, Heinsohn was compelled to conclude that the Neo-Assyrian and Neo-Babylonian monarchs were Achaemenid Persians using Semitic names.

Accepting that this may be correct, Emmet Sweeney, a long-time supporter of Heinsohn's method, had, by the early 1990s, and by the simple process of working backwards from the final Neo-Babylonian and Persian kings, come to the following identifications: Tiglath-Pileser III = Cyrus; Shalmaneser V = Cambyses; Sargon II = Darius I; Sennacherib = Xerxes; Esarhaddon =

---

1 See for example Heinsohn *Perserherrscher gleich Assyrerkonige?* (Mantis Verlag, Frankfurt, 1996).

Artaxerxes I; Ashurbanipal = Darius II; Nabopolasser = Artaxerxes II; Nebu-chadrezzar = Artaxerxes III; and Nabonidus = Darius III.[1]

Before the age of archaeology the aforementioned Neo-Assyrian and Neo-Babylonian kings were known to us almost exclusively through the Bible, where they are apparently placed before the age of the Persians. It was then naturally assumed that they were identical to the Assyrian and Babylonian monarchs mentioned in the various Greek histories. But this is not the case, and the misidentification of these rulers and their subsequent misplacement two centuries before their proper time has had the effect of dislocating the whole of ancient history.

How could this have happened?

Before answering that question we should note that the Bible, as noted by Heinsohn, has its own "dark age" between the Persian Age and the Hellenistic: between roughly 420 and 200 BC the Jews, most assiduous of record-keepers, seem to have left virtually nothing. No book of the Old Testament treats of this epoch. Thus Ezra, Nehemiah, Haggai and Zachariah, along with one or two other Old Testament prophets and scribes, are said to have flourished in the first century or so of the Persian period: These men organized the return of the Jewish exiles from captivity in Babylon, a return which finally got underway, supposedly, around 450 BC and was completed by about 400 BC. After them however there is absolutely nothing until the time of the Maccabees, around 175 BC! How is it that the Jews, most careful of record-keepers, left nothing for over two hundred years of their history, two centuries rich in events from where we might have expected copious chronicles? This is a question that has long perplexed scholars, but to which none could provide a plausible answer.

Nor could archaeology, it seemed, shed any light on the issue: For just as the written history of the period was a blank, so was the archaeological. Try as they might, excavators have signally failed to find almost anything in the land of Israel between roughly 400 BC and 175 BC! This problem elicited the following comment from two eminent scholars at a recent conference: "The topic of our symposium, 'Judah and the Judeans in the Persian Period,' leads us into the realm of mystery. The word mystery evokes a twofold feeling of sadness and hope: Sadness, because we know so little and would like to know so much more; hope, because there is still much work to be done in this area. ... The Hebrew Bible contains very few passages that address Achaemenid rule over Judah and the Judeans (539–332 BCE). Very few events

---

1 These identifications are defended in detail in Sweeney's *Ramessides, Medes and Persians*, op cit.

are illuminated or given any kind of value judgement. ... The existing extra-biblical sources contain little or no reference to the Judeans or Judah. There are [in addition] only a few archaeological and epigraphic finds. Thus, Herbert Donner justifiably refers to the Persian era as the 'dark ages.'"[1]

But if the archaeological and the written records can find nothing to fill this 225-year gap there are innumerable clues in Jewish literature which have always suggested a solution. Thus for example Talmudic tradition generally placed the Babylonian Exile in the fourth century rather than the sixth, as per conventional chronology; and this is strikingly supported by the Gospel of Matthew, where the birth of Jesus is placed 14 generations after the deportation to Babylon. Allowing 25 years per generation (a generous figure, given the early marriages and deaths of the time), this would place the Exile around 350 BC.

Assuming then that the Gospel of Matthew and the Talmud are correct, we are compelled to conclude that Israelite history has been artificially stretched by just over two centuries immediately before the time of the Maccabees and that all dates prior to the latter epoch need to be reduced accordingly, with the Babylonian Exile commencing not in the early-sixth century, but in the mid-fourth. But having stated that, we are again thrown back on the vexed question: How could such a colossal error have occurred?

The student of this confused epoch is immediately drawn to the central catastrophe of Jewish history prior to the deportations carried out by the Romans; and that is the Babylonian Exile itself. Almost the entire population of Judah was uprooted from its ancestral home and taken — often in chains — to Mesopotamia; where it remained for well over a century. During this time the Jewish people lost their language and even their Phoenician-style written script. Those who finally returned from Babylon, in a gradual trickle that seems to have lasted a century, adopted the language of the Syrians and Samaritans amongst whom they now settled — Aramaic. They also devised a new script for their sacred texts, the old Phoenician one having fallen out of use. We cannot doubt that they continued to keep records and family genealogies: Of all peoples the Jews were the most attached to charting their ancestry and family histories. Yet the disruption caused by the removal to Babylon and the subsequent return to a ruined Israel cannot be over-estimated. The king who deported them was a Persian, the notoriously brutal Artaxerxes III; but he was a Persian who ruled from Babylon and who used the Babylonian name Nebuchadrezzar. The Book of Judith tells us of his gen-

---

1 Oded Lipschits and Manfred Oeming (eds.) "Judah and the Judeans in the Persian Period," Conference, Winona Lake, Indiana: (Eisenbrauns, 2006), No. XXI, p. ix

eral Holofernes and his eunuch Bagoas; whilst the Greek historian Diodorus tells us of Artaxerxes III's general Holofernes and of his eunuch Bagoas.[1] The Jews, being of Semitic speech themselves, seemed to have known the king of the Exile primarily by his Babylonian name, and to have subsequently imagined him to be an actual Babylonian.

At this point another factor entered the equation: Artaxerxes III/Nebuchadrezzar was the penultimate ruler of the Persian Empire. When he died he was — after a series of assassinations — succeeded by Darius III (who also ruled from Babylon and called himself Nabonidus), the last of the Persians. It was he, and not Darius I, who threw Daniel into the lions' den. Only five years after mounting the throne, Darius III was dead and his empire ruled by the victorious Alexander of Macedon. We know from various Jewish sources that Alexander was a religious liberal and sympathetic to the Jews. According to Josephus he worshipped the Hebrew God at Jerusalem and was on good terms with the Hebrew priestly class. It must then, as Emmet Sweeney has argued, have been Alexander and his Greek successors who freed the Jews from their Babylonian Exile and who facilitated the return to Judea and the reconstruction of the Temple.[2]

Yet here there arose a problem: Assuming that it was the early Seleucids who began the process of resettling the Jews in the land of Israel, say between 300 and 225 BC, they had to have been friends and benefactors of the Israelites. Yet by 175 BC another scion of the Macedonian dynasty, Antiochus IV Epiphanes, sought to eliminate the Jewish religion and began his ruthless campaign of Hellenization, which eventually brought forth the Maccabean Rebellion. This was to be one of the most ruthless wars ever fought by the Jews, and the massacres committed by Antiochus and his forces lived long in the memory of the people. Now, it so happens that what we call the Jewish Bible or the Old Testament was written in the century after the Maccabees. The compilers of that body of literature had available to them a huge mass of texts, written in Hebrew, which only a few members of the priestly class could read fluently. In it, they learned of a king with a Babylonian name, Nebuchadrezzar, who enslaved their ancestors and deported them to Mesopotamia. There were also texts which told of their liberation by the Greeks under Alexander. But these Greeks seemed very different from the forces of Antiochus, which they had so recently opposed on the field of battle. It may have been with some reluctance that the compilers of the bibli-

---

1 The true identity of Nebuchadrezzar is examined in detail in Sweeney's *Ramessides, Medes and Persians* op cit.

2 Sweeney, *Ramessides, Medes and Persians*, op cit.

cal texts recalled that it had been Antiochus' own ancestors who had freed their ancestors from Babylonian captivity. In time it was entirely forgotten. The Persians, who had been the real enslavers of the Jews, were then transformed into benefactors, and the Greeks, the actual liberators, effaced from the record entirely. This was all the more easily done because, as we saw, the Achaemenid Persians had used Assyrian and Babylonian names, whilst conversely the early Seleucid Greeks had on occasion used Persian names such as Darius and Artaxerxes.

The end result then was a stretched history, with events that had occurred in the fourth century backdated to the sixth, and a period of phantom time, spanning over two centuries, inserted into Hebrew chronology. Since the history of the Hebrews became extremely important following the conversion of the Roman Empire to Christianity, this error was then incorporated into the general pre-Christian history of the ancient Near East.

It is evident then, if we are on the right track, that all Jewish history before the time of the Maccabees must be shortened by about two and a quarter to two and a half centuries. The Babylonian deportation therefore occurred around 340 BC rather than 586 BC, whilst Isaiah, whose book of prophecies mentions both Tiglath-Pileser III and Cyrus, rightly belongs in the time of the latter, who was himself an alter-ego of the former. Thus Isaiah would have flourished not in the eighth century but in the sixth; roughly between 550 and 530 BC.

Looking a little further into the past we see that Solomon, and his contemporary Hatshepsut, cannot have reigned in the tenth century but in the eighth (or, to be more precise, in the early seventh: the erroneous gap in history increases somewhat the farther back in time we go). Thus Hatshepsut made her memorable visit to Jerusalem around 680 BC rather than 950 BC.

The evidence then, viewed as a whole, suggests that Egyptian New Kingdom dates need to be reduced by around five to five and a half centuries in order to bring them in line with those of the Bible, but that all of these dates then need to be reduced by a further two to two and a half centuries to bring them in line with the chronology of the classical historians. Thus a double adjustment, to correct a double mistake, is necessary; and this is clearly reflected in Velikovsky's historical works: In *Ramses II and his Time* and *Peoples of the Sea* he reduced Egyptian dates by almost eight centuries to bring them in line with classical chronology, but in *Ages in Chaos* Vol. 1 he reduced Egyptian dates by just over five centuries, thereby bringing the Eighteenth Dynasty into line with the Bible. One part of his reconstruction was therefore synchronized with the Bible, and the other part with the Greek histories. Hence the strange and incomprehensible gap he opened between the Eighteenth Dynasty and the Nineteenth. Nonetheless, Velikovsky was on the right track, and it was the trail he blazed which should have been followed.

The pharaohs of the Eighteenth Dynasty really were contemporaries of the early Hebrew monarchs, and the two kingdoms did indeed arise simultaneously on the ruins of the Hyksos Empire. But the Hyksos Empire was that of the Assyrians (or "Old Assyrians"), not of the Amalekites, as Velikovsky believed.[1] Saul in Israel and Ahmose in Egypt had been minor players in a far greater game, which saw the Mitanni/Medes under Parsatatar (Parsattra/Phraortes) attack the Assyrians/Hyksos and strip them of their empire. Princes with Indo-Iranian names, members of the *mariyanna* aristocracy, now established themselves in many of the city-states throughout Syria/Palestine, where we find them in the earliest records of the Eighteenth Dynasty.

In subsequent years the destruction of Assyria would be completed by Shaushtatar/Shaushattra, who conquered their greatest cities and established his own empire in their Mesopotamian heartland. This Shaushattra can only be Cyaxares, the Great King of the Medes who completed the conquest of Assyria after the inconclusive war waged by his predecessor Phraortes.

Three generations after Shaushattra the land of Mitanni was ruled by a king Tushratta, who wrote several letters to Amenhotep III. This Tushratta was apparently murdered by one of his own sons. The murderer, or the man suspected of the murder, whose name is read as Shattiwaza, subsequently fled to the court of the Hittite king Suppiluliumas, who placed an army at his disposal. With these forces the fugitive returned to Mitanni, which he subdued. From the ruins of the Mitannian state Assyria reawakened, and its new king Ashuruballit became an important player in the politics of the region. He wrote at least two letters to Akhnaton, in the second of which he requested "gifts" equal at least in value to those the pharaoh had previously sent to the "Hanigalbatian." Hanigalbat was another word for Mitanni.

---

1 The Amalekites, an Arabian tribe, may indeed have been allies of the Assyrians and acted as their mercenaries in the Canaan region. There is certainly strong evidence to show that the Assyrians recruited local peoples to enforce their authority in that part of the world, and the Philistines too seem to have been Assyrian agents.

As we saw in Chapter 1, dating Ashuruballit's letters, as well as the others in the Amarna archive (from a biblical perspective), is facilitated by the fact that several characters and settlements named in the Letters were associated with the generation of Solomon's grandchildren and great-grandchildren. Thus we recall how Abdi-Astarte of the Letters is almost certainly the same person as Abdastartus, grandson of Solomon's ally Hiram of Tyre. All of this evidence indicates that the Letters were written in the time of King Asa of Judah and Kings Baasha and Omri of Israel. The latter three monarchs are recognized as contemporaries of the Neo-Assyrian king Ashurnasirpal II, father of the well-known Shalmaneser III, who was a contemporary and opponent of King Ahab of Israel. If this is the case, if the Amarna Letters were written in the time of Ashurnasirpal II, it can only mean that the latter character was one and the same person as Ashuruballit, the Amarna correspondent.

It should be noted that both Ashuruballit and Ashurnasirpal (II) are regarded as having initiated a new epoch of Assyrian power and prosperity, and both were great builders. Strangely, however, virtually nothing of what Ashuruballit built has been found, whilst there are abundant remains associated with Ashurnasirpal. Furthermore, archaeologists have discovered that the Assyrian cities typically have a Mitanni stratum followed immediately and without any intervening gap, by a Neo-Assyrian one. The Mitanni remains end with Tushratta, and the Neo-Assyrian ones begin with Ashurnasirpal II. So, in the very spot where we might expect to find the settlements and artifacts of Ashuruballit (who rose to power immediately after the death of Tushratta), we find instead the settlements and artifacts of Ashurnasirpal II.

The evidence indeed shows, as Sweeney has outlined in some detail in his *Empire of Thebes* (2006), that neither Ashuruballit nor Ashurnasirpal were real Assyrians — both are identical to Shattiwaza, the parricide son of Tushratta who fled to Suppiluliumas after the death of his father. Suppiluliumas helped Shattiwaza conquer the Mitanni land and establish him as "King of Assyria." But the "new era" of Assyrian power under Ashuruballit/Ashurnasirpal was just a new phase of Mitanni/Mede power. In fact, during the time of Ashurnasirpal II's son Shalmaneser III, the people of Assyria, led by Ashur da'n apla (Sardanapalus) rebelled, and a great war for leadership of the Near East (called by Ctesias of Cnidus the Battle of the Nations) commenced. All the powers of the region, including Egypt, the Hittite Land, and Babylon, were drawn into the conflict. The Hittites allied themselves with the Assyrian rebels, whilst the Egyptians supported the Medes. To this end pharaohs Seti I and then Ramses II led armies towards the Euphrates, where they clashed with the Hittites and their most important confederates, the "people of Naharim [Assyria]." The outcome of this sixth century World War was victory for the Medes, but only after Shalmaneser III's son Shamshi-Adad (IV) had forged an alliance with Babylon through his marriage to Queen Samurammat (Semiramis), a woman as renowned in antiquity as the Queen of Sheba herself.

Shalmaneser III's Mede name was Hvakhshatra (also written as Khwakhshatra) which was Hellenized as Cyaxares — as indeed was the earlier Shaushattra. Shalmaneser III must then be listed among the great kings of antiquity as Cyaxares II. His son Shamshi-Adad was known by the Mede name Arbaku (Arbaces), and his grandson Adad-Nirari (III) bore the Iranian name Ishtumega (Astyages).

The great struggle in which Shalmaneser III, Shamshi-Adad IV, Sardanapalus and Semiramis were involved commenced around 580 BC.

We thus return full circle in the "Ages in Chaos" to Velikovsky and the line of enquiry he indicated all those years ago. The great war conducted by Ramses II against the Hittites, which Velikovsky placed in the early sixth century, did indeed occur at that time; for in *Ramses II and His Time* and in *Peoples of the Sea* he reduced Egyptian dates by almost eight centuries to bring them in line with classical chronology,[1] but, to repeat what we said earlier, in *Ages in Chaos* Vol. 1 he reduced Egyptian dates by just over five centuries, thereby bringing the Eighteenth Dynasty into line with the Bible. In this way he opened a strange and puzzling gap in the sequence of Egyptian history. Nonetheless, having recognized this very understandable error and corrected it, we can see that Velikovsky was ultimately on the right track, and it was the path he pointed to which should have been followed. In the end, the abandonment of that trail by the scholarly establishment and by various revisionist historians such as Peter James and David Rohl must be seen as a tragic error which has set the study of ancient chronology back by several decades.

The revised chronology may be schematically represented thus:

---

1 Note however that in *Ramses II and his Time* Velikovsky partially incorporated biblical timescales, thus making the book something of a hybrid. Thus he identified Ramses II's Hittite opponent Hattusilis with the Neo-Babylonian Nebuchadrezzar. As noted above however Hattusilis is rightly seen as an alter-ego of the Lydian king Alyattes, whilst Nebuchadrezzar is an alter-ego of the Persian Artaxerxes III, and cannot have been a contemporary of Ramses II.

Date BC.	EGYPT	ISRAEL/ JUDAH	ASSYRIA/MEDIA
720	Ahmose	David	Shamshi-Adad I/Deioces
	Thutmose I		Adad-Nirari I/Parsatatar/ Phraortes
670	Hatshepsut	Solomon	
	Thutmose III	Rehoboam	Shalmaneser I/Shaushtatar/ Cyaxares I
650	Amenhotep II	Asa	
	Amenhotep III	Asa	Tukulti-Ninurta II/Tushratta
625	Akhnaton	Jehoshaphat	Ashurnasirpal II/Shattiwaza
	Horemheb	Jehoram	Shalmaneser III/Cyaxares II
590	Seti I	Ahaziah	Shalmaneser III/Cyaxares II
	Ramses II	Uzziah	Shamshi Adad IV/Arbaces
560	Ramses II		Adad-Nirari III/Astyages
	Merneptah	Jotham	Tiglath-Pileser III/Cyrus
525	Amenmose/Amasis	Ahaz	Shalmaneser V/Cambyses

BIBLIOGRAPHY

Abdel-Aziz Saleh, "Some Problems Relating to the Pwenet Reliefs at Deir el-Bahari," *Journal of Egyptian Archaeology* 58 (1972)

Aharoni, Y. *The Land of the Bible: A Historical Geography* (John Knox Press, London, 1966)

Akurgal, Ekrem. *The Birth of Greek Art* (Methuen, London, 1968)

Albright, W. F. "An Archaic Hebrew Proverb in an Amarna Letter from Central Palestine," *Journal of Near Eastern Studies*, 98 (1943)

Albright, W. F. "The Chaldaean Inscriptions in Proto-Arabic Script," *Bulletin of the American Schools of Oriental Research*, 128 (1952).

Baikie, James. *A History of Egypt* Vol. 2 (London, 1929)

Bimson, John. "Hatshepsut and the Queen of Sheba: A Critique of Velikovsky's Identification and an Alternative View", *Society for Interdisciplinary Studies; Review*, 8 (1986)

Birch, K. Letter in *Society for Interdisciplinary Studies: Catastrophism and Chronology Workshop* No. 2 (1987)

Blanford Edwards, Amelia Ann. *Pharaohs, Fellahs and Explorers* (New York, 1891)

Breasted, James Henry. *A History of Egypt from the Earliest Times to the Persian Conquest*, Vol. 2 (London, 1951)

Breasted, James Henry. *Ancient Records of Egypt: Historical Documents from the Earliest Times to the Persian Conquest* Vol. 2 (London, 1922).

Budge, E. A. Wallis. *The Kebra Nagast* (London, 1932)

Burke, Aaron A. "Canaan under Siege: The History and Archaeology of Egypt's War in Canaan during the Early Eighteenth Dynasty," in J. Vidal (ed.) *Studies on War in the Ancient Near East: Collected Essays on Military History* (Alter Orient und altes Testament, Ugarit Verlag, Munster, 2010)

Butzer, K. W. "Physical Conditions in Eastern Europe, Western Asia and Egypt Before the Period of Agriculture and Urban Settlement", in *The Cambridge Ancient History* Vol. 1, part 1 (3rd ed)

Claude Schaeffer, Claude. *The Cuneiform Texts of Ras Shamra-Ugarit* (Oxford University Press, London, 1939)

Danelius, E. and H. Steinitz, "The Fishes and other Aquatic Animals on the Punt Reliefs at Deir el Bahri" *Journal of Egyptian Archaeology*, 53 (1967)

Danelius, Eva. "Did Thutmose III Despoil the Temple in Jerusalem?" *Society for Interdisciplinary Studies; Review*, 2 (1977/78)

Danelius, Eva. "The Identification of the Biblical 'Queen of Sheba' with Hatshepsut, 'Queen of Egypt and Ethiopia,'" *Kronos* I, 4 (1977)

Davis, Theodore M. *The Tomb of Hatshopsitu* (London, 1906)

Doresse, J. *Ethiopia* (Elek Books, London, 1959)

Drower, Margaret S. "Syria before 2200 BC," in *The Cambridge Ancient History*, Vol.1 part 2 (3rd ed.)

Edwards, I. E. S. "The Early Dynastic Period in Egypt," in *The Cambridge Ancient History* Vol. 1 part 2 (3rd ed.)

Erman, Adolph and Hermann Grapow, eds. *Wörterbuch der aegyptischen Sprache*, Vol. 5, (Leipzig, 1926-1963).

Ewing, Rev. W. "Syria" in *Countries of the World*, Vol. 6 (Waverley Books, London)

Fakhri, Ahmed. *Siwa Oasis* (American University in Cairo Press, 1992)

Finkelstein, Israel and Neil Asher Silberman. *The Bible Unearthed: Archaeology's New Vision of Ancient Israel and the Origin of its Sacred Texts* (Free Press, New York, 2001)

Finkelstein, Israel. "The Rise of Jerusalem and Judah: The Missing Link," in Andrew G. Vaughan and Ann E. Killebrew (eds.), *Jerusalem in Bible and Archaeology: The First Temple Period* (Atlanta, Georgia, 2003)

Fossing, P. *Glass Vessels before Glass Blowing Vessels before Glass Blowing* (Ejnar Munksgaard, Copenhagen, 1940)

Fox, M. V. *The Song of Songs and Ancient Egyptian Love Songs* (University of Wisconsin Press, 1985).

Gardiner, Alan. *Egypt of the Pharaohs* (Oxford University Press, London, 1961)

Ginenthal, Charles. *Pillars of the Past*, Vol. 3 (Ivy Press Books, New York, 2011) Vermeulen U. and D. de Smet, *Egypt and Syria in the Fatimid, Ayyubid and Mamluk Eras* (Leuven, Belgium, 2005)

Ginzberg, L. *Legends of the Jews*, Vol. 1 (Philadelphia, 1909).

Giveon, R. *Les Bedouins Shoshou des Documents Egyptiens* (Leiden, 1971)

Goetze, A. "Anatolia from Shuppiluliumash to the Egyptian War of Muwatallish," in *The Cambridge Ancient History*, Vol. 2, part 2 (3rd ed.)

Graves, Robert. *The Greek Myths*, 2 Vols. (Penguin Books, 1955)

Greenfield, R. *Ethiopia: A New Political History* (London, 1965)

Hayes, W. C. "Egypt: Internal Affairs from Tuthmosis I to the Death of Amenophis III," in *The Cambridge Ancient History* Vol. 2, part 2 (3rd ed., 1971)

Heinsohn, Gunnar. *Die Sumerer gab es nicht* (Eichborn Verlag Ag, 1995).

Heinsohn, Gunnar. *Perserherrscher gleich Assyrerkonige?* (Mantis Verlag, Frankfurt, 1996)

Insoll, Timothy. *The Archaeology of Islam in Sub-Saharan Africa* (Cambridge University Press, 2003)

Irvine A. K. "The Arabs and Ethiopians" in D.J. Wiseman (ed.) *Peoples of Old Testament Times* (Oxford, 1973)

Jack, J. W. *The Ras Shamra Tablets* (T & T Clark, Edinburgh, 1935)

Jones, A. H. M. and E. Munroe *A History of Ethiopia* (Oxford, 1935)

Juergens, Ralph E. and Lewis M. Greenberg, "A Note on the Land of Punt," *KRONOS*, Vol. 1, no. 2 (June, 1975).

Kitchen, Kenneth. *Ramesside Inscriptions*, Vol. 2 (Blackwell Publishing Limited, London, 1996)

Layard, A. H. *Discoveries in the Ruins of Nineveh and Babylon* (Harper and Brothers, London, 1853)

Lepsius, Karl Richard. Denkmäler aus Aegypten und Aethiopien nach den Zeichnungen der von Seiner Majestät dem Koenige von Preussen, Friedrich Wilhelm IV., nach diesen Ländern gesendeten, und in den Jahren 1842—1845 ausgeführten wissenschaftlichen Expedition auf Befehl Seiner Majestät. Vol. 3 (Nicolaische Buchhandlung, Berlin, 1846).

Lewy, Jules. "The Sulman Temple in Jerusalem," *The Journal of Biblical Archaeology*, 59 (1940)

Lorton, David. "Hatshepsut, the Queen of Sheba, and Immanuel Velikovsky" (1984) on the world-wide web at www. geocities. com/Athens/Academy/1326/hatshepsut. html.

Luke, H. C. "Palestine" in *Countries of the World*, Vol. 5 (Waverley Books, London)

Maccoby, Hyam. "The Queen of Sheba and the Song of Songs," *Society for Interdisciplinary Studies, Review*, Vol. IV, No. 4 (Spring, 1980)

MacQueen, J. G. *The Hittites and their Contemporaries in Asia Minor* (Westview Press, London, 1975)

Maspero, Gaston. *History of Egypt*, Vol. V (Grolier Society, London, 1906)

Maspero, Gaston. The Struggle of the Nations: Egypt, Syria and Assyria (S. P. C. K. Books, London, 1896)

Meeks, Dimitri. "Locating Punt," in David B. O'Connor and Stephen Quirke (eds.) *Mysterious Lands (Encounters with Ancient Egypt)* (University of California Press, 2003)

Millar, Naomi F. *The Archaeology of Garden and Field* (University of Pennsylvania Press, 1984)

Montet, Pierre. Tanis, douze années de fouilles dans une capitale oubliée du delta égyptien (Payot, Paris, 1942)

Montgomery, J. A. *Arabia and the Bible* (Philadelphia, 1934)

Morenz, Siegfried. *Egyptian Religion* (Cornell University Press, 1973)

Murray, A. S. "Excavations at Enkomi," in A. S. Murray, A. H. Smith, and H. B. Walters, *Excavations in Cyprus* (London, British Museum Press, 1900)

Murray, Margaret A. *Egyptian Temples* (Sampson Low, Martson and Co., London)

Naville, Edouard. *The Mound of the Jew and the City of Onias*: Egyptian Exploration Fund, 1887 (Kegan Paul, London, 1890)

Naville, Edouard. *The Temple of Deir el-Bahari*, Part III (London, 1907)

Newberry, P. E. "Three Old Kingdom Travelers to Byblos and Punt," *Journal of Egyptian Archaeology* 24 (1938)

Nibbi, Alessanrda. "The Shipwrecked Sailor Again", *Göttinger Miszellen* 24 (1977)

Nielsen, Kjeld. *The Incense of Israel* (Leiden, 1986)

Niemi, Tine M., Zvi Ben-Avraham and Joel Gat, (eds.) *The Dead Sea: The Lake and its Setting* (Oxford University Press, 1997)

Olmstead, A. T. *History of Assyria* (New York and London, 1923)

Petrie, Flinders. *A History of Egypt*, Vol. 2 (London, 1896)

Petrie, Flinders. *The Making of Egypt* (Macmillan, London, 1939)

Pritchard, John. *Ancient Near Eastern Texts* (Princeton, 1950)

Rawlinson, George. *History of Ancient Egypt* Vol. 2 (London, 1881)

Reid, Joyce M. H. and H. H. Rowley (eds) *Atlas of the Bible* (London, 1956)

Rice, Michael. *Egypt's Making: The Origins of Ancient Egypt, 5000–2000 BC* (Routledge, London, 1990)

Rohl, David. *Legend: The Genesis of Civilization* (London, 1998)

Rothernberg, B. *Timna, Valley of the Biblical Copper Mines* (Thames and Hudson, London, 1972)

Rullkötter, J. and A. Nissenbaum, "Dead Sea asphalt in Egyptian mummies: Molecular evidence," *Naturwissenschaften*, December (1980)

Saggs, H. W. F. *The Greatness that was Babylon* (London, 1962)

Sayed, A. M. "Discovery at the Site of the 12th Dynasty Port at Wadi Gawasis on the Red Sea Shore," *Revue d'Egyptologie*, 29 (1977)

Schaeffer, Claude. *The Cuneiform Texts of Ras Shamra-Ugarit* (Oxford University Press, London, 1939)

Stager, L. E. "The Archaeology of the Family in Ancient Israel," *Bulletin of the American School of Oriental Research*, Vol. 260, Issue 260 (1985)

Stannard, Brendan. *The Origins of Israel and Mankind: A Unified Cosmogonic Thoery* (Carib Publications, 1983)

Stiebing, William H. "Rejoinder to Velikovsky," *Pensee* 5 (Autumn, 1973)

Sweeney, Emmet. *Arthur and Stonehenge: Britain's Lost History* (Domra Publications, England, 2001)

Sweeney, Emmet. *Empire of Thebes, or Ages in Chaos Revisited* (Algora, New York, 2006)

Sweeney, Emmet. *Ramessides, Medes and Persians* (Algora, New York, 2008)

Sweeney, Emmet. *The Genesis of Israel and Egypt* (2nd ed. Algora, New York, 2007)

Thornhill, Wallace and David Tablott. *The Electric Universe* (Mikamar Publishing, 2007)

Tilman, H. W. *Eight Sailing/Mountain-Exploration Book* (Leicester UK, Seattle WA, 1987)

Tyldesley, Joyce. *Hatchepsut: The Female Pharaoh* (Penguin Books, 1998)

Van Beek, G. W. "Recovering the Ancient Civilization of Arabia," *Biblical Archaeologist* XV: 1 (1952)

Van Seters, John. *Abraham in History and Tradition* (Yale University Press, 1987)

Velikovsky, Immanuel. *Worlds in Collision* (New York, 1950)

Velikovsky, Immanuel. *Ages in Chaos* (New York, 1952)

Velikovsky, Immanuel. *Oedipus and Akhnaton* (New York, 1960)

Velikovsky, Immanuel. *Peoples of the Sea* (New York, 1977)

Velikovsky, Immanuel. *Ramses II and his Time* (New York, 1978)

Virolleaud, Charles. "Les Inscriptions cunéiformes," *Syria*, X (1929)

Weigall, Arthur. *A History of the Pharaohs: The Twelfth to the Eighteenth Dynasties* (T. Butterworth Limited, London, 1927)

White, John B. *A Study of the Language of Love in the Song of Songs and Ancient Egyptian Poetry*, (SBL Dissertation Series 38, Scholars Press, Missoula, Montana, 1978).

Wright, George Frederick. "The Jordan valley," *International Standard Bible Encyclopedia*, (1915)

Yahuda, Abraham Shalom. *The Language of the Pentateuch in its Relation to Egyptian* (Oxford, 1933)

INDEX

A

Abdi-Ashirta/Abdi-Astarte), 16, 176
Abdi-Hiba, 159
Abraham, 15, 20, 59, 61, 68-69
Abyssinia, 2, 41-42, 44, 83-84
Adad-Nirari III, 164, 177-178
Adonis, 66, 85
Ahab, King of Israel, 16, 176
Ahiram, 168
Ahmose, 7, 9-11, 21, 40, 164, 175, 178
Akhnaton, 13-14, 16, 20, 40-41, 164-165, 167, 175, 178
Akkadian(s), 14-15, 159, 167
Al Kuds (Jerusalem), 132
Alyattes, 169, 177
Amalekite(s), 21, 153, 165, 175
Amarna Letters, 6, 14-16, 30, 129, 159, 165, 167-168, 176
Amenhotep II, 9, 38, 45, 105-106, 164, 178
Amenhotep III, 6, 14, 16, 18, 72, 159, 164, 167, 175, 178
Amu, 29, 91, 99, 105, 107, 110
Amurru, 16
Ano, princess, 7
Antiochus IV Epiphanes, 173-174
Aqaba, Gulf of, 5, 101-102, 104, 107
Arabah, 5, 7, 64, 83, 102-103, 105-107, 110
Arbaces, 177-178
Artaxerxes III, 171-173, 177

Aruna, 145-149
Asa, King of Juda, 6, 15-17, 45, 147, 160, 164, 176, 178
Ashurnasirpal II, 18-19, 164, 176, 178
Ashuruballit, 175-176
Assyria, 19, 37, 77, 82, 133, 159-160, 164, 166-167, 175-178
Astyages, 177-178
Ati, wife of Perehu, 50, 90, 103, 107
Avaris, 100
Azariah, 164

B

Bagoas, 172-173
balm (of Gilead), 65, 84
Barkay, Professor Gabriel, 139
Beth Horon, 146-147
Bimson, John, 3, 5, 32-33, 35-36, 38, 50, 62, 71, 73, 77, 79-82, 88, 94, 116
bitumen, 59, 99, 107
Botrys, 16
Burke, Dr Aaron A., 122-123, 138-139
Byblos, 4, 47-48, 56-59, 62, 66-68, 76, 78-79, 85, 99, 113, 137, 168

C

Canaanite(s), 15, 17, 22, 124, 133, 137, 140, 159-160
Caucasian(s), 90
Cleopatra, 13, 65
Cosmic Pillar, 60-61
Cyaxares, 166-167, 175, 177-178
Cybele, 169
Cyprus, 72, 168

D

Dan, 137-138
Danelius, Eva, 5, 38, 52, 78, 87, 90, 102, 146, 149
Darius I, 37, 170-171, 173
Darius III, 171, 173
date-palms, 55-56, 103-104, 107
Dead Sea, 5, 7, 59, 83-84, 86, 99, 101-103, 107, 110-111
Diodorus Siculus, 160
Djed Pillar, 59-60
Djeser-djeseru (Hatshepsut's temple), 14, 24-25
Djeser-kau, 161-162

E

Edom, 7, 76, 108, 138, 140
Edomite(s), 7
Ein Gedi, 64, 107, 110-111
Elat, 7, 92, 98, 101-103, 105, 107-109
elephants, 82, 84, 100, 152
Enkomi, 168
Eritrea, 32, 55-56, 65, 76, 78, 80, 86, 89, 93-95, 97, 99-100
Ethbaal, 16
Ethiopia, 1-2, 23-24, 32, 35, 37-38, 41-42, 44-45, 52, 84, 94-95, 98-99, 131, 153
Ethiopian(s), 17, 23, 38, 40-44, 84, 94, 125, 132, 141, 147, 164-165

F

frankincense, 4, 26, 32, 56, 63-65, 84-85, 99, 111, 125

G

gazelles, 83, 110
Genubath, King of Edom, 7
Ghor (Jordan Valley), 5, 64, 83-84
Gilead, 65, 84
Ginenthal, Charles, 95-97
giraffes, 50, 81, 84-85, 87, 110

H

Hadad, King of Edom, 7
Hamitic, 71, 89-90, 94
Hamite(s), 80, 89
Harmachis, 41
Hathor, 4, 7, 11, 14, 25, 50, 53, 56, 66, 79-80, 99, 105-109, 113-115, 117, 121, 124, 127
Hatti, 77
Hattus-ili, 169
Hazor, 124
Heinsohn, Gunnar, 60, 120, 166, 170-171
Herodotus, 37-38, 86, 133, 160, 162, 166, 170
Hiram, King of Tyre, 16, 26, 29-30, 92, 103, 176
Hittite(s), 18-19, 139, 166-167, 169, 175-177
Holofernes, 172-173
Horemheb, 18-19, 164, 178
Horus, 41, 71, 81, 149, 161-162
Hulah, Lake, 102
Hyksos, 9, 11, 21-22, 91, 100, 120-122, 127, 175

I

incense, 11, 25-26, 28-29, 32, 47-48, 50-52, 55, 57, 62-64, 85, 94, 107, 110, 113, 118, 129, 133, 135, 152, 154-155, 157
Ineni, 10
Ishmaelites, 65
Ishtar, 70, 127

J

Jebus, 15
Jebusite(s), 138, 146, 148, 159
Jericho, 7, 27, 64, 84, 99, 107, 111
Jeroboam I, King of Israel, 7, 15, 31, 132, 143-145

U

V

W

X

Z